SEED TO PLATE SOIL TO SKY

PINTO
BEANS
$5.00

BOLITA
BEANS
$8.00

ANASAZI
BEANS
$8.00

SEED TO PLATE SOIL TO SKY

MODERN PLANT-BASED RECIPES USING NATIVE AMERICAN INGREDIENTS

LOIS ELLEN FRANK

Native American Culinary Advisor
WALTER WHITEWATER

Recipe Testing & Development Advisor
MARIANNE SUNDQUIST

Go
hachette
BOOKS

Author's Note: Some foods in this book may be unfamiliar to you, especially to anyone who has never been to the Southwest. I urge the readers of this book to be absolutely certain to properly identify wild edible plants, herbs, flowers, fungi, and vegetables before harvesting and eating them as some plants look alike and are not edible. Please adhere to any special instructions or warnings I have included in the recipes with the handling of wild plants. Most states have laws against the removal of native plants from their natural habitat and have restrictions on the collection of these plants including collecting their seeds and fruits. Check regulations in your own state and national law to see if any plants are protected or endangered before harvesting them and anything that grows in the wild. This ensures and protects these plants and makes them available for future generations. Please follow any traditional protocols when harvesting plants in the wild. Thank you.

Hachette Go, an imprint of Hachette Books
Hachette Book Group
1290 Avenue of the Americas
New York, NY 10104
HachetteGo.com
Facebook.com/HachetteGo
Instagram.com/HachetteGo

First Edition: August 2023

Hachette Books is a division of Hachette Book Group, Inc. The Hachette Go and Hachette Books name and logos are trademarks of Hachette Book Group, Inc.

The Hachette Speakers Bureau provides a wide range of authors for speaking events. To find out more, go to hachettespeakersbureau.com or email HachetteSpeakers@hbgusa.com.

Hachette Go books may be purchased in bulk for business, educational, or promotional use. For information, please contact your local bookseller or Hachette Book Group Special Markets Department at special.markets@hbgusa.com.

The publisher is not responsible for websites (or their content) that are not owned by the publisher.

Print book interior design by Diahann Sturge.

Library of Congress Cataloging-in-Publication Data has been applied for.

ISBN: 9780306827297 (hardcover); 9780306827303 (ebook)

Printed in China

APS

10 9 8 7 6 5 4 3 2 1

DEDICATION

To my mother, Jeanne Allen West Frank Richman. You were the best mother I could have ever asked for. Thank you for instilling in me the ethics and ideologic values that gave me the foundation to be who I am today. You taught me to be kind, generous, compassionate, empathetic, and passionate about my life and my life's work. You told me I could do anything if I just set my mind to it. Without you, I would not be me. And to my dad and stepmom who always believed in me and were so very proud of me and who I turned out to be. Thank you, Mom, Dad, and Arlene, I know you are still watching over me from the Spirit World and helping me with all that I continue to do.

And to Chef Walter Whitewater, for all the food he has cooked with me on this project and over the many, many years we have worked together. And for all the cooking he continues to do in the field and in the kitchen with Native American Ancestral foods, Native American Cuisine, and his traditional foodways. Thank you, Walter, for working with me to keep alive Native Ancestral foods for health and wellness.

To my family for their unyielding love and support in all that I do and throughout my life.

And to all the Native elders, Native American cooks, Native American chefs, and chefs preparing Native American Cuisine, who shared their traditional foodways, dishes, Ceremonies,

and Feasts, and opened their homes and hearts, invited me into their kitchens to cook and to eat at their tables, and to all those who carry, share, revitalize, and re-indigenize the knowledge of Ancestral Native American food traditions.

Thank you.

Top: *Walter Whitewater with the author, Lois Ellen Frank.* Bottom: *Lois Ellen with farmer Matt Romero.*

CONTENTS

ACKNOWLEDGMENTS

Many people contributed to this project, more than I ever could have imagined, and I am grateful to each and every one of them for their support and help.

The spirit of this book comes from the need to eat more plants for health and wellness in Native communities. Therefore, I am deeply indebted to all the Grandmas, Aunties, Sisters, and women who invited me into their kitchens to learn traditional recipes from which I have developed plant-based modern versions. Thank you for sharing with me your traditional dishes and traditional ways of cooking these Ancestral ingredients.

I would like to express my deepest gratitude to the following people:

Walter Whitewater for his Native American Cuisine culinary advice, for helping test the recipes for this book (sometimes many times), for his amazing food styling and beautiful artistic plating of each dish that we photographed for this cookbook, and for sharing all his knowledge on the Ancestral and traditional foods in his family, family lineage, and from his people. He worked many tireless hours on the completion of this cookbook. Thank you, Walter, I am forever indebted to you, and we couldn't have done it without you.

To Marianne Sundquist for coming in at the perfect time in the process of this cookbook, for taking on testing all the recipes, sometimes multiple times, for helping to develop creative ways and easy methods for readers to prepare them, and for helping me simplify recipes with complicated directions. All with a smile and always willing to do whatever it took to get it all done. For reading through all the recipes with me and helping to edit them, and for being one of the most organized chefs I have ever worked with. For coming to the photo shoots and making the recipes, in some cases double to triple the recipe so that Walter could style the food for the beautiful photographs throughout this cookbook. And for helping me plan recipes on the photo shoot days so that we could eat balanced meals. Thank you.

To Aurora Fernandez, whom I have known since she was a teenager, and who got us started early on in the cookbook process and helped to test some of the first recipes and develop some of the recipes in the cookbook and work with us on the beginning photos and first photo shoot of the cookbook. Thank you, Aurora.

To Daphne Hougard, with whom I went to Brooks Institute of Photography and who is one of the most talented location photographers I know. She was the digital supervisor and location photographer creating beautiful photos of me at the Santa Fe Farmers' Market, Matt Romero's farm, and Jose Gonzalez's farm. She skillfully worked

Adobe Lightroom to keep the team on track, allowing us instant feedback on our work. You are so talented, Daphne, we could not have done this cookbook without you.

To Terri Graves, a very creative and talented woman and friend who did the props and prop styling for the photographs. Terri, you were always able to find the perfect plate, perfect bowl, the perfect background. Thank you for all the tireless hours you spent in the studio with us creating magical photos with our dream team.

To Melissa K. Nelson for writing a beautiful foreword. You are so eloquent with your words, an amazing Native academic, a creative, kind educator and patient teacher, and so supportive of all the work I do. Thank you.

To everyone at The Cultural Conservancy (TCC) for supporting us with the permission to use the words *Seed to Plate and Soil to Sky*, which is so much a part of the work you do.

To Matt Romero and José Gonzalez, two of my favorite local farmers, for letting us come out to your farms and make beautiful photos of all the amazing food that you grow and that I use in my cooking. Thank you.

To my wonderful and talented cookbook agent, Leigh Eisenman, of Wolf Literary Services, who worked tirelessly with me on the cookbook proposal and then got me the best cookbook contract with the best publisher and editor ever.

To my wonderful, amazing, heartfelt, and easy-to-work-with editor, Renée Sedliar, who helped me articulate the words and flow of the cookbook. Thank you. I enjoyed working with you every step of the way to create this cookbook that I am so proud of.

To everyone at Hachette Book Group that helped create this beautiful book. Diahann Sturge, the designer; Sara Pinsonault, the cookbook cover designer; Cisca Schreefel, senior production editor; Martha Whitt, copyeditor; Lauren Rosenthal, of the publicity department. Thank you. To Anna Campagna, the designer who did Red Mesa Cuisine's logo almost twenty years ago, who came in at the end of this cookbook process and helped me with proofreading and typography tweaks.

To Wilmer (Chibbon) Kavena, for helping me with making the hominy corn and culinary ash and for making me tons of culinary ash to use for testing the recipes that use ash. Thank you.

To Angela Smith Kirkman of Paseo Pottery in Santa Fe, who made the beautiful platter for the photo on page 141. Thank you. And to all the Native American artists whose beautiful pottery appears throughout this cookbook, thank you.

To all the many tribes, Pueblos, and people who have been a part of my life since I started working with Native Ancestral foods and Native American Cuisine in the 1980s and who taught me about the traditional foods and Native American foodways in this cookbook. Thank you.

And to all those who are not mentioned here but impacted me and my life on this path of using Ancestral Native American foods for health and wellness. Thank you.

We respectfully acknowledge that we are based on traditional lands of the Tewa People, O'gah'poh geh Owingeh (white shell water place) now known as Santa Fe, New Mexico.

Friendship and Collaboration Through Native Foodways

I first met Lois Ellen Frank and Walter Whitewater in 2003 at a Slow Food meeting. I was there to learn more about the emerging Slow Food movement in the United States and see how to respectfully include Native American communities who have been practicing "slow food" for millennia. At that time, I was less familiar with the extraordinary agrobiodiversity of the Southwest Indigenous farming traditions. I was in awe of the diversity of foods and seeds Lois and Walter brought to share, multiple varieties of corn, chiles, squashes and gourds, and several beautiful red, brown, and white beans. After a whirlwind virtual tour with gorgeous photos, engaging stories, and chef demonstrations, we tasted and savored some of the magnificent foods we just learned about. Summer squash–stuffed Hatch chiles with moist mushroom tamales and tepary bean dip with blue corn bread were absolutely mouthwatering. After their talk and our meal, we connected personally, and it was like meeting a long-lost sister and brother.

We have been deep friends and colleagues ever since and have worked together, in various contexts, for the health and well-being of Indigenous communities through Native foodways. Many of our food projects have been

through The Cultural Conservancy, the Native-led Indigenous rights organization for which Lois and I both serve on the board of directors and that I directed from 1993 to 2021. Through our Native Foodways Program, we have worked with various urban and rural tribal communities. Lois has helped us create recipes and has taught in-person and online cooking classes to our tribal partners.

It's been enriching to also dive into growing Native foods and learning together as we share heirloom seeds and gardening practices. The Cultural Conservancy now manages two Indigenous farms in Coast Miwok territory in Northern California. At these sites we grow most of the "magic eight" Lois writes about so beautifully in this book: corn, beans, squash, chiles, tomatoes, and potatoes, but not cacao and vanilla. It's important to honor these sacred foods of the Americas; this book does just that as it takes us on a historical, culinary, nutritional, and cultural journey through their complex genealogies and pathways to our plates.

It is ironic and sadly typical that these foods were identified, cultivated, and loved by Indigenous ancestors for thousands of years before being "discovered" by European nations. Everyone on the planet knows and eats these foods, often daily. But very few know and understand the Indigenous Traditional Ecological Knowledge (TEK) and deep kinship relationships that Indigenous Peoples historically had and still have today for these "life sustainers" as the Haudenosaunee refer to the Three Sisters (corn, beans, and squash).

Lois has a very practical approach to getting more culturally relevant, nutrient-dense, plant-based foods onto Native people's plates; she is famous for helping people find affordable Three Sisters ingredients like organic corn at Walmart or Trader Joe's to feed their families on a budget. This pragmatism is essential and complemented with a deeply reverential approach to these first foods, as she holds them in high esteem, respecting each nation's unique cultural relationship with the foods. "Seed to Plate" honors the practical side of growing Indigenous heirloom seeds to fruition. Lois demonstrates how to respect the whole life cycle of these foods by processing and cooking them with reverence, so when they end up on our plate and in our bellies, they are true medicine. This book shows us how we can decolonize our diets, one seed and meal at a time. "Soil to Sky" helps us to recognize the spiritual dimensions of our foods and their essential and holy bond with the soil, the very body of Mother Earth that gives us all life. This cycle is complete when we move from soil to Father Sky and recognize the cosmological dimensions that animate our lifeways. This book honors Native American food wisdom and transforms the way we think about daily nourishment.

Melissa K. Nelson
(Turtle Mountain Chippewa)
Professor of Indigenous Sustainability,
Arizona State University
Chair of the Cultural Conservancy
Salt River Valley,
Akimel O'odham/Piipaash Territory
April 24, 2022

Joel Gonzalez making a New Mexican traditional roasted sweet corn called chicos *in the earthen oven on the Gonzalez Family Farm in Lynden, New Mexico.*

INTRODUCTION

The Magic Eight: The Plants That Native Peoples Shared with the World

I always knew I wanted to work with food. It was a part of my dreams and visions growing up. I grew up with an innate knowledge that food was the nourishment and medicine we need to sustain ourselves.

My family ancestry and cultural heritages are mixed. My mom always told me that all people were like the different colors of corn. She told us that since we had mixed ancestry, we were like the beautifully multicolored speckled corn, and I always thought that this was a wonderful way to describe who we were. I grew up on Long Island in New York, mostly with my dad's side of the family. My mom always had a garden. I remember her growing corn, beans, squash, tomatoes, and other crops, using straw as mulch to keep the moisture and nutrients in the soil and placing leftover vegetables scraps in the garden under the straw to decompose, before it was called compost. She always instilled in us to care for the earth and the land and that the earth would care for us.

I am the chef/owner of Red Mesa Cuisine, a small catering company where I cook and work with Chef Walter Whitewater. Walter is Diné from the small town of Pinon, Arizona, on the Navajo Reservation. We have been cooking together since the early 1990s, and our mission has always been to educate people on the history of Native American Cuisine and the contributions that Native Peoples have given to some of the foods we eat every day. Eight of these foods—corn, beans, squash, chile, tomato, potato, vanilla, and cacao—which I call the Magic Eight, were given to the world by Native Peoples of the Americas. Part of Red Mesa Cuisine's mission is to provide Indigenous foods and cultural education. We like to call it Native American Cuisine with a modern twist.

Walter's family adopted me into their way of being in the world, and my family adopted Walter into our family. He is truly considered a brother to me and my siblings, and a son to my parents when they were alive. We have both had tremendous impacts on each other's lives. Learning and living the traditions of Walter's family has been influential to my work and has taught me about many foods and dishes that have been in the Whitewater family lineage for millennia. I have worked with Diné (Navajo) families from many different communities and learned many different traditional recipes from them. I have also worked with many Pueblo communities and Native families in New

Chef Walter Whitewater and the author

Mexico and Arizona. Through increasing my own personal knowledge on Native foods and foodways, my work is focused on and dedicated to health and wellness, improving diets with Native American Ancestral foods, and passing this information on to future generations.

Through decades of working with Native American communities in the Southwest on traditional foods and foodways, the elders have taught me where to find, how to harvest, and how to prepare Native American foods. I have had the honor of cooking alongside generations of Native women in their kitchens. Through them I have learned traditional methods of cooking and, from that, while honoring tradition, created new approaches to these traditional foods.

Throughout this cookbook I use the terms *Native American, American Indian, Indigenous, Native,* and *Native Peoples*—all of which are how the People here in the Southwest refer to themselves. I refer to the People here as they call themselves first and then provide the names by which they may be commonly called by others.

Please note that there are many recipes not included in this book and that I do not represent all Peoples of this region and all foodways that have existed here for thousands of years. What I do present in this book is a sample of the abundance of foods and recipes of Native American Southwestern cuisine and a snapshot of how intricate and diverse the cuisine in the Southwest is. Some of the recipes are presented as they have been prepared for millennia, while others are contemporary versions of traditional dishes. Still others are creative, nutritious, and delicious recipes featuring the ingredients of this region. For example, Walter grew up eating Navajo kneel down bread (*nitsidigo'i'*), which is traditionally made with just sweet corn, but he wanted to add a modern twist to the recipe, so he added golden raisins, which were part of the food distribution program foods he grew up with; dried currants, which he remembers hand-harvesting; and apples, which are nutritious, delicious, and easily accessible. Some recipes like Grilled Sweet Corn may be familiar to you but perhaps not without butter, and the recipe I present here features red and green chile with some citrus and sunflower oil for an emulsion that doesn't have the saturated fat that butter has.

Other recipes you may be familiar with, but you may not know that they are made here in the Southwest and are a part of Southwestern cuisine. For example, enchiladas are made on many of the Pueblos and have been for generations. Jemez Pueblo is famous for their version, called the Jemez Enchilada. A variation of this dish is served at the Indian Pueblo Kitchen located in the Indian Pueblo Cultural Center kitchen in Albuquerque and at many Pueblo Feast Days. Tamales are another Southwestern staple that are made in a variety of ways with an assortment of ingredients. Some food historians estimate that Native Americans have been preparing corn soaked and cooked in wood ash for thousands of years, combining this corn masa with beans, squash, chiles, and other ingredients and then wrapping them in corn husks to make the first tamales that are a Native American dish and served throughout the Americas. I've included some yummy plant-based versions of both enchiladas and tamales in this book, recipes that I've tasted over the years and then put my own spin on them. And some recipes, like the Native American Wild Rice & Sweet Corn Sauté (Manoomin) (page 52), include hand-harvested wild rice from the Great Lakes area of the United States and portions of Canada, which is a Native ingredient but not native to the Southwest. However, because it is very nutritious and an important part of a healthy Native American diet, I've included it in the chapters that follow as well. I'm an advocate for purchasing this wild rice and other native ingredients from Native-owned suppliers to support important Native American Indigenous foods (see the Source Guide for Native Foods on page 277).

Another example is the Blue Corn Pasta recipe (page 43). Because I love pasta, Chef Marianne Sundquist (who is Italian and helped test and develop some of the recipes in the cookbook) and I created a blue corn pasta recipe that features blue corn, doesn't use eggs, and preserves the integrity of the blue corn. Chef Walter has been the culinary advisor on all the recipes and helped to modernize some of the traditional recipes for the home cook while keeping the essence of the traditional version intact.

The focus solely on plant-based recipes in this cookbook is for several reasons. Chef Walter and I want to encourage people to use plants that are nutritious and delicious, and that can be incorporated into our lives as part of a healthy lifestyle and healthy diet without losing flavor. I think that cooking with plants is harder to do than with meat proteins, and the challenge here has been to make delicious plant-based recipes to help incorporate more plants into all our diets. More and more health professionals are promoting a plant-forward diet, and this has been an important mission to me and Chef Walter in our cooking. If any information has been excluded in the body of work I present here or it has offended any of the Peoples that share this region, this has not been our intention.

The foods and plants celebrated in this book were not only important in the past but are crucial to the future. The food traditions here are alive and vibrant, and their importance is realized by many different cultural groups that now share the Southwest. Food has always been more than something just to eat. Some of the foods we focus on in this book are used in Ceremony, as medicine, and to heal. For me, food has always been something that is meant to be shared, even when there is only a small amount to go around. My mother always revered food and told us to share all that we had. She said that when we share something with others, in this case food, that more will be bestowed upon us through the act of sharing. Thus, the act of sharing gives something to the sharer, more than the food itself. She grew up without much and she never wasted anything. All food was saved, and she had a zero-waste policy, which I now continue to this day at Red Mesa Cuisine. Everything is used and everyone is fed.

Please join us in rediscovering the nutritional benefits of these foods and honoring their heritage. Whether you gather your own foods and cook with these recipes or simply read to educate yourself, I hope you take away how important these foods are and how they will help you appreciate and honor the Southwest and the Native communities that live here. And I hope that this book inspires you to pursue knowledge and an understanding of the importance of these foodways for the health and wellness of the generations that are still yet to come.

The Foods That Native Peoples Gave to the World

Seed to Plate, Soil to Sky is the story of eight plants that Native peoples gave to the world: corn, beans, squash, chiles, tomatoes, potatoes, vanilla, and cacao. Prior to 1492, these plants existed *only* in the Americas. Once these plants were introduced to cultures of the world outside of the Americas, sometimes referred to as "Old World,"[1] those cuisines were changed forever.

The originators of agriculture in the Americas were, of course, the Indigenous Peoples here. By the time Europeans reached this land, many of the Native cultures had made the transition to growing and cultivating plants, using hunting and gathering to supplement the produce from their fields. Native communities were cultivating these eight plants in different regions throughout the Americas, creating a Native American Cuisine that I think is one of the most underrepresented cuisines in the world, yet a cuisine that is rich in flavor, nutritious, and extremely diverse in origin.

These eight plants, now found in almost every cuisine all over the world, are inherently

Native American and are the foundation to the foods we cook at Red Mesa Cuisine. And they are an important part of Native American Cuisine. Think about this: the Italians didn't have the tomato until after 1492. The Irish didn't have the potato. In Britain, they had fish but no chips. The Russians didn't have the potato, nor did they have vodka or distilled spirits from the potato. Corn, beans, and squash were not a part of any of the world's cuisines. There were no chiles in any East Indian cuisine dishes, including curries, and no chiles existed in any Asian cuisines at all. As a matter of fact, chiles weren't introduced into South Asia until the 1500s, when they would come to dominate the world spice trade in the sixteenth century. Vanilla and cacao weren't used in

any confection dishes prior to 1492. Ecuador, Belize, and the United States are also known for making some of the world's finest chocolate; however, Belgium, Switzerland, France, the United Kingdom, Italy, and the Ivory Coast, which are now known for making some of the best chocolates in the world, didn't have cacao.

Cacao was first cultivated some four thousand years ago in ancient Mesoamerica by pre-Olmec cultures, the first known civilizations to turn the cacao plant into chocolate. They cultivated cacao plants found in the tropical rain forests by fermenting, roasting, and grinding the cacao beans into a paste that is thought to have been mixed with water, vanilla, honey, chile, and other spices to brew a frothy chocolate drink. They used their chocolate

during rituals but also as medicine. Olmec, Mayan, and Aztec cultures found chocolate to be an invigorating drink, a mood enhancer, and an aphrodisiac. These beans were so coveted that they were used as a form of currency.

What's so fascinating is that the average American today, even those who cook with these foods regularly, doesn't know this history. Many people are unaware of the contribution Native peoples have made to the foods we eat every day; the story of these eight ingredients is an important one that needs to be told. And so, this book relays the little-known history of these magical plants and so much more. I believe this food has a story of how it nurtured the Ancestors of the Americas and sustained generations. Corn, beans, and squash, also called the Three Sisters, are connected to the culture of Native peoples. The Three Sisters are considered to be a sacred gift from the Great Spirit to support the health of the People. Besides providing nearly all the nutrients needed to sustain human life, the way these vegetables grow together is a perfect example of permaculture, creating a self-sufficient and sustainable ecosystem. The understanding of sustainability is based on the philosophy that all things are integrally connected. For instance, corn draws nitrogen from the soil while beans replenish it. The tall cornstalks provide climbing poles for the bean tendrils. And the broad leaves of squashes grow low to the ground, shading the soil, keeping it moist, and deterring the growth of weeds. Many Native communities hold that a healthy environment means a healthy culture, which ultimately means a healthy people.

Originating in Mesoamerica, these three crops were brought northward, up through river valleys over generations, to tribes in what is now the United States and Canada, where they were used for food and trade. The Iroquois or Haudenosaunee ("People of the Longhouse") of the northeastern United States refer to the Three Sisters in their stories, describing how these plants emerged from the first garden as sisters to help and support one another. The term *the Three Sisters* also refers to the companion agricultural practice of planting corn, pole beans, and squash (such as pumpkins) together in mounds.

Kaylena Bray, who is Seneca from Cattaraugus Territory in western New York along Lake Erie, and the former Native Foodways Program director at The Cultural Conservancy, as well as an academic now living in Piermont, New York, talks about how she was taught about these Sisters, spirits collectively referred to as *Jöhéhgöh* (meaning "those who support us" or "our sustainers"). Kaylena, along with her parents, Wendy and David Bray, shared their sacred Seneca white corn with The Cultural Conservancy, and it now grows in Northern California in Marin County.

And Clayton Brascoupe (Mohawk/ Anishnabeg) of the Iroquois Confederacy, a founding member and program director of the Traditional Native American Farmers Association (TNAFA), a nonprofit intertribal association of Indigenous farmers, gardeners, educators, and health professionals with a mission to revitalize traditional agriculture for spiritual and human need, and who lives at New Mexico's Tesuque Pueblo, just north of Santa Fe, has practiced traditional agriculture here in the Southwest for many years now and emphasized that there have always been multiple varieties of corn, beans, and squash planted together in fields here as well.

The Ancestral Puebloans of the Southwest have grown corn, beans, and squash for thousands of years; even today, the technique of planting the three types of vegetables in the same proximity, mound, or waffle garden (an ecological method of conserving water in dry land environments) is found at many Pueblos and on some farms in Northern New Mexico. This sophisticated, sustainable system cares for both the People and the earth, providing a healthy diet and long-term soil fertility.

Many people are unaware of the contribution Native Peoples have made to the foods we eat every day. When Chef Walter and I prepare these foods, we revitalize everything associated with them. And when we feed people, we nurture them while still honoring the Native American Ancestors.

A Timeline of Native American Cuisine

There are four distinct food periods that now make up this cuisine:

First, the **Precontact Period**, beginning from over twenty thousand years ago[2] and evolving until contact with Europeans. The People from this period used petroglyphs and pictographs to document historical events, such as epidemics, food shortages, droughts, and other important events, such as how to harvest, how to plant, what to plant, etc. This vital information is a part of a form of Indigenous Science called Traditional Ecological Knowledge (TEK) that is passed down through generations via traditional songs, stories, and beliefs; it is the foundation of Native communities today. TEK is a form of food sovereignty that includes food security and environmental justice. It connects Native Peoples to their land, their community, and culture. (For more on TEK and food sovereignty, see pages 13–17.) Ceremonies have always honored many of the sacred foods that are a part of this period, giving gratitude to everything that is harvested, hunted, and procured. Thus, the health of the land and the health of the People are inextricably linked.

Some of the foods from the precontact period include corn, beans, squash, chiles, tomatoes, potatoes, vanilla, and cacao, along with wild foods including carrots, celery, onions, garlic, greens, spinach, purslane greens, cacti, mushrooms, and all types of wild fruits, grains, and nuts including sunflower seeds, piñon nuts, pecans, acorns, mesquite beans, amaranth—and many more. Wild animals were a part of the precontact period diet, as well as lots of medicinal plants used for teas, tinctures, and other healing uses.

Extensive trade routes have been documented, especially with Mesoamerica, but primarily dried goods were traded. In 2009, an analysis of ceramics in Pueblo Bonito, the largest site in Chaco Canyon in northwestern New Mexico, documented for the first time the presence of theobromine, a marker for *Theobroma cacao,* or chocolate, indicating that cacao was consumed in the American Southwest around A.D. 1000 to 1125.[3] Items such as seeds, shells, beads, turquoise, and feathers were traded between the tribes from this region and tribes to the south, which supports the idea that several trade mechanisms operated simultaneously.[4] Sometimes trade occurred because items were not available locally, but the exchange also confirmed social bonds between groups. With the use of grinding stones, seeds, nuts, and corn were ground into flour for breads, mush, and other uses. As much as 85 to 90 percent of the Ancestral Pueblo diet consisted of calories consumed from agricultural products, with wild fruits, greens, nuts, and small game making up the balance. Because larger game was scarce, textiles and corn were traded with the Plains tribes for bison meat.[5]

The precontact period is probably the most diverse and most important part of Native American Cuisine. Activities related to foods were, and still are, central to many Native communities in the Southwest. What are now classified as art forms in these communities were originally made for purposes centered around food. Chef Walter stated that plants are not picked randomly or wastefully. In his Navajo way of being, the Diné direct a prayer to the plant to explain why its neighbor will be harvested. An offering is made and then the harvester picks only what they need to use. After the plant is harvested, and then prepared into food, the plant remains are put back to the earth with a final prayer. A good example are the corn husks used to cook corn in the oven: Chef Walter uses these burned corn husks after the corn has been cooked as a garnish on his beautifully designed plates, so as not to waste these husks and to create art from the ingredients he cooks with. These corn husks are not wasted. Chef Walter and I follow a traditional protocol with any of the wild foods we harvest for any culinary event in which we prepare and use these foods. Each plant is considered sacred, and they must be respected if they are to continue to be effective in helping to heal and feed humans. Chef Walter states, "Plants were and are harvested not only as medicine but also as food, for making tools, and in some instances for making clothing."

Second, the **First Contact Period**, with foods introduced to Native communities from Europe after 1492. In the 1500s the Spanish entered the American Southwest from Mexico. In 1540, the Spanish conquistador Francisco Vasquez de Coronado and his party arrived at the cornfields of Zuni Pueblo, demanding food, and the departure of Pueblo life as they had known it had begun. The Spanish changed the traditional way of life and altered an Ancestral food history that would never be the same.[6] Probably the biggest and most profound introduction was that of domesticated animals and their by-products. Because Native Peoples only hunted wild game, there was no dairy. The Spanish also brought additional varieties of chiles, tomatoes, potatoes, cultivated prickly pears, epazote, and so on, north from the tribes of Mesoamerica to the South. Bread made from wheat was introduced to the New Mexico Pueblos in horno ovens, constructed from adobe and earth, further changing the corn-based diet here. Once these foods were woven into the Native American diet, in many instances, they became inseparable from the identity of the People.

Third, **Government-Issue Period**, during which foods were imposed onto Native communities during the relocation and Indian reservation era of the 1800s. The most historically traumatic and the most detrimental in terms of Native foods and traditional foodways, this is the period of forced relocation of Native Peoples from their Ancestral lands onto Reservations and the issuing of commodity foods by the US government. Some Native communities remained on and in their Ancestral areas, but the land mass and size of those areas was drastically reduced. When Congress initiated the Federal Indian Removal Act of 1830, more than one hundred thousand Native Americans east of the Mississippi River were evicted and forced to Indian Territory in Oklahoma, disrupting traditional ways of life, Ceremonial calendars, and foodways. The loss of lands was devastating. Native Peoples have always called the earth their Mother, or Turtle Island, and revered their association with the land and all that the land provided for them. The United States government would ultimately determine where Native tribes could live, hunt, fish, farm, gather, harvest, and eat.[7]

On August 10, 1864, Captain John Thompson and Colonel Christopher "Kit" Carson destroyed countless crops, including roughly four thousand Navajo peach trees in Canyon de Chelly, on their way to Fort Canby, Arizona (formerly Ft. Defiance), after overtaking Barboncito, the leader of the de Chelly Navajos, who had no choice other than to finally surrender. After the majority of their sheep were slaughtered, their crops burned, and their orchards cut down, the Navajo people surrendered and accepted deportation to the Bosque Redondo Reservation at Fort Sumner, in southeastern New Mexico.[8] They were marched at gunpoint from their traditional lands, and this approximately four-hundred-mile walk is known as the Long Walk of the Navajo. The entire period of incarceration on the Bosque Redondo Reservation at Fort Sumner is called *Hwéeldi* in Navajo. Between 1863 and 1868, thousands died from the inhumane conditions at the camp. In 1865, more than 450 of the Ndé (Mescalero Apaches) escaped, but the Diné (Navajo) remained there for another three years until the US government intervened and allowed them to make the return walk home, with nearly one-third of the People dying before being permitted to return to their homelands.[9]

Foodways and life among Native peoples changed dramatically during this period. Foodways are particularly entrenched in cultural identity. They are the earliest layers of culture to form and the last to erode.[10] During the relocation and incarceration period, the government-issued food rations to relocated tribes which originally included beans, beef (sometimes bacon), lard, flour, coffee, and sugar, which were distributed twice a month. The Native American diet during this period included foods that Native communities struggled to incorporate into dishes and recipes. As time passed, additional foods were issued as part of the commodity food program, such as cheese, egg mix, nonfat dry and evaporated milk, pasta, rice, other grains, dehydrated potatoes, peanut butter, crackers, corn syrup, vegetable shortening, and canned or frozen meat, poultry, and fish.

Top: *Monument Valley (Tse'Bii'Ndzisgaii), Totem Pole, and Yei Bi Chei.* Bottom: *Canyon de Chelly, Navajo Fortress.*

Top: *Monument Valley, Mittens buttes.* Bottom: *Canyon de Chelly, White House Ruins.*

Today, as noted on USDA's website, the Food Distribution Program on Indian Reservations (FDPIR), a food and nutrition service, "provides USDA Foods to income-eligible households living on Indian Reservations and to Native American households residing in designated areas near reservations or in Oklahoma." FDPIR offers a wide variety of fresh fruits and vegetables, frozen meats, whole grains, and traditional foods.[11] Participating tribal communities today can select from more than seventy products to help them maintain a nutritionally balanced diet. Chef Walter and I work with several of these programs, showing community members how to use some of the distributed foods in healthy recipes that are nutritious and taste good.

Fry bread and the Indian Tacos (both now pan-Indian dishes) were born from the government-issue period. This period is the most painful and most difficult in terms of health and wellness in Native American Cuisine history. I, along with some other academics working in Native Studies, sometimes refer to this initial period as one of nutritional genocide.

Fourth, **New Native American Cuisine**, contemporary times, which have seen Native communities returning to and reclaiming the healthy foods of their past to move forward into the future for their own health and wellness. For the first time in history, Native American chefs and cooks are defining what foods should be included in this category. Chef Walter's focus is on using Ancestral Native American ingredients along with healthy introduced foods from all the other periods (primarily the precontact and first contact periods), which he and I now serve with a modern twist at Red Mesa Cuisine. However, some Native American chefs are presenting precontact or solely precolonial ingredients on their menus; others serve a combination of precontact and first contact foods, and still others are presenting a combination of all three of the historic food periods on their menus. It's now up to each Native American community and each Native American chef to decide what the New Native American Cuisine is and what they are going to serve on their plates.

Tocabe, an American Indian Eatery in Denver where diners can build-their-own Indian tacos, is the only American Indian–owned and –operated restaurant in Metro Denver specializing in Native American Cuisine. According to their website, as part of the Osage Nation, Tocabe utilizes American Indian roots to help educate people on Indigenous culture. In Minneapolis, founder/CEO Chef Sean Sherman and co-owner/COO Dana Thompson opened Owamni, by the Sioux Chef, a modern Indigenous James Beard–award winning restaurant serving foods from the precontact period. And Brian Yazzie (a.k.a. Yazzie the Chef) defines himself as cooking in two worlds: he has a catering company, Intertribal Foodways, and is now the executive chef at the Gatherings Café located in the Minneapolis American Indian Center. Crystal Wahpepah, chef and owner of Wahpepah's Kitchen in Oakland, California, features foods that she views as a portal to food sovereignty and a reclamation of Ancestral knowledge in Native and Indigenous communities. At Thirty Nine Restaurant at First Americans Museum in Oklahoma City, chefs Bard Harris and Loretta

Barrett Oden serve Modern Indigenous Cuisine. Sherry Pocknett is the executive chef and owner of Sly Fox Den in Charlestown, Rhode Island, a Native American restaurant serving East Coast regional specialties promoting local seasonal foods and traditions of the Mashpee Wampanoag. And Chef Nephi Craig opened Café Gozhóó a Western Apache Cafe in Whiteriver, Arizona, integrating the tastes and flavors of Apache foodways. For Craig, it's the end of a long journey and the beginning of a new one—one of healing, reciprocity, restoration, and nutritional recovery.

There are Native American chefs all over the United States opening restaurants, cafés, and eateries both in urban areas and on Ancestral tribal lands. Today is a great time to be a chef, especially for Native American chefs, and I hope that young Native chefs will be inspired to continue the legacy of these important foods and Native American Cuisine. Today there is a Native foods movement focusing on food sovereignty, the revitalization of Native American foods, and the re-indigenizing of Ancestral Native American foods, and it is growing.

Reclaiming Indigenous Foods and Foodways

Traditional Ecological Knowledge (TEK) is one of the most important terms I have used when I have taught the Indigenous Concepts of Native American Food class over many years at the Institute of American Indian Arts (IAIA). Also sometimes called Indigenous Knowledge, or Native Science, TEK is the foundation to understanding Native American Food Sovereignty and how Native American communities and community members can re-indigenize their bodies, minds, and way of being in the world. TEK is an Indigenous Science that has accumulated over thousands of years' experience and observations of relationships among living beings that are a part of a specific ecosystem, including the myriad of interactions with people, plants, animals, landscapes, and environmental factors.[12] An important way to understand ideological concepts of what it is to be Native and how to live sustainably in the world, TEK is the perpetuation of the wisdom of the ancestors, information that is handed down through generations by traditional songs, stories, beliefs, and a part of Native American physical, mental, emotional, and spiritual wellness. It is used for life-sustaining knowledge and ways of living in the world, and its application here, specifically surrounding food and foodways, includes traditional methods of food procurement and other types of knowledge systems surrounding food. And it is a vital method to implement positive change surrounding health and wellness in Native communities today.

Oral accounts taught by the elders in Native communities imprint this vital information on the younger generations. Where foods are concerned, elders have traditionally served as the tribal historians. They commit to memory a body of past experiences and cultural traditions relating to food—how to prepare specific dishes, how to find wild plants, which plants are edible, their names

Canyon de Chelly, Spider Rock

and their uses for food and medicine, when to plant and how to grow crops, how to prepare and store them—as well as a multitude of other information relating to food and its uses. Food is indeed more than something to eat. Food is medicine. The foods that make up Native American Cuisine are the Indigenous cultural traditions that are woven together into the fabric of life in Native American communities, like a beautiful blanket, of what it is to be Native American.

In the book *Original Instructions: Indigenous Teachings for a Sustainable Future*, edited by Melissa K. Nelson, PhD, a colleague and friend, she states, "There's no time like today to decolonize and re-indigenize our bodies, minds, and communities by taking back our food sovereignty. Our very survival, individually and collectively, may depend on us taking back control over the quality and production of the food we put into our bodies."[13] The phrase "Decolonizing Our Bodies, Nourishing Our Spirits" has become a central theme in Dr. Nelson's work.

Chef Walter and I like to say that in order to move forward to the future for health and wellness, everyone has to go back to the past to understand what happened, when it happened, and how it happened. That's why it is so vital and important to understand the history of what happened in the past and investigate why the Indigenous diet deviated from a healthy precontact diet—a diet that I call a "Nativevore Diet"—to the diet that exists today and what that means in terms of the future and Native American health and wellness. TEK, therefore, does not stand alone in understanding how

to move forward in the future. By using the ancient Ancestral foods of the past in contemporary kitchens, Native communities can reclaim a new Native American Cuisine based on the wild and cultivated foods of the past for health and wellness, and to solve contemporary health problems, now and in the future.

In *Recovering Our Ancestors' Gardens*, Devon A. Mihesuah says, "Even if we have access to our precontact foods today, often those nutritious foods are contaminated with pesticides, farm animal wastes, and genetically modified organisms. Still prior to the introduction of sugar and wheat flour, Indigenous peoples appeared to have suffered fewer food-related maladies than they do today—maladies such as type 2 diabetes, obesity, high blood pressure, and celiac disease. How can we become healthy?"[14] Her book offers a way to get started, and I often use parts of it when teaching the Indigenous Concepts of Native American Food class at IAIA.

In order to truly move in the direction of health and wellness in Native communities, there is a need to understand the concept of Native American Food Sovereignty and how this sovereignty is intricately tied to and a part of each Native American community's TEK. But what is Native American Food Sovereignty, anyway? Chef Walter Whitewater and I have this conversation on a regular basis. He believes, like some other Native American activists, that the word *sovereignty* is rooted in and comes from a European and Eurocentric system that is not Native at all. He doesn't like to use the word to define *what* Native American communities are reclaiming and *how* they are revitalizing their Indigenous foodways; he says that most of the Native American community members he knows don't know what the term means and that it is better to discuss how to do this in Native terms as opposed to non-Native terms. And Chef Whitewater believes that each Native community has their own way of doing this.

The Food Sovereignty definition includes prioritizing local agricultural production in order to feed the People, the right of farmers to produce food and the right of consumers to be able to decide what they consume, and how and by whom it is produced, the right of countries and Indigenous nations to protect themselves from too-low-priced agricultural and food imports, agricultural prices linked to production costs, populations taking part in the agricultural policy choices, and the recognition of the rights of women farmers, who play a major role in agricultural production and in food.[15] If I were to try to simplify the meaning of food sovereignty, it would mean the right to sufficient, healthy, culturally appropriate food. And I would emphasize the word *right*. Yet Native American Food Sovereignty can be localized even more so, with a focus on food justice, food security, environmental justice, knowledge that is dependent on TEK, and a means by which Native American communities can produce, grow, and harvest their own food and buy these foods from Native vendors and growers, and ultimately to acknowledge that all these factors help to reconnect these communities to their land, community, and culture.

In an interview for the Healthy Roots Project by Chelsea Wesner (Choctaw) at the University of Oklahoma's American Indian Institute (Aii), Joseph (Joey) Owle from the Eastern Band of Cherokee Indians stated, "Having attended the second annual Food Sovereignty Summit in Wisconsin hosted by the Oneida Nation, the motto of the conference really impacted me. It simply stated, 'How sovereign are we . . . if we can't feed ourselves?'" Mr. Owle went on to state, "As our tribe progresses with gardening and agricultural initiatives, I would like to see all families and individuals of this tribe create their own garden. At least with their own garden, a family or individual would then be producing some of the food they consume within a year. The ultimate goal is to have all the food we consume in a year be produced within our boundary. It is a lofty goal, but nonetheless, a goal to strive towards."[16] And many Native communities all over the Americas are now working on health and wellness initiatives to include gardens, educate their youth on planting traditional crops, and then follow up with cooking classes on how to prepare these foods.

So what are the next steps in terms of sustainability? Where do Native communities go from here? There is no exact formula for what to do and how to do it. Each Native community is working on creating their own steps that are relevant for their own community. And this to me seems like a good way to move forward. Some of the steps that communities are taking include objectives surrounding food and foodways and how to pass on culinary information in their own communities. These include:

- Reclaiming Ancestral foods for physical, mental, emotional, and spiritual wellness;

- Revitalizing traditional cooking techniques and the recipes associated with them;

- Educating and teaching children, teens, and adults of all ages the importance and role Ancestral foods play in health and wellness;

- Developing well-rounded culinary professional programs in both the theory and technique of food, foodways, and cuisine;

- Developing specialized workshops tailored toward individual and group needs that include but are not limited to health, nutrition, team-building, youth development, and technical skill enhancement, and other social and professional development;

- Creating an overall awareness of traditional and contemporary Native American culinary customs and technologies that include concepts of sustainable agriculture, health, and nutrition; and

- Emphasizing how the benefits of incorporating an Ancestral diet can improve health and connect Native American community members to their culture.

These educational steps lead to new outcomes and paradigm shifts. Chef Walter and I now use the following steps as teaching tools in the work we do in Native American communities, and I also use these steps in my academic teaching work, as well. These steps include:

- Activating Ancestral knowledge utilizing TEK and understanding the interactions with land and culture to inform practice;

- Creating and embedding Indigenous cultural links into standards of Indigenous cuisine;

- Recovering social values through Indigenous foods;

- Transitioning from a Western or Euro modern culinary methodology to one that reclaims Native traditional values for food, food practice, and food presentation surrounding Native American foodways;

- Using teaching methods and strategies that incorporate the history of Native American foods, including agricultural practices, wild food–harvesting techniques, food as medicine, and other methods to prepare Native foods that inform a cook's decisions on health and wellness for their community members all from a Native American perspective;

- Strengthening community partnerships with local, tribal, state, and federal programs and services that support food systems for health and wellness in Native American communities; and

- Identifying resources that assure accessibility to safe, fresh, and healthy foods.

I believe that there is room for everyone to participate in this Native American

Foods Movement and a place for everyone to become part of the sustainable future. Dr. Melissa K. Nelson has framed this as an Indigenous partnership, which she defines as short- and long-term reciprocal alliances between Indigenous groups, Native American tribes, communities, and organizations and other ethnic or Euro-American groups, organizations, and institutions where the Indigenous agenda(s) take priority. Dr. Nelson provides essential ingredients for these partnerships that include (1) Listening—what does the community really want and need; how do they want to work together? (2) Self-knowledge—each partner is rooted in an ethnic background, cultural identity, and useful position, (3) Acknowledging positions of power—there is explicit acknowledgment about differential positions of power and privilege, (4) Respect—for Indigenous cultural traditions and diverse worldviews including cultural privacy and intellectual property rights, (5) Time—to commit to a collaborative process, to building trust; to making a real difference; to both short- and long-term goals, (6) Reciprocity—mutual respect and shared decision-making process; all partners are learners and teachers, and finally, (7) Benefit-sharing—tangible and intangible benefits are outlined and a system for equity and sharing is outlined as part of the partnership.

Today is the time that is not only exciting but empowering for Native communities. To realize that everyone can play a role in the health and wellness of all people is a wonderful place to be. There is so much hope for the future. The time for re-indigenizing these foods in Native communities is now. The time for a sustainable future is now. The time for reclaiming and revitalizing Indigenous foods and foodways for Native American community members is now. Joseph Brophy Toledo, a cultural leader from Jemez Pueblo, and a wise and wonderful advocate for traditional foods and foodways, stated in 2021 that we are all "Earth People" and Indigenous to the earth and that in order for any of us to work toward health and wellness in any of our communities, we need to work together as caretakers and stewards of our Mother Earth.

What can you do? Buy ingredients from Native producers and growers to support these efforts and to support the Native American Foods Movement. There are some wonderful Native American food producers listed in the source guide (at the back of this book) where you can purchase wild rice, culinary ash, and cornmeal. Get involved and donate your time to a Native non-profit or organization, and/or your resources to a Native-run non-profit. My hope and wish is that everyone can work together toward a sustainable future and that these recipes inspire you to cook with these amazing nutritious and delicious Indigenous Ancestral plants for health and wellness.

Lois Ellen Frank, PhD,
Santa Fe, New Mexico

Monument Valley, East and West Mitten Buttes, and Merrick Butte

Corn

The story of corn begins about nine thousand years ago. The ancestor of corn, *teosinte* (meaning "God's corn" in Nahuatl), is actually a form of a wild grass. Yet how corn arose from *teosinte* has long been a subject of dispute among scientists and academics. I wonder how the Native American ancestors knew that it was edible and how they were able to grow it and develop it into the most important grain of the Americas, one that would become the essence of life to tribes from as far south as it will grow to as far north as it will grow. The domestication of corn was probably a rapid process, which took place over a sizable portion of Mexico and Guatemala, where the greatest number of cultivated maize varieties are grown today.

By the time of Columbus's voyage to the Americas—often referred to as the "New World"[17]—maize had been established throughout most of the continental North America east of the Colorado River, Central America, and the Caribbean Islands, where Columbus first encountered it. Corn was the only staple grown in both the Northern and Southern Hemispheres and still today grows virtually everywhere humans can grow crops.[18]

Because of the beauty of corn's colors and form, many Indigenous Peoples of the Americas developed around it a great culture of art, science, literature, and religion in addition to its importance as a food source. The significance of corn in these cultures' rituals and creation narratives is also a part of the story of corn. Each tribe has its own explanations for its origin and its variously colored strains. The story of corn is essentially the story of Old America and its many Native cultures. Corn is believed to be the plant of the greatest spiritual significance to the tribes of the Southwest. Some tribes consider corn to be Mother. Rituals using corn can be seen in pottery, jewelry, carvings, paintings, a variety of textiles, and in the Native cuisine of this region. The first harvest of corn is celebrated by some tribes in the East with the Green Corn Festival. These tribes share a tradition to honor the beginning of the yearly corn harvest with this festival, which usually takes place in July or August, depending locally on when the corn crop ripens.

Growing up, I was told that there are four significant colors of corn: yellow, white, blue or black, and red. Speckled corn is a blending together and mix of the four significant colors of corn. Some Native communities believe that the People are the caretakers of the corn and that they would be taught how to plant and harvest the corn, and how to use corn for food, medicine, prayer, and in ceremony.

Chef Walter Whitewater uses a special corn pollen as an offering to a new day beginning every morning and to the setting sun every evening. He greets the sun and thanks the Creator for the new day, and in the evening, he thanks the Creator for the day that is ending. Corn, to him, is medicine and he often uses the metaphor "food is our medicine," with corn being the first and foremost ingredient in his food. You'll see some of his uses of corn in recipes we collaborated on throughout this book. Corn to Chef Walter is not only food, it is medicine, with stories and songs, and it is art.

Corn is the most important ingredient in Native American Cuisine. The miracle of corn is that it grows only with the interaction of humans. It cannot grow without humans. And the fact that it grows at all in arid regions of the desert Southwest without irrigation is even more amazing. The corn plant itself represents the life cycle of the human being, from the planting of the seed to the stalks that are left in the fields to dry and wither until it is planted again in the spring, beginning a new cycle the following year. Corn leaves behind new kernels on each cob that can be planted again and become new life for future generations. Corn is woven into the culinary traditions of all the tribes in the Americas that revere it and is truly considered to be the essence of life. I know for me corn is a very sacred and a dominant ingredient in my cooking. I have been to many Pueblo dances in New Mexico over the years that honor corn. Each dance is unique to the specific Pueblo that performs it. The summer Corn Dances honor the Corn Mothers and are a part of some of the Feast Days from the nineteen Pueblos, many of which line the Rio Grande in New Mexico, and several others that are to the west of the river. The dances are magical. Standing in the plaza of a Pueblo watching dancers hold corncobs while they dance methodically to the beat of the drum is sacred. I feel honored and blessed to have been able to have seen these dances over the years. The rattles and drum are mesmerizing, and the sounds stay with me for days after the dances end.

The Indian Pueblo Cultural Center's website (www.indianpueblo.org) lists all the nineteen Pueblos of New Mexico's Feast Days and is a great resource for planning how and when to visit to see dances that are a part of the Native culture here in New Mexico. Always consult with each individual Pueblo to learn about the proper etiquette and appropriate dress for the Pueblo you intend to visit.

NIXTAMALIZED CORN OR ASH CORN

One of the biggest accomplishments by Native Peoples surrounding corn is the traditional Indigenous process called nixtamalization. Corn is soaked in an alkaline solution, like culinary ash, or treated with limewater, then it is washed, cooked, and hulled. Once processed, the whole corn kernels can be ground into a masa and used fresh for a variety of dishes including corn tortillas and tamales. When the kernels are left whole and dried, they become hominy corn (as it is called in most parts of the United States) or *posole*, named by the Spanish (and the term traditionally used here in New Mexico). The dried, treated corn kernels can then be ground into masa harina (corn flour).

Nixtamalization has been used by Indigenous Native communities for thousands of years. It is referred to as lye corn by the Iroquois or Haudenosaunee in the northeastern part of the United States and Canada, and it is commonly called nixtamalized corn by many of the Indigenous tribes to the south in Mexico and Central and South America. According to Chef Walter Whitewater, the Navajo refer to this type of treated corn as Nakai bi naadą́ą́, translated in Navajo to mean "Mexican corn." Many of the Pueblo people as well as the Diné (Navajo) people add the ash to the ground untreated corn, making a pudding or mush. Some Navajo communities make corn bread, pancakes, corn dumplings, and other dishes from the cornmeal and ash. The Hopi and some Pueblos make a blue corn bread dish called Piki or paper bread, where the culinary ash is added to ground untreated cornmeal.

The easiest way to get hominy corn is to buy it (see source guide); however, Chef Walter and I think it is important to know how to make it because it is such a key ingredient in so many traditional Native American dishes and an Ancestral process that is an integral part of many Native American cultures and communities. I was originally taught how to make hominy corn with culinary ash from Juanita Tiger Kavena, who has since passed, many years ago in the 1980s in First Mesa, Arizona, after her cookbook, *Hopi Cookery*, was released and her son, Wilmer (Chibbon) (Creek for little boy) Kavena, worked with me on the ash to corn ratio for this recipe.

There are many ways to nixtamalize corn, but it is generally a long process. It may be helpful to watch a video, so you have an idea of what to do. There are many videos on the internet. Native American dried corn or field corn is most commonly used, and the preferred color is white; however, blue, red, and yellow can also be processed this way (I tested this recipe with white corn, blue corn, and red corn. All worked, although the best result came from the white corn). Some of the farmers at the Santa Fe Farmers' Market who sell posole treat their corn with a food-grade lime (calcium hydroxide). However, most Native American communities use a culinary ash that they prepare themselves for this process.

Because the ash is so alkaline, you cannot use a metal or aluminum pot or spoon. The lye in the ash reacts strongly with metal. I make this corn using an enamel pot and a wooden spoon. Many cooks used a ratio of two to one, dried corn to ash, or one to one, dried corn to ash.

For Soaking the Corn Overnight:
1 cup dried white, blue, or red whole corn kernels
8 cups warm water

For the Cooked Hominy Corn:
Soaked corn
8 cups water, plus additional hot water as needed
½ cup culinary ash (page 255, or see source guide)

First soak the dried corn in a bowl filled with water and let it sit overnight. In the morning, drain the water and place the soaked corn into an enamel pot with 8 cups of water. Bring the soaked corn and water to a boil. Once it comes to a boil, add the culinary ash and stir. Continue stirring until the ash has completely mixed into the corn and water. When you add the ash, the corn will turn to an orange-yellow color if you are using the white corn. As the corn cooks, it will change back to a white color. Cover the pot, reduce the heat, and simmer for approximately 3 hours, or until the hulls become loose and the corn has turned white again. Check the cooking corn every hour or so to ensure that there is enough water in the pot. If the water becomes low, add some additional hot water, and continue to cook.

Once the hulls become loose on the corn (you can check this by removing a couple of kernels and rubbing them between your fingers), remove from the heat and drain. Rinse the ash from the corn in a colander under cold running water for several minutes. Then place the cooked corn in a large plastic bowl or plastic tub filled with cold water. Rub each kernel with your fingers to remove the hulls. Drain the corn again through a colander and then fill the bowl a second time. The skins, germs, and hulls will separate from the hominy corn. Drain the water again, pouring off any hulls, skins, or the germ that has separated from the corn. Do this process of rinsing at least three times.

After the corn has been completely cleaned, drain and set aside. The corn can be used immediately in a soup or stew, it can be ground into a masa, or it can be placed in a freezer bag, once it is completely cool, or airtight container and frozen for future use.

WHITE CORN TORTILLAS

Corn tortillas are readily available in most supermarkets; however, homemade corn tortillas are the best. In the time it takes you to go to the store and buy them, you could have made them. It's easy to do, and the more you do it, the quicker you get. For cooking my corn tortillas, I use a cast-iron *comal* or a large cast-iron pan. A *comal* is a smooth, flat cooking surface or griddle that is used throughout the Americas. It is commonly used to cook corn tortillas, but it is also used to cook spices and sear meat. It was traditionally made of pottery but is more often made of cast iron today. For pressing the corn masa, you will want to use a tortilla press. These are inexpensive to purchase and a worthwhile investment if you are going to make corn tortillas on a regular basis.

MAKES 12 TO 13 TACO-SIZE TORTILLAS

2 cups dried corn masa flour
   (see source guide, page 277)
½ teaspoon kosher salt
1½ cups warm water

In a medium mixing bowl, combine the corn flour, salt, and warm water. Mix with a spoon or your hands until you have formed a moist dough.

After the corn flour and water are completely mixed, use your hands to form balls just smaller than a Ping-Pong ball and set aside.

Preheat your *comal* over high heat until it is hot but not smoking.

In a tortilla press, place one ball in the center, and then press to make one corn tortilla. I use a plastic freezer bag that I cut in a circle to match the size of my tortilla press so that I have two pieces. I place the corn masa ball in between the two pieces of plastic so that it doesn't stick to the tortilla press. If you don't have a tortilla press, you can use a rolling pin and roll out the dough between the two pieces of plastic.

Gently remove the tortilla by peeling it off the plastic and place it on the hot *comal*. Cook the first side of the tortilla for 1½ minutes, then turn it over and cook until it puffs, for about 1½ minutes, until the tortilla is done.

Place the cooked tortilla in a kitchen towel inside a basket or bowl and prepare the next tortilla following the same steps. Stack the tortillas on top of one another to keep them warm inside the towel.

Serve warm with your favorite soup, stew, or tacos.

BLUE CORN TORTILLAS

Made just like a white corn tortilla, this recipe adds blue corn flour, making these tortillas a beautiful blue color and changing the flavor slightly to one that is both rich and earthy. Blue corn also has a nutty flavor, and you can taste that flavor in these corn tortillas. This recipe explains how to toast the blue corn flour, but you can also buy it already roasted. See source guide for where to find blue corn flour.

MAKES 10 TO 12 TACO-SIZE TORTILLAS

½ cup finely ground blue cornmeal
1½ cups dried corn masa flour (see source guide)
1 to 1¼ cups water
½ teaspoon kosher salt

First toast the blue cornmeal. To do this, heat a cast-iron skillet or heavy-bottomed pan over medium heat, add the cornmeal, and toast for approximately 8 to 10 minutes or until it turns a golden blue brown, stirring frequently to prevent burning and to ensure that the cornmeal toasts evenly. It will turn from a light-blue color to a light-blue, golden blue-brown color. Remove from heat and reserve.

In a medium mixing bowl, combine the toasted blue cornmeal, the corn masa flour, water, and salt and mix with your hands or a spoon until you have formed a moist dough. After it is completely mixed, form balls just smaller than a Ping-Pong ball and set aside.

Preheat your *comal* over high heat until it is hot but not smoking.

In a tortilla press, place one ball in the center, and then press to make one corn tortilla. I use a plastic freezer bag that I cut in a circle to match the size of my tortilla press so that I have two pieces. I place the corn masa ball in between the two pieces of plastic so that it doesn't stick to the tortilla press.

Gently remove the tortilla by peeling it off the plastic and place on it the *comal*. Cook the first side of the tortilla for 1½ minutes, then turn it over and cook again until it puffs, for approximately another 1½ minutes, until the tortilla is done.

Place the cooked tortilla in a kitchen towel inside a basket or bowl and prepare the next tortilla following the same steps. Stack the tortillas on top of one another to keep them warm inside the towel.

Serve warm with your favorite soup, stew, or recipe for tacos.

GLUTEN-FREE BLUE CORN BREAD

There is nothing like a warm, freshly made blue corncob bread right out of the oven. On a cold fall day with a nice bowl of soup or stew these breads are a sure bet with guests or for your family. This recipe is easy to make. It uses chia, an ancient grain indigenous to the Americas that now, with its many health benefits, is considered a superfood. I use an antique corncob-shaped cast-iron bread pan; new ones are also available. If you don't have a corncob bread pan, you can use a round cast-iron frying pan or square baking dish, it just takes longer for the corn bread to bake. Blue corncob bread can be served alongside lunch or dinner and for breakfast with fruit sauces and jellies.

MAKES 1 PAN OF CORN BREAD (APPROXIMATELY 8 X 8 INCHES) OR APPROXIMATELY 21 CORN STICKS IN A CORNCOB PAN

For the Dry Mix:
1¼ cups finely ground blue cornmeal
1¼ cups gluten-free all-purpose flour (I use the Trader Joe's brand because it can be used as a 1:1 substitute for all-purpose flour)
1 teaspoon kosher salt
¼ cup organic unbleached sugar
1 teaspoon baking soda

For the Wet Mix:
3 tablespoons ground chia seeds
1¾ cups oat milk
2 teaspoons apple cider vinegar
8 tablespoons vegan butter, melted
½ cup unsweetened applesauce

Preheat the oven to 425°F and place whatever size pan you are using—an 8 x 8-inch baking pan, a round cast-iron skillet approximately the same size, or cast-iron corncob pans—in the oven to heat while you are preparing the batter.

In a large mixing bowl, mix the dry ingredients. In another bowl, whisk together the wet ingredients. Let the wet mixture sit for 10 minutes. After 10 minutes, add the wet ingredients to the dry and fold together with a rubber spatula or spoon until a wet dough is formed.

Carefully grease the hot pan with a gluten-free baking spray or brush with olive oil. Transfer the batter to the prepared pan, reduce heat to 350°F, and bake for approximately 40 minutes, or until a paring knife inserted comes out clean. If you are making the bread in the corncob pans, cook for approximately 20 minutes until done and a toothpick or paring knife comes out clean. The baking time depends entirely on the baking dish size. Let rest for 10 minutes before slicing or removing from corncob pans.

Note:
If you cannot get blue cornmeal (although it is widely available on the internet and from many grocers), you can also use yellow or white cornmeal for this recipe.

BASIC TAMALE MASA

Some food historians estimate that Native Americans have been preparing corn soaked and cooked in wood ash and then ground into a corn masa for thousands of years. Combining this masa with fresh corn, beans, squash, chiles, and other ingredients and then wrapping the stuffed masa into a corn husk is now referred to as a tamale. The word *tamale* is derived from its Nahuatl root, *tamalli*, meaning "wrapped," and the Mexican Spanish word *tamal*. Today, tamales are traditionally steamed before they are eaten; however, in the Ancestral past, large tamales were slow cooked in large earthen pits in the ground. This recipe is a good and easy basic tamale masa for making a variety of tamales.

MAKES ABOUT 4 CUPS OF MASA, WHICH WILL YIELD 24 TO 28 TAMALES

1 cup all-vegetable shortening, nonhydrogenated (organic if possible, see Note)
4 cups dry white corn masa harina flour
2 teaspoons baking powder
2 teaspoons kosher salt
2¼ cups warm water

In a stand mixer with the paddle attachment or in a medium mixing bowl with a hand mixer, whip the shortening for 1 minute. Scrape down the sides with a rubber spatula and whip for another minute to add air into the shortening.

In a separate bowl, combine the corn flour, baking powder, and salt.

With the mixer on low, add 1 cup of the dried masa mixture at a time to the shortening, alternating with about ½ cup of water. You will do this a total of four times. Scrape down the sides with the spatula as you go to ensure all the ingredients are completely mixed. If mixing with a handheld electric mixer (I have one that my mom used to use while I was growing up), or by hand, mix completely until a soft moist dough has formed.

The goal is to form as moist a dough as possible without it sticking to the sides of the mixing bowl, yet dry enough to form a cohesive ball that comes off the sides of the mixing bowl.

Because masa dries out quickly, it should be used immediately or placed in a plastic freezer bag and stored in the refrigerator for 1 to 2 days or in the freezer for up to a month. To defrost frozen masa, transfer the frozen dough to the refrigerator overnight to thaw. Once thawed, use as per recipe instructions.

Note:
For the all-vegetable shortening I use Spectrum culinary brand. It is Rainforest Alliance Certified, Fair Trade Certified, certified sustainable palm oil, Non-GMO Project Verified, USDA organic, and available in most supermarkets.

THREE SISTERS TAMALE WITH GREEN CHILE

This tamale features corn, beans, and squash. It is a classic combination of ingredients and a favorite of mine. The green chile adds a little spice and some additional nutrients. I have made this tamale using the Sweet Potato Tamale Masa (page 199), and it works well with that tamale masa as well. I've also served it with the Red Chile Sauce (page 129). However, I'm a green chile girl and this is my favorite way to prepare this tamale. The robust Green Chile Sauce (page 131) complements the subtlety of the Three Sisters. You will need to purchase dried corn husks to make tamales. They usually come in either Natural Dried Corn Husks or Premium Dried Corn Husks. The premium variety is more expensive, but it means that someone has already picked out the best corn husks for you to use for your tamales. Either variety will work here. These are available in the Latin food section of most supermarkets or online. Some Native families make their own dried corn husks from the corn that they grow, but they are easy to purchase.

MAKES APPROXIMATELY 28 TAMALES

1 recipe Green Chile Sauce (page 131)
1 recipe Basic Tamale Masa (page 31)
30 dried corn husks
28 dried corn husk ties (see directions)

For the Tamale Filling:

2 teaspoons blackened garlic (page 253)
2 to 3 New Mexico or Anaheim green chiles, roasted, peeled, and chopped (approximately ½ cup) (page 250)
1 tablespoon sunflower oil
1 medium yellow onion, diced (approximately 2 cups)
2 zucchini, cut into ¼-inch cubes (approximately 2 cups) (each zucchini approximately 7 inches long by 1½ inches wide)
1½ cups cooked pinto or Anasazi beans (or one 15.5-ounce can pinto beans, drained and rinsed with bean juice reserved for other recipes)
1 cup corn kernels, fresh cut from the cob or frozen
2 teaspoons kosher salt, or to taste

Prepare the Green Chile Sauce and set aside.

Next prepare the Basic Tamale Masa and set aside. Because the masa dries out quickly, place it in a plastic freezer bag or covered bowl to keep it moist.

Soak the corn husks in hot water until soft, for approximately 10 minutes. I place a dinner plate on top of the soaking husks to keep them immersed in the hot water. Then remove them from the warm water and place in a mixing bowl.

To make the corn husk ties, tear a few corn husks into long strips, approximately 8 inches long by about ¼ inch wide.

For the filling, prepare the blackened garlic, then prepare the green chiles and set aside.

Preheat a cast-iron skillet on high heat until it is hot but not smoking. Add the sunflower oil, then the onion, and sauté until clear, for approximately 3 to 4 minutes. Add the garlic and cook for 1 more minute, stirring to prevent burning. Add the zucchini and sauté for another 3 minutes, stirring to prevent burning. Add the beans and corn and stir. Add the green chile, cook for another 2 to 3 minutes, stirring constantly until the vegetables are cooked. Season with salt. Remove from heat and set aside.

Open a corn husk lengthwise, spread about 2 tablespoons of the masa on the bottom part of it and press evenly over the bottom side (wide side) of the husk, leaving at least 1 inch of husk on each side (left and right side) uncovered and several inches or approximately half on the top so that you can fold over the remaining corn husk to make the tamale. Spoon approximately 1 heaping tablespoon of the filling on the center of the pressed-down masa and then fold each side of the corn husk over the filling, rolling it together so that the masa wraps around the filling. Holding and bringing up both sides of the husk, gently press the masa up and around the filling as much as possible. Fold the left side, then the right side of the corn husk covering the masa so that the tamale is sealed inside the corn husk and is fully wrapped. Fold down the remaining corn husk on the top without the filling in it in half over the filled portion of the tamale with the bottom part still open and then tie it with a corn husk tie.

Tie each strip into a knot and trim any excess corn husk hanging out from the piece that is tucked in. I use pieces of corn husks that are not large enough for wrapping to make my ties.

Repeat the process with the rest of the ingredients until all the tamales are filled and tied.

Next, using a pasta pot with an insert or a large pot with a steamer basket, add water and fill to the bottom of the insert or the steamer basket. Bring to a boil, then place the tied tamales open side up into the insert or steamer basket and line with the completed tamales. Take a clean kitchen towel and run under hot water, then wring it out and lay it over the top of the tamales. Cover with a lid. Steam for 45 minutes for frozen tamales or 35 minutes for fresh tamales. After cooking, turn off the heat and let rest for 5 minutes. Remove the lid and remove the towel, and then remove the tamales and serve plated with the Green Chile Sauce, or place the tamales in a bowl and serve family style with the heated Green Chile Sauce on the side.

Serve immediately.

Note:
The tradition of making tamales is always to eat some immediately and freeze the rest to enjoy later. This recipe makes approximately twenty-eight tamales. For an entrée, serve two to three per person; for an appetizer, serve one. Freeze any leftover tamales in a plastic freezer bag marked with the date you made them. They will last for a month or more in the freezer.

THREE SISTERS ROLLED ENCHILADAS

The Three Sisters—corn, beans, and squash—are often used together, especially here in the Southwest. Many Native gardeners say that they are a family and that they prefer to grow together in the garden, exemplifying their interconnectedness. I happen to agree and think that they do best when planted together. This is a lovely dish featuring these three plants that will not only feed the body but also nurture the soul.

I've written this recipe to feature these enchiladas with Green Chile Sauce (page 131), but we tested them with Red Chile Sauce (page 129) and Mole Sauce (page 228), and they were delicious with these sauces as well.

MAKES 21 ROLLED ENCHILADAS, SERVING 6 TO 8

2 teaspoons sunflower oil

2 small zucchini, cut into ½-inch cubes (approximately 2 cups) (each approximately 7 inches long by 1½ inches wide)

2 small yellow summer squashes, cut into ½-inch cubes (approximately 2 cups) (each approximately 7 inches long by 1½ inches wide)

¾ teaspoon kosher salt, divided

1 cup yellow sweet corn kernels, fresh or frozen

¼ teaspoon freshly ground black pepper

3 tablespoons water

1 recipe Green Chile Sauce (page 131)

1 recipe Red Mesa's Refried Pinto Beans (page 74)

21 corn tortillas

4 green onions, sliced, for garnish

Preheat a medium cast-iron or heavy-bottomed skillet over medium to high heat until it is hot but not smoking. Add the sunflower oil, zucchini, and yellow summer squash and ½ teaspoon of the kosher salt (to bring out the moisture of the squashes) and sauté for 7 minutes, stirring to prevent burning, so that the squash begins to turn golden brown and caramelize. Add the corn kernels, remaining ¼ teaspoon of salt, pepper, and water. Stir and cook for an additional 2 minutes to deglaze the pan and incorporate all the ingredients together. Remove from the heat, then place cooked ingredients in a bowl and reserve.

Make the Green Chile Sauce and reserve.

Make the Refried Pinto Beans and reserve.

Heat the tortillas for approximately 30 seconds on each side using an open flame on a grill or in a very hot seasoned cast-iron pan. Place in a basket lined with a clean kitchen towel to hold and keep warm. Repeat until all the tortillas have been heated.

Preheat the oven to 350°F. To assemble the enchiladas, place a warmed open tortilla on a flat work surface. Spoon 2 tablespoons of the refried pinto bean mixture onto each tortilla and spread evenly across the center portion of the tortillas. Top with 1 tablespoon of the squash mixture and spread evenly over the

refried bean mixture. Roll each side of the tortilla toward the center, turn it over, and place open side down onto a lightly oiled baking dish or sheet tray.

Spoon approximately 2 tablespoons of the Green Chile Sauce over each rolled enchilada and place the baking dish in the oven. Cook for 20 to 25 minutes or until hot all the way through. Remove from oven.

Serve immediately, garnished with the green onions and any additional Green Chile Sauce.

POSOLE WITH RED CHILE

Posole is the word used in New Mexico to describe corn that has been nixtamalized, also known as hominy. Posole when eaten on its own is also a simple, rustic stew common throughout many Native communities. Traditionally made from dried hominy corn, vegetables, spices, dried red chile, and meat (wild game is common), this stew is usually cooked in large quantities because it is almost always served for large family gatherings, Ceremonies, and at Pueblo Feast Days. I make it without any meat, deviating from the traditional version, as I love the flavor of the corn perfectly paired with the spices.

Hominy (posole) can be found in four colors: yellow, white, blue, and red. I love both the white and the blue, and I think the blue is uniquely delicious. It is usually sold dried; white hominy corn is also sold in cans already cooked, although I always prefer to cook it from dried corn because it has a more delicious and delicate flavor.

For the Cooked Hominy Corn:

1 cup dried hominy corn (white, blue, or both)
    (approximately 5 cups cooked for the
    blue corn and 6 cups cooked for
    the white corn)
12 cups water (divided)

For the Posole Stew:

2 teaspoons sunflower oil
½ large yellow onion, diced
    (approximately 1⅓ cups)
1 tablespoon finely chopped garlic
1 dried New Mexico red chile pod, mild, seeded,
    stemmed, and broken into small pieces
1 tablespoon New Mexico red chile powder, mild
1 tablespoon azafran (Mexican safflower or
    Native American saffron; see source guide)
4 cups corn liquid or water
¼ teaspoon dried Mexican oregano
⅛ teaspoon dried thyme
1 teaspoon kosher salt, or to taste
6 lime wedges, for garnish
1 tablespoon chopped fresh cilantro, for garnish

To cook the corn, soak it overnight in 4 cups of water.

The following day, drain and discard the water. Place the corn (posole) in a larger pot filled with the remaining 8 cups of water. The water should cover the corn by at least 3 inches; if it does not, add a little more water.

Bring to a boil over high heat, then reduce heat and simmer, uncovered, for about 3 hours, and cook until the kernels are puffy and tender, when tasted. Check throughout the cooking process, adding additional water if needed.

Once the corn has cooked, drain it, reserving the corn liquid, and set aside. You should have approximately 3 to 4 cups of water left after draining the corn. White corn tends to puff the most.

You can also cook the corn in a slow cooker or Crockpot. This is how I like to cook my hominy corn (posole). See instructions in Pantry Staples (page 259).

In a separate heavy-bottomed soup pot, heat the sunflower oil over medium to high heat until it is hot but not smoking. Add the onion and sauté until clear, for approximately 3 to 4 minutes, stirring occasionally to prevent burning but allowing the onion to begin to caramelize. Add the garlic and sauté for another 3 to 4 minutes, stirring occasionally to prevent burning. Add the chile pod pieces, the chile powder, and the *azafran*. Stir and continue to cook for another 3 minutes. Add the corn water and corn and bring to a boil.

Once it has boiled, reduce the heat and simmer for 15 minutes until all the flavors have melded together. Add the Mexican oregano, thyme, and salt and continue cooking on low for another 5 minutes.

Serve hot in large soup bowls as a main course or as a side dish with warm bread. Garnish with a slice of lime and the chopped cilantro.

Note:

New Mexico red chile pods and powder come in mild, medium, and hot. For those of you who want a spicier posole, use a hotter chile.

WALTER'S HOMINY CORN VEGETABLE

On the Navajo Reservation, Chef Walter Whitewater grew up calling this dish vegetable hominy. He likes to prepare it this way and eat it as a vegetable side, but if you add homemade vegetable broth (page 264) or vegetable stock (page 265) to it, it becomes a delicious and nutritious stew. This is one of Chef Walter's new favorite versions of this dish; it is savory and not spicy like a traditional Pueblo or Northern New Mexican posole.

MAKES 4 TO 6 SERVINGS

½ cup (4 ounces or ¼ pound) dried hominy corn (white) (approximately 2½ cups cooked)

8 cups water

2 teaspoons sunflower oil

1 small yellow onion, diced (approximately ¾ cup)

2 teaspoons finely chopped garlic (3 to 4 large garlic cloves)

2 tomatoes, diced (approximately ¾ cup)

3 cups fresh baby spinach

3 cups total liquid (corn liquid, plus the remaining liquid in water, or you can use all water)

1½ teaspoons kosher salt

½ teaspoon dried thyme

½ teaspoon dried Mexican oregano

½ lemon, squeezed (approximately 1 tablespoon)

Place the corn in a slow cooker or Crockpot with 8 cups of water.

Bring to a boil over high heat, then reduce the heat to low, cover, and simmer for approximately 6 hours, or until the corn has puffed and is tender.

After the corn has cooked, drain it, keeping the corn liquid, and set aside. You should have approximately 1 to 2 cups of water left after draining the hominy corn.

Heat a separate 6-quart pot, add the sunflower oil over medium to high heat until hot, then add the onion and sauté until clear, approximately 3 to 4 minutes. Add the garlic and sauté for another 3 minutes. Add the tomatoes and cook for another 5 minutes, stirring to prevent burning. Add the spinach and the cooked hominy corn with the corn liquid. Stir. Bring to a boil, then reduce heat and simmer for approximately 5 minutes until the spinach has wilted. Add the salt, thyme, Mexican oregano, and the lemon juice. Taste and adjust the seasoning if desired.

Serve hot as a vegetable side or add 3 cups of vegetable stock (page 265) or 3 cups of vegetable broth (page 264) and serve as a main course stew with warm bread.

HOMINY HARVEST STEW

This wonderful and treasured hominy corn stew is both healthy and delicious. Unlike the Posole with Red Chile (page 37), which tends to be a little spicy, and Walter's Hominy Corn Vegetable (page 39), which is not spicy at all, this stew is not too spicy, has lots of vegetables in it, and is very filling. Blending some of the stew gives it a thicker texture that both Chef Walter and I love. I've made it with just the blue hominy corn, just the white hominy corn, or with a combination of both types of corn, which is my favorite way to make it.

This stew is usually cooked in large quantities to feed extended family or lots of people at a Ceremony or traditional foods gathering. Here, I've scaled down the recipe to feed approximately eight people as an entrée stew (it will feed approximately ten as a side dish or first course) as it makes 12 cups or 3 quarts of stew. If you have a small family, this is perfect the following day for lunch or dinner, and it freezes well for a future meal.

SERVES 8 TO 10

For the Cooked Hominy Corn:
1 cup dried hominy corn (white, blue, or both) (will yield 5 to 6 cups cooked)

12 cups water

For the Stew:
1 tablespoon sunflower oil

1 yellow onion, chopped (approximately 2 cups)

1 tablespoon blackened garlic (page 253)

4 Roma tomatoes, diced (approximately 2 cups)

2 medium-size zucchini, cut into ½-inch cubes (approximately 2 cups) (each approximately 7 inches long by 1½ inches wide)

2 medium-size yellow summer squashes, cut into ½-inch cubes (approximately 2 cups) (each approximately 7 inches long by 1½ inches wide)

1 dried New Mexico red chile pod, mild, seeded, stemmed, and torn or cut into small pieces (add a second chile for a spicier stew)

3 tablespoons New Mexico red chile powder, mild

2 bay leaves

1 tablespoon azafran (Mexican safflower or Native American saffron; see source guide)

½ teaspoon dried Mexican oregano, or to taste

½ teaspoon fresh thyme leaves, finely chopped

5 cups total liquid (corn liquid, plus the remaining liquid in water, or you can use all water)

2 teaspoons kosher salt, or to taste

1 tablespoon freshly squeezed lime juice (approximately ½ lime)

2 teaspoons agave sweetener (optional)

½ cup cilantro leaves, finely chopped, for garnish

Place the corn in a slow cooker or Crockpot with 8 cups of water.

Bring to a boil over high heat, then reduce the heat to low, cover, and simmer for approximately 6 hours, or until the corn has puffed and is tender.

After the corn has cooked, drain it, keeping the corn liquid, and set aside. You should have approximately 1 to 2 cups of water left after draining the hominy corn, which you will reserve and use with water for the stew.

In a separate large, heavy-bottomed soup pot, heat the sunflower oil over medium to high heat and sauté the onion until clear, approximately 3 to 4 minutes. Add the garlic and cook for another minute. Add the tomatoes and sauté for another 4 minutes, stirring to prevent burning. Add the zucchini and the yellow summer squash, sauté for another 4 minutes. Add the

chile pod, chile powder, bay leaves, *azafran*, Mexican oregano, and thyme. Stir so that all the spices are completely mixed with the vegetables. Add the corn and corn liquid and bring to a boil, then reduce heat, add salt, lime juice, and agave (if using), and simmer for 15 minutes or until the vegetables are cooked. Carefully remove several cups of the stew, place in a blender, and process until smooth. Return the mixture back to the pot and stir. If you want the stew thicker, blend a little more until you have the desired thickness. The stew will be a nice thick consistency with lots of texture and flavor from the remaining unblended ingredients. Garnish with chopped cilantro.

Serve immediately with No Fry Frybread (page 266) or White Corn Tortillas (page 27). Top with a little homemade Red Chile Sauce (page 129) or Green Chile Sauce (page 131) if desired.

BLUE CORN PASTA

This recipe is easy to make and has the delightful nutty flavor of blue corn and a nice texture. While you might not think of pasta as Native, pasta has been and still is distributed through the FDPIR food program. I wanted to make a contemporary pasta using blue corn without using eggs, so Chef Marianne (who is Italian and grew up making pasta) and I experimented with several different versions of a pasta that features blue corn. This is our favorite and if you love pasta, like I do, I think you will enjoy this recipe. It can be used fresh or frozen for future use. Making your own pasta is a fun family activity to do for an afternoon, but not something I recommend trying to do if you are pressed for time. This pasta pairs well with Heirloom Tomato Sauce (page 171) and the Butternut Squash with Arugula Pesto & Pasta (page 115).

MAKES 4 SERVINGS

1½ cups all-purpose flour
¾ cup finely ground blue cornmeal
1 teaspoon kosher salt
2 tablespoons sunflower oil
½ cup water

Line a sheet pan with a piece of parchment paper and lightly flour it. Set aside.

In a large bowl whisk together the flour, cornmeal, and salt. Make a well in the center of the bowl and add the sunflower oil and water. Using a fork, whisk in the flour mixture until it incorporates. Once it forms a kneadable ball (add a little more water if it is too dry or a little more flour if it is too wet), transfer it to a dry, lightly floured work surface and knead the dough by hand for approximately 10 minutes, or until it's smooth. You can also use a stand mixer with a dough hook to knead the dough if you have one available.

Once the dough is a smooth ball, wrap with plastic wrap and let it rest for 30 minutes. After the dough has rested, divide the ball of dough into quarters. You will work with one piece of dough at a time, so be sure to keep the others covered in plastic or in a clean kitchen towel until ready to use.

If using a pasta machine, roll it through the largest "0" setting. Using your hands, fold the right side of the dough in toward the center, then the left side. This step of folding will only need to be done the first time and is just like folding a piece of paper to fit inside an envelope. It creates a uniform rectangle shape that is easy to roll out.

Place this folded piece of dough through the next "1" setting on the pasta machine, making sure to keep the dough lightly floured between rollings. Repeat this process for settings "2," then "3," then "4," and finally "5."

Cut each strip of finished pasta dough in half down the center. You should have a total of eight pieces of pasta.

Next, using the fettuccini attachment on your pasta machine, run the long thin strip through the pasta machine to make the noodles. Gently form them into a circle and place on the lined sheet pan. The noodles should be formed into what looks like a small bird nest. Repeat until you have eight bird nest piles of the blue corn pasta and you have used all the dough. Place in the refrigerator until ready to cook or freeze for later use.

If you do not have a pasta machine, you can also cut the dough into pieces and roll each piece out into thin rectangles approximately 4 inches wide by 12 inches long. Slice the dough into ¼-inch wide slices approximately the size of a fettuccini noodle. Gently form them into a circle and fold the noodles into what looks like a small bird nest. Place on a lightly floured parchment-lined sheet tray to freeze, or store in the fridge for up to 2 days.

Cook just like you would any fresh pasta, until it rises to the top of a pot of boiling water, approximately 3 minutes, depending on the thickness of the pasta. If you allow the pasta to dry, which I did with some of the batches of pasta we tested for this cookbook, you will need to cook the pasta slightly longer—approximately 5 to 7 minutes at sea level and slightly longer at altitude. Follow the Note below for proper cooking time.

Gently rinse the cooked pasta in cold water to stop the cooking process, being careful not to break the pasta. Serve immediately with the Heirloom Tomato Sauce, pesto and butternut squash, or other sauce of your choosing.

Note:

When cooking any pasta at altitude, the rule of thumb is to add about 1 minute of cooking time per thousand feet of altitude. In Santa Fe, New Mexico, which is 7,199 feet, for instance, you will need to add 7.2 minutes of cooking time to the pasta.

NAVAJO KNEEL DOWN BREAD (NITSIDIGO'I')

Chef Walter made this Navajo corn recipe based on the traditional recipe that his grandmother, Aunties, and relatives have always made. It is called kneel down bread because you have to kneel down to grind the fresh corn on a grinding stone and because the cook had to tend to this traditionally earthen-pit-cooked bread while kneeling. Walter's dad, Thomas Mike, was the farmer in the family and grew corn and other crops, including squashes, sunflowers, and melons. This dish was always made with the fresh corn that his dad grew, before he passed. Technically, it is not a true bread but a fresh corn dish that is baked in a corn husk.

While this recipe is traditionally made with fresh corn, it can be made with frozen corn kernels as well. The corn kernels are lightly ground, traditionally on a stone, but today can be made in a food processor or blender. Walter always sings during this process of preparing the corn to put the Ancestral songs into the breads before they bake, and he sang as we tested this recipe.

The moist meal or a version of a type of masa is seasoned with a little salt, sometimes herbs, and then the masa is placed in either fresh or dried corn husks that are soaked and baked. In the past, and for some Ceremonial occasions, these breads were baked in the ground overnight on the embers of a fire that has burned down, but many people today bake them in their kitchen oven. This dish truly celebrates corn in one of its purest forms.

MAKES APPROXIMATELY 6 KNEEL DOWN BREADS FOR THE CORN VERSION AND 9 KNEEL DOWN BREADS FOR THE FRUIT VERSION

For the Kneel Down Bread:
8 to 9 corn husks, fresh or dried, soaked in hot
    water for 10 minutes until soft
3 cups fresh or frozen sweet white corn kernels
    (cut from the cob or a 1-pound bag of frozen
    corn kernels)
1 cup blackened corn (page 252)
½ cup water
½ teaspoon kosher salt
About 6 corn husk ties (see directions)

For the Corn Sauce:
1½ cups fresh or frozen white corn kernels
½ cup water or vegetable broth (page 264)
½ teaspoon kosher salt
1 teaspoon pure maple syrup

For the Fruit Version of Kneel Down Bread:
8 to 9 corn husks, fresh or dried, soaked in hot
    water for 10 minutes until soft
3 cups fresh or frozen sweet white corn kernels
    (cut from the cob or a 1-pound bag of frozen
    corn kernels)
¼ teaspoon kosher salt
1 small apple, seeded and diced with skin on
    (approximately 1 cup)
¼ cup golden raisins
¼ cup dried currants
1 teaspoon pure maple syrup
About 9 corn husk ties (see directions)

Preheat the oven to 400°F. Soak the dried corn husks in hot water for 10 minutes. If using fresh corn, cut both ends of the fresh corn off, first the top and then the bottom. Gently remove the fresh husks, keeping them as intact as possible. Wash the husks to remove any dirt and place in warm water to soak for 10 minutes. Cut the kernels from the cob.

Prepare the blackened corn.

In a food processor, place 3 cups of the uncooked corn kernels, add the water, and process on low until you have a rough masa. It should not be completely puréed but have some texture to it.

Remove from the blender or food processor and place in a bowl. Add the salt and the blackened corn kernels and stir together. This is your masa for the kneel down breads.

Take a soaked corn husk and place approximately 6 tablespoons of the masa into the center of the husk. Roll the husk first from the left side and fold over, then from the right side and fold over so that it covers the masa. Next take another soaked corn husk and roll over the open side of the bread, covering it. Fold over the bottom (wide side) of the corn husk and tie using a piece of the corn husk. Then fold the top (narrow side) over and tie with a torn piece of corn husk. To make the ties, rip a piece of corn husk lengthwise that is approximately 1 inch wide by whatever the length of the husk is (which should be about 8 to 9 inches long). Tie a knot on the thick end of the torn husk and tear it into two pieces that will be tied together at the end by the knot. Now you should have two pieces of tie that are ½ inch in width and held together by the knot at the end.

This should be long enough to tie around the kneel down bread.

Chef Walter's breads were about 5½ inches long by 2 to 2½ inches wide. Place on a sheet pan and bake in the oven for approximately 60 minutes until the breads are done and firm to the touch.

While the breads are cooking, make the sauce. Place the corn kernels, water, salt, and maple syrup in a blender and mix on high until completely smooth, for approximately 2 minutes. Pass through a fine strainer and discard or compost the contents of the strainer. Place the sauce in a small saucepan and heat on low for approximately 10 minutes just before serving, stirring to prevent burning.

Remove the baked kneel down breads from the oven and serve immediately with the corn sauce.

To try the fruit version of this bread, make the masa as directed above in a food processor or blender. Remove from the blender or food processor and place in a bowl. Add the salt, apples, raisins, currants, and maple syrup, and stir together. You should have approximately 3 cups of lightly ground corn mixture. This is your fruit version masa for the kneel down breads. Follow the instructions for preparing the tied breads. Place approximately 5 tablespoons of the mixture in each corn husk. Place on a sheet pan and bake in the oven for approximately 60 minutes until the breads are done and firm to the touch.

Serve these kneel down breads as a dessert with corn sauce or with the Vanilla Peach Sauce (page 211) or the Chokecherry Syrup (page 271).

GRILLED SWEET CORN

Fresh grilled sweet corn on the cob is one of the best dishes to showcase summer. The Santa Fe Farmers' Market sells sweet corn for a limited time, and this is the perfect recipe to use to enjoy grilled fresh sweet corn when it is available. Terri and Brian Graves, of Anasazi Roasted Corn, sell roasted corn on the Santa Fe Plaza; folks line up for blocks to get their perfectly roasted fresh sweet corn. The biggest dilemma has always been providing a good marinade other than melted butter. When we tested this recipe on the grill, Terri was amazed at how delicious our alternative to butter is. The flavor of the corn has a little spice to it from the chile, the lemon brightens the emulsion, the blackened garlic adds a savory component that is not overpowering to the corn, while the salt brings out the sweet corn flavor, making a delightful grilled sweet corn without losing the essence of fresh sweet corn on the cob.

MAKES 4 SERVINGS

For the Emulsion:

1 tablespoon lemon juice
(approximately ½ lemon)
½ cup sunflower oil
1 teaspoon New Mexico green chile powder
(mild)
1 teaspoon New Mexico red chile powder (mild)
1 tablespoon blackened garlic (page 253)
1 teaspoon kosher salt, or to taste
1 tablespoon water

For the Sweet Corn:

4 pieces fresh white or yellow sweet corn

For the emulsion, place all the ingredients into a blender and mix, starting on low, and then turn up to high, for approximately 30 seconds. Pour the emulsion into a bowl and reserve.

For the fresh corn, peel down the husk from the top and remove the corn silk from the corncob. Compost, discard, or save and dry the corn silk for later use. Tie the outer corn husk leaves together using a piece of the fresh corn husks as a tie so that it holds together on the bottom of the corn. This is what you and your guests will use to hold the corn so you can eat it right off the grill.

Brush on some of the emulsion and place the corn on the grill. Rotate it four times, cooking approximately for 45 seconds to 1 minute, brushing a little more of the emulsion onto the exposed corn with each rotation, so it blackens but does not burn. Corn will be ready in approximately 3 to 4 minutes, depending on the size of the corn and the heat of your grill.

I use a charcoal grill and charcoal wood pieces. Look for a locally made charcoal in your area. I let the charcoal burn down so that it has just the hot embers to cook the fresh corn on the cob. And because you are using fresh corn, you don't want to overcook it; you just want to cook it enough so that it remains sweet and tender.

Once the corn has cooked, remove it from the grill and serve immediately.

Note:

For those of you with a spicier palate, you can increase the amount of chile or use a hotter chile in the emulsion.

WALTER'S FRESH CORN SALAD

Fresh corn reminds me of summer. This simple salad features sweet corn and purslane. Purslane, also called *verdolagas* in Spanish, is an annual weed, from the family Portulacaceae, the genus *Portulaca* and of the species *P. oleracea* that grows wild in disturbed soil areas all over the United States as well as in other parts of the world. It is a succulent-looking plant with green flat leaves that are tender, edible, and very nutritious that are often eaten in salads, soups, and stews. It is not as bitter as arugula but similar in flavor. If you can't find or harvest purslane, substitute arugula as it has a similar flavor and is readily available. While I recommend making it with summer sweet fresh corn from your local farm stand or farmers' market, it works perfectly with organic sweet frozen corn any time of year.

MAKES 4 SERVINGS

For the Vinaigrette:

2 tablespoons elderberry balsamic vinegar
    (see source guide) or any balsamic vinegar
1 tablespoon water
1 teaspoon smooth Dijon mustard
1 teaspoon whole-grain Dijon mustard
1 teaspoon agave sweetener
¼ teaspoon kosher salt
¼ teaspoon freshly ground black pepper

For the Salad:

½ small red onion, thinly sliced
    (about ½ cup)
½ pound cherry tomatoes, halved
    (approximately 2 cups)
2 cups fresh organic white or yellow sweet corn
    kernels (or frozen if fresh is not available)
1 cup purslane (in summer) or arugula
    (in winter)
1 tablespoon minced fresh chives, for garnish

In a large bowl, whisk together all the vinaigrette ingredients. Add the onion, tomatoes, corn, and purslane and gently toss together.

Garnish with the chives. Serve immediately.

NATIVE AMERICAN WILD RICE & SWEET CORN SAUTÉ (MANOOMIN)

Manoomin, or wild rice, is a Native American grain that is part of Native communities in northern Minnesota, Wisconsin, Michigan, and Canada. According to Anishinaabe writer Tashia Hart, author of *The Good Berry Cookbook: Harvesting and Cooking Wild Rice and Other Wild Foods*, stories told in oral traditions of the Seven Fires Prophecy spoke of "the food that grows on the water." And this food was wild rice, which translates to "good berry" and is revered by the Peoples who use it. True wild rice can only be harvested by hand using traditional methods and following the traditions of the Ancestors. This dish is wonderful on its own as wild rice has a wonderful nutty flavor that is perfect with the earthiness of the mushrooms, tartness of the dried cherries or cranberries, and sweetness of the corn; however, it pairs nicely with the Roasted Sweet Potatoes (page 187) as a main course.

MAKES 4 TO 6 SERVINGS

For the Cooked Wild Rice:
½ cup dried hand-harvested Native American wild rice (see source guide) (will yield 1½ cups cooked wild rice)
1½ cups water
¼ teaspoon kosher salt

For the Sauté:
2 teaspoons sunflower or olive oil
1 small yellow onion, diced (approximately ¾ cup)
1 teaspoon blackened garlic (page 253)
1½ cups white mushrooms, washed, dried, and thinly sliced (approximately 6 mushrooms or about half an 8-ounce package)
1½ cups brown cremini mushrooms, washed, dried, and thinly sliced (approximately 6 mushrooms or about half an 8-ounce package)
⅓ cup dried tart cherries or dried cranberries
½ cup yellow corn kernels, fresh or frozen

½ teaspoon kosher salt, or to taste
⅛ teaspoon freshly ground black pepper, or to taste
3 to 4 green scallions, finely sliced (approximately 3 tablespoons)

Rinse the dried wild rice several times in running water. In a medium saucepan, bring the rice, water, and salt to a boil, then reduce heat, cover, and simmer on low for approximately 40 minutes or per the instructions on the package, until the rice is cooked and all the water absorbed. Remove from the heat and set aside. Let sit, covered, for 5 minutes. Reserve.

Preheat a medium to large seasoned cast-iron pan over medium to high heat until it is hot but not smoking. Add the sunflower oil, then the onions and sauté, stirring to prevent burning, for approximately 4 minutes. Add the garlic and sauté for 2 more minutes, stirring constantly to prevent burning. Reduce the heat to medium and then add the mushrooms and sauté, stirring to prevent burning for approximately 6 minutes. You will want the mushrooms to start to caramelize and turn brown. Add the dried cherries and stir. Cook for another 2 to 3 minutes and then add the corn kernels. Stir and cook for another 1 to 2 minutes. Add the cooked rice, salt, and pepper. Stir. Taste and adjust seasoning, if necessary. Cook for 2 more minutes or until completely hot, stirring constantly. Remove from heat, stir in the freshly sliced scallions, and serve immediately.

Wild Rice Sauté with Roasted Sweet Potato with Maple Chile Lime (page 187)

SWEET CORN SOUP WITH CHIPOTLE PAINT

I usually make this soup from fresh corn during the warm weather of summer months and at the summer harvest time when corn is at its sweetest, but it can be made at any time of the year with frozen sweet corn—organic is my choice if it is available. The chipotle garnish made from roasted red bell peppers, white beans, and chipotle chiles adds a robust and spicy flavor to the sweet corn, making a sweet and spicy soup. Chef Walter and I use this garnish as a paint to incorporate symbols onto the soup when we serve it. We like to paint a spiral design with four dots. The spiral is one of the oldest symbols in the Southwest and found on many petroglyphs throughout the world. The spiral design that we use represents the Indigenous knowledge of the Native American Ancestors; the four dots represent the four generations, child, adolescent, middle-aged, and elder, and the importance of passing on the knowledge of the Ancestors so that this knowledge is not lost. It takes only one generation for a language, song, story, or recipe to be lost. It is vital that all traditions, all over the world, be carried on, and the symbols that we paint onto this soup are a reminder to ourselves and our patrons of this importance.

MAKES APPROXIMATELY FOUR 1-CUP SERVINGS

For the Soup:

4 ears fresh corn (approximately 3 cups corn kernels), cobs reserved, or 3½ cups frozen corn kernels (approximately a 1-pound bag)

2 teaspoons sunflower oil

½ white onion, diced (approximately 1 cup)

1 tablespoon blackened garlic (page 253)

2 cups corn broth if using fresh corn, or water

½ teaspoon kosher salt

1 teaspoon agave sweetener (optional)

For the Chipotle Chile Paint:

1 red bell pepper, roasted, peeled, and seeded (see directions)

1 can (15.5 ounce) white kidney beans (cannellini beans), strained

1 teaspoon dried chipotle chile powder (more if you want it spicier)

1 tablespoon New Mexico red chile powder, mild

1 teaspoon blackened garlic (page 253)

½ teaspoon kosher salt

½ lime, freshly squeezed (approximately 1 tablespoon)

Prepare the corn by cutting the kernels from the cob. Save the corncobs and set aside. The cobs will add additional corn flavor to the soup. If using frozen corn, measure 3½ cups or a 1-pound bag of frozen corn kernels.

If using fresh corn, place the corncobs in a saucepan and cover with 4 cups of water. Bring to a boil, then reduce heat to medium and allow the mixture to reduce by half, which will take about 15 to 20 minutes. This is the liquid you will use instead of the water when preparing this soup from fresh corn. After the corncob liquid has reduced by half, remove the corncobs and compost them, reserving the corn broth.

In a medium cast-iron pan over medium to high heat, add the oil and heat until it is hot but not smoking. Add the onions and sauté for approximately 4 minutes, stirring to prevent burning, until they turn a little brown, then add the corn kernels and garlic and sauté for 2 to 3

Opposite: *Sweet Corn Soup with Gluten-Free Blue Corn Bread (page 29)*

minutes. This brings the corn kernels to a hot temperature without too much heat or cooking, as you will lose some of the corn flavor if you cook the corn kernels for too long. Add the corn broth and turn off the heat.

Pour the mixture into a blender and purée for 2 minutes. Add the salt, blend again to mix the salt into the corn mixture, and then pass it through a fine strainer. Compost or discard the contents in the corn strainer, placing the corn soup into a small saucepan. Heat until hot just before serving.

Taste the soup and adjust for sweetness. Add the agave, if needed (if the corn isn't at its peak sweetness).

To make the paint, roast and peel the red bell pepper over an open flame, allow to cool, then peel and de-seed the pepper. Place the bell pepper, beans, chipotle chile powder, New Mexico red chile powder, garlic, salt, and lime juice into a blender and mix until smooth. Place the contents into a squirt bottle for painting onto the soup and set aside.

Pour the warm soup into a bowl and paint a design onto the top of it.

Serve the soup immediately.

Note:
This soup can also be served cold during the summer months. Follow the recipe instructions and then chill in the refrigerator before serving.

BLUE CORN PANCAKES WITH PIÑON BUTTER

I grew up on Long Island eating pancakes on many Sundays. One of my best friends, Cat Taylor, lived in a house that was constructed of beautiful cedar wood that had been in their family for over fifty years. It was situated on a bay in Quiogue, Long Island; we loved the serenity and beauty of the land that surrounded her house and would walk around for hours. Cat's grandfather made us pancakes every weekend.

These blue corn pancakes are a tribute to the ones I loved so much while growing up. Here, the earthy, nutty flavor of the blue corn pairs perfectly with the sweetness of the piñon butter, making a filling breakfast. I buy blue cornmeal from Santa Ana Pueblo (Tamaya), but you can easily purchase blue cornmeal online from any source although I recommend purchasing Native American–grown cornmeal whenever possible. Piñon nuts (as they are called in the Southwest) are the same as pine nuts and available at most supermarkets. I serve these with a plant-based piñon nut butter that Marianne Sundquist and I developed for these delicious pancakes. They are easy to make, and the perfect dish for a weekend morning, as Cat's grandfather always knew.

MAKES APPROXIMATELY 16 PANCAKES

For the Piñon Nut Butter:

½ cup piñon nuts
2 tablespoons solid coconut oil
1 tablespoon maple syrup
½ teaspoon kosher salt

For the Pancakes:

1½ cups all-purpose flour
1 cup finely ground blue cornmeal
2 tablespoons baking powder
¼ cup brown sugar, packed
1 teaspoon kosher salt
2 teaspoons vanilla bean paste
2½ cups unsweetened almond milk
    (vanilla or plain)
1 tablespoon freshly squeezed lemon juice
    (approximately ½ lemon)
Sunflower oil for cooking pancakes

To make the piñon butter, add the piñon nuts to a food processor and pulse until they are almost a powder. Add the coconut oil, maple syrup, and salt and process for another 30 seconds until it looks like a spreadable butter. Transfer to a jar or container and place in the fridge, making sure to bring to room temperature before serving so that it is soft enough to melt onto the pancakes.

To make the pancakes, preheat a griddle or seasoned cast-iron pan over medium heat until hot. In a large bowl, combine the flour, cornmeal, baking powder, brown sugar, and salt. In a separate bowl, whisk together the vanilla, almond milk, and lemon juice. Let this mixture sit for 5 minutes. Then pour the almond milk mixture into the dry ingredients and stir well to combine, making sure there are no lumps.

Drizzle a little sunflower oil on the griddle or cast-iron pan and wipe evenly over the surface with a paper towel. Spoon batter to make any size pancakes you want. I like making the silver-dollar size that I grew up with. Flip over when the bottom of the pancake turns golden brown, after approximately 1 minute, and finish cooking the other side. Repeat this process until all the batter is used up.

Serve warm with the piñon butter and additional pure maple syrup, if desired.

NATIVE AMERICAN CORN PUDDING PARFAIT

This is one of my most favorite traditional-yet-modern recipes using blue corn. The corn mush, a very traditional Ancestral corn dish, is lightly sweetened with agave, making it more like a sweet pudding than a savory dish. The corn naturally thickens as it cools, which is perfect for layering together with the mixed-berry fruit compote.

This parfait uses two traditional corn mushes, one blue and one white, that are layered together with a berry compote, then topped with nuts, making a Native version of the classic French recipe. I make it all the time and not only serve it warm (my favorite way to eat it) but also chilled. Many of the students who made this as part of the Indigenous Concepts of Native American Food class at the Institute of American Indian Arts (IAIA) froze it in hard plastic cups and it was delicious as a frozen dessert as well. But don't eat this dish only for dessert; it also makes a healthy breakfast and is perfect for a snack at any time of the day.

MAKES 4 TO 6 PARFAITS (DEPENDING ON THE SIZE OF YOUR DISHES)

For the Mixed-Berry and Fruit Compote:

2 to 3 Fuji, Honeycrisp, or Gala apples, peeled, cored, and cut into ½-inch cubes (approximately 2 cups)

½ cup unfiltered apple juice or cider

2 cups frozen mixed berries (I use a mixed-berry medley with blueberries, blackberries, raspberries, and Bing cherries)

1 cup unsweetened applesauce

1 tablespoon agave sweetener, plus more if needed to taste

For the Blue Corn Mush Layer #1:

1 cup water

¾ cup cold water

½ cup finely ground blue cornmeal (untoasted) (see source guide)

½ teaspoon culinary ash (optional) (see source guide)

¼ teaspoon kosher salt

1 to 2 tablespoons agave sweetener, or to taste

For the White Corn Mush Layer #2:

1 cup water

¾ cup cold water

½ cup finely ground white cornmeal (untoasted)

½ teaspoon culinary ash (optional)

¼ teaspoon kosher salt

1 to 2 tablespoons agave sweetener, or to taste

½ cup chopped pecans (toasted) for garnish

1 small Fuji, Honeycrisp, or Gala apple, thinly sliced, for garnish

6 fresh mint sprigs, for garnish (optional)

To make the compote, in a medium saucepan combine the apples and apple juice. Bring to a boil, stir, then add the frozen mixed berries. Bring to a boil again, then reduce the heat and simmer on low, covered, for about 15 minutes, or until fruit is tender when pierced with a fork.

Add the unsweetened applesauce and the agave and mix well. It should be thick but not too thick. Taste. If it is not sweet enough, add an additional tablespoon of the agave, then taste again. If you still want it sweeter, then add an additional tablespoon of agave. Return to heat and simmer on low, uncovered, for 10 minutes. My palate is not too sweet, so I only add 1 to 2 tablespoons of agave, depending on whom I am cooking for. Remove from heat and set aside.

To make the first corn mush layer, in a small saucepan over medium to high heat, bring the 1 cup of water to a boil. In a separate bowl mix the ¾ cup cold water, cornmeal, culinary ash (if using), and salt, stirring constantly with a whisk until there are no lumps.

Slowly add the ground cornmeal mixture into the saucepan of boiling water, stirring to prevent any lumps from forming. Reduce heat to low and continue to cook for 3 minutes, stirring constantly, until the mixture has a nice thick consistency. Add the agave and mix well. Taste to make sure you like the sweetness; if it is not sweet enough, add a little more agave. Continue to cook for approximately another 3 minutes, on low, stirring constantly as the mixture spits, until it turns smooth and is thick like pudding. It will become quite thick at this point, and this is how you know it is done. Remove from heat.

In glass dishes or hard plastic cups add a little of the warm cornmeal pudding (several tablespoons to coat the bottom of your glass or cup) as your first layer, using up all the first batch of corn mush and spreading it equally into the dishes. Next add the same amount of the mixed-berry fruit compote on top of the corn pudding mixture once it has thickened in the glasses. You will want to use half of the cooked berry compote, leaving the remaining half for the final layer.

Repeat the process to make the corn mush for the second layer and then add another layer of the white corn pudding, allowing it to thicken in the glass. Then add the final layer of the mixed-berry compote, dividing it evenly over the white corn pudding.

Top with the nuts and several apple slices. Here we garnish the corn pudding with a Juniper branch. Serve immediately warm, or refrigerate for several hours or overnight and serve as a cold dessert.

Notes:
If you are using sweetened applesauce, you may not want to add the agave. Adding unsweetened berries is a good way to dilute the sweetness and make it a healthier dish. Many things can be added to the corn mush as a topping. Try sliced apple, toasted piñon (pine) nuts, or any kind of granola. You can also add as a topping any kind of natural syrups, including prickly pear syrup, Chokecherry Syrup (page 271), and maple syrup.

GRACE'S CORN ICE (DA'YIS TIIN)

Before there was refrigeration on the Navajo Reservation, this dish was prepared and then put outside in the snow overnight. In the morning, kids would eat the frozen corn mush for breakfast. Chef Walter remembers his grandmother, Grandma Susie Whitewater Begay, making this for him when he was a child.

Plant-based Navajo cook Grace Tracy shared her version of this corn dish with me and said that it was a variation of a popsicle she likes. She said, "The elder teaching is 'Ash repels evil, as it has spiritual significance to protect. White corn is our identity and a gift from the Creator.'"

The delicate flavor for this corn ice is lightly sweet from the corn and maple syrup, and the texture is a lot like shaved ice. For those of you with a sweeter palate, drizzle some additional maple syrup onto the plate when serving. This recipe was inspired by both Grace, whose recipe I adapted, and Chef Walter's memory of this dish while growing up.

MAKES 3 (5 X 8-INCH) FROZEN CONTAINERS

2 cups finely ground white cornmeal
5 cups water
¾ cup pure maple syrup, plus more for drizzling
½ teaspoon kosher salt
½ teaspoon culinary ash (optional)
  (see source guide)

First toast the cornmeal. To do this, heat a large cast-iron skillet or heavy-bottomed pan over medium heat, then add the cornmeal and toast for around 10 minutes or until it turns a golden brown, stirring frequently to prevent burning and ensuring that the cornmeal toasts evenly. The cornmeal will turn from a white color to a light brown. Remove from heat and reserve.

In a large saucepan over medium heat, bring the water, maple syrup, salt, and culinary ash (if using) to a boil. Whisk in the toasted cornmeal, lower the heat to a simmer, and cook for 30 minutes, stirring frequently with a heatproof rubber spatula or whisk to prevent burning.

After 30 minutes, transfer the mixture to a heatproof container or containers so that it comes up the sides approximately 1 inch. Let cool to room temperature before covering and freezing overnight. Place in an oblong, flat, hard plastic container so that it is easy to cut into small squares for serving after it has frozen, and then freeze.

Remove from the freezer and let thaw for approximately 40 minutes before turning it out on a cutting board and slicing into small squares. Serve with a drizzle of additional maple syrup.

Note:
I used three hard plastic to-go containers that were approximately 5 x 8 inches in width and length. One container served four people.

Beans

I love beans. They are a staple in my diet and a very important part of Southwest cuisine. They are an essential Ancestral Native food and easy to make. Because beans are relatively easy to grow and they dry very well, these seeds became historically very important to the survival of Native Peoples. Archaeological excavations in the Tehuacán-Cuicatlán Valley in central Mexico show that beans were first domesticated between 7000 and 3000 B.C. and are indigenous to the Americas.[19] The common bean (*Phaseolus spp.*) was cultivated between 5000 and 3500 B.C.E. Sometimes called the American bean, or New World bean, these varieties include kidney beans, pinto beans, navy beans, wax beans, and lima beans; jack beans and tepary beans were cultivated later.

Starting with the second voyage of Columbus in 1493, beans were taken from the Americas to Europe, Africa, the Mediterranean basin, and Asia. Beans are now widely used in many parts of the world over five hundred years after their introduction. The cannellini bean is a great example. Now considered an Italian bean and used in many Italian dishes, it is a white kidney bean, and its origin begins in the Americas.

Of course, we can't talk about beans without addressing the gastrointestinal side effects that many people experience when they eat "the musical fruit." Many Native Peoples have traditionally used herbs, such as epazote (*Dysphania ambrosioides*), to take out the gaseous effect of beans. There are many other ways to mitigate this effect. Soaking and cooking beans and increasing the amount of beans you eat slowly over time, letting your body adjust to the enzymes, can all help with minimizing the gaseous effect of beans. And taking digestive enzymes like alpha-galactosidase can help prevent gas from beans as well.

While you are probably familiar with beans such as pinto and kidney, you may not know of tepary beans. Tepary beans (*Phaseolus acutifolius*) are an Ancestral Akimel O'odham (River People) and Tohono O'odham (Desert People) small heirloom bush bean found throughout northwestern Mexico, Arizona, and New Mexico. There are two types of tepary beans that I primarily use: the white tepary bean (*S-totoah Bavi*), which has a unique sweet buttery flavor and creamy texture, and the brown tepary (*S-oam Bavi*), which has a more earthy flavor with a nutty taste, although Ramona Farms, where I buy my tepary beans, sells a black tepary bean (*S-chuuk Bavi*) that is also delicious, when available (see source guide).

Beans are still a part of a nutrient-dense healthy diet: they provide high quantities of protein and fiber and are a good source of essential vitamins and minerals needed for cell growth and formation, bone formation, and immunity. A diet that includes beans may help to reduce the risk of certain types of cancers and heart disease and may also lower blood pressure and help to manage type 2 diabetes. So there are tons of reasons to eat this tasty legume. They are super healthy, they are cheap, and they are nutritious.

Throughout the Americas, tribes, nations, and Indigenous communities combined corn and beans together. In the Narraganset language a dish called *m'sickqquatasch* was made of dried beans boiled with fresh corn kernels. Today this dish is known as succotash. You'll find some delicious corn and bean recipes here.

BLACK BEAN & CORN SALSA

This is a great salsa to serve as a side dish with tortillas or chips, or as part of a meal. You can make a tasty and nutritious taco with this recipe by adding freshly made My Favorite Guacamole (page 165) or just serve with fresh perfectly ripened avocado slices. It is easy to make, and I recommend that in the summer months you make this salsa instead of buying it premade. The longer this salsa sits, the hotter it will get due to the chiles releasing the capsicum they contain. I like to make it and eat it immediately, but it will last for a couple of days in the refrigerator.

MAKES APPROXIMATELY 4 CUPS

½ medium-size red onion, minced
    (approximately ¾ cup)
2 Roma tomatoes, diced (approximately 1 cup)
1 cup blackened corn kernels (page 252)
1 tablespoon blackened garlic (page 253)
1 can (15.5 ounces) black beans, rinsed and
    drained (or 1½ cups cooked black beans)
1 jalapeño, seeds and veins removed, minced
    (or more for a spicier salsa)

1 small lime, juiced (approximately
    1½ tablespoons, or to taste)
2 teaspoons New Mexico red chile powder, mild
1 teaspoon kosher salt, or to taste
¼ cup chopped fresh cilantro

In a medium mixing bowl, combine all the ingredients and gently toss together. Serve immediately or refrigerate for later use.

A TRIO OF BEAN SPREADS

Featuring the Southwest staple of pinto beans, white kidney beans (also known as cannellini beans), and black beans, these spreads are high in protein, healthy, inexpensive, easy to make, and very flavorful. Serve them together with warm No Fry Frybread (page 266) or freshly cut vegetables. These spreads are also great to use with sandwiches or on your morning toast. I use them on almost everything and make several versions with different beans.

PINTO BEAN SPREAD

Chef Walter grew up eating pinto beans all the time, and he loves this bean spread served on sandwiches, toast, No Fry Frybread (page 266), and with freshly cut vegetables for a family gathering or celebration. I use this spread on my toast in the morning for a quick, nutritious breakfast. For an Ancestral twist, try making these versions with brown tepary beans (*S-oam Bavi*), white tepary beans (*S-totoah Bavi*), and black tepary beans (*S-chuuk Bavi*) (see source guide), which I like to make as well. The tepary beans will need to be cooked in advance, but it's worth the effort.

MAKES APPROXIMATELY 3 CUPS

1 tablespoon blackened garlic (page 253)

2 cans (15.5 ounces each) pinto beans, drained, with half the liquid reserved

2 tablespoons freshly squeezed lemon juice, or to taste

1 teaspoon kosher salt, or to taste

⅛ teaspoon freshly ground black pepper, or to taste

2 teaspoons chipotle en adobo, or to taste

1 teaspoon New Mexico red chile powder, mild (optional)

In a food processor, purée the garlic with the beans until it is a smooth purée. Add the lemon juice, salt, pepper, and chipotle en adobo. Process until it is completely mixed and creamy, using 1 to 3 tablespoons of the reserved bean juice to make the mixture creamy and smooth, adding 1 tablespoon at a time to the food processor until you reach your desired texture.

Transfer the mixture to a medium-size serving bowl. Garnish with the red chile powder, if desired, and serve. Place in an airtight container and store in the refrigerator for up to several days.

Notes:
Three cups of cooked pinto beans with 3 tablespoons of reserved bean juice can be used instead of the two cans of beans for this recipe.

Chipotle en adobo are smoked and dried jalapeños that are rehydrated and made into a purée with tomato, vinegar, garlic, and spices, which have some nice heat, and lots of body. It can be purchased in a can or jar, and there are many brands available from your grocers.

WHITE BEAN &
ROASTED RED BELL PEPPER SPREAD

Cannellini beans are large white kidney beans, with a buttery and nutty taste, that are very popular in Central and Southern Italy, especially in Tuscany. I love the texture of these beans and use them a lot in my sauces. Some people substitute navy beans or Great Northern beans, but I prefer this bean for both flavor and texture. However, try this with three cups of cooked white tepary beans (*S-totoah Bavi*) (see source guide) for an Ancestral twist.

MAKES APPROXIMATELY 3 CUPS

1 head of garlic
½ teaspoon sunflower oil
1½ teaspoons kosher salt, or to taste
1 red bell pepper, roasted, peeled, seeded,
    and diced (see directions)
2 cans (15.5 ounces each) cannellini or another
    white bean, drained and rinsed, or 3 cups
    cooked white tepary beans
Zest of 1 organic lemon
1 tablespoon freshly squeezed lemon juice
Pinch of freshly ground black pepper, or to taste

Preheat the oven to 400°F. Remove the loose outer leaves from the head of garlic. With a sharp knife, slice the top ½ inch off the head, exposing the inner cloves. Place the head of garlic in a small baking dish with the sunflower oil and a sprinkle of kosher salt and cover. Bake for 30 minutes until the cloves are soft. When the garlic is cool enough to safely handle, squeeze from the base of the bulb to press out the roasted garlic, or you can remove each clove with a small fork. Reserve.

Roast the red bell pepper using the open flame method or carefully under a broiler until it is charred all over. Transfer the bell pepper to a bowl with a splash of water in the bottom and cover tightly. Let sit at room temperature for 10 minutes to steam. Peel with your hands or a paring knife, remove the seeds and stem, and dice.

In a food processor, add the garlic, bell pepper, beans, lemon zest, and lime juice. Process until mixture is completely smooth, around 1 minute. Season with the remaining salt and pepper to taste.

Transfer the mixture to a medium serving bowl. Serve with No Fry Frybread (page 266) or freshly cut vegetables. The bean spread can be placed in an airtight container and stored in the refrigerator for up to several days.

BLACK BEAN & GARLIC SPREAD

Black beans give a different texture than the other two spreads; the beans are a little chunkier and their flavor a little more distinct than the other two beans, almost like a savory earthy flavor. This paired with the roasted garlic makes a lovely combination, and it has a beautiful color. It is the perfect accompaniment to the other two bean spreads.

MAKES APPROXIMATELY 3 CUPS

1 head of garlic
½ teaspoon plus 1 tablespoon sunflower oil
1½ teaspoons kosher salt, or to taste
1 yellow onion, diced (approximately 1½ cups)
2 teaspoons New Mexico red chile powder, mild
2 cans (15.5 ounces each) black beans,
    drained and rinsed
⅛ teaspoon freshly ground black pepper,
    or to taste

Preheat the oven to 400°F. Remove the loose outer leaves from the head of garlic. With a sharp knife, slice the top ½ inch off the head, exposing the inner cloves. Place the head of garlic in a small baking dish with ½ teaspoon of the sunflower oil and a sprinkle of kosher salt and cover. Bake for 30 minutes until the cloves are soft. When the garlic is cool enough to safely handle, squeeze from the base of the bulb to press out the roasted garlic, or you can remove each clove with a small fork. Reserve.

In a large skillet over medium heat, add the 1 tablespoon of sunflower oil. Once the oil is hot but not smoking, add the onion, stir, and cook for approximately 6 minutes, stirring occasionally to prevent burning, until the onion is caramelized brown and all the water from the onion has evaporated.

Add the chile powder, garlic, and beans. Let cook for a few minutes, stirring frequently. Season with the kosher salt and pepper before transferring to a food processor and pulsing until completely smooth.

Transfer the mixture to a medium serving bowl. Serve immediately with No Fry Frybread (page 266) or freshly cut vegetables, or serve chilled. The bean spread can be placed in an airtight container and stored in the refrigerator for up to several days.

THREE BEAN SALAD

I have made this salad with my students in the Indigenous Concepts of Native American Food class at the Institute of American Arts (IAIA). Leaving the romaine leaves whole keeps them crisp and fresh; however, you can cut the leaves and mix them together with the three beans and serve immediately. This salad can be made in advance and dressed at the last minute, then plated with the lettuce leaves.

MAKES 4 SERVINGS

2 small heads romaine lettuce
(20–30 lettuce leaves plus 5–8 leaves
each serving)

For the Salad:
½ cup pinto beans, cooked or canned
(rinse if using canned)
½ cup red kidney beans, cooked or canned
(rinse if using canned)
½ cup garbanzo beans, cooked or canned
(rinse if using canned)
1 cup blackened corn (page 252)
3 to 4 fresh vine tomatoes, small to medium size,
diced (approximately 1 cup)
4 green onions, sliced on a bias
(approximately ½ cup)
2 tablespoons cilantro, finely chopped

For the Salad Dressing:
6 tablespoons red chile agave (page 269)
2 tablespoons plus 2 teaspoons smooth Dijon
mustard
½ cup freshly squeezed lime juice
(approximately 3 limes), or to taste
1 teaspoon ground cumin
1 teaspoon kosher salt, or to taste
⅛ teaspoon freshly ground black pepper

Cut the bottom off of the heads of romaine lettuce, wash and dry, and set aside.

In a medium mixing bowl, gently mix the beans, corn, tomatoes, green onions, and cilantro. Toss with a large spoon to make sure they are completely mixed.

In another mixing bowl, whisk together the red chile agave, mustard, lime juice, cumin, salt, and pepper. Chef Walter likes a little less lime juice in his dressing, so add it in small amounts, tasting as you go, until you think it has enough lime in it. However, I love lime juice and use all the amount listed.

Pour ½ cup of the salad dressing over the bean salad mixture. Toss together so that the dressing completely covers the bean mixture.

To serve, place approximately five to eight romaine leaves on a salad plate. Top with a portion of the bean salad mixture (½ cup to ¾ cup). Drizzle a little amount (about 2 tablespoons) of the remaining salad dressing over the romaine leaves. Serve immediately on a large platter or individual plates.

RED MESA'S REFRIED PINTO BEANS

With its complex flavors, this refried bean recipe is my go-to. It can be used on its own or as a part of other dishes like the Pinto Bean & Mushroom Rolled Enchiladas (page 148) and the Three Sisters Rolled Enchiladas (page 35) or wrapped in a tortilla for a mouthwatering taco served with Lois's Pico de Gallo (page 164) and My Favorite Guacamole (page 165). As with cooking hominy corn, I cook my beans in a Crockpot overnight. This way I can make additional bean juice, which I use to cook with. It's easy to do and the beans come out perfectly. You can also use an Instant Pot if you prefer.

MAKES 4 TO 6 SERVINGS

1½ cups dried pinto beans, or 4 cups cooked beans
½ teaspoon dried Mexican oregano
½ teaspoon cumin seed
½ teaspoon coriander seed
2 teaspoons sunflower oil
1 small to medium yellow onion, finely chopped (approximately 1½ cups)
1 tablespoon blackened garlic (page 253)
2 tablespoons water
1 tablespoon New Mexico red chile powder, mild
1½ teaspoons kosher salt, or to taste
2 cups bean juice, reserved from cooking the beans

To Make the Beans in a Crockpot:

Add beans to 7½ cups of water. Bring the beans and water to a boil in the Crockpot and then turn it down to low and let them cook for approximately 8 hours. Check to make sure the beans are cooked and soft but not mushy, then strain the beans from the bean juice, reserve the beans and the liquid, and let them cool. Once they have cooled, use them as instructed below.

To Make Beans on the Stove Top:

Soak the beans overnight in water to cover. In the morning, rinse the beans with cold water and place them in a saucepan with enough fresh water to cover. Bring to a boil over high heat, then reduce the heat and simmer for 2 to 3 hours until the beans become soft, the skins begin to split, and the beans are completely cooked. Taste one to make sure that they are completely cooked. Add water when necessary and stir occasionally to prevent the beans from sticking to the bottom of the pot. Remove from the heat, strain the beans from the juice, and reserve the bean juice and the beans separately. Once the beans have cooled, use as instructed below.

To prepare the bean purée, toast each dried spice (Mexican oregano, cumin, and coriander) separately in a dry small sauté pan over medium heat until lightly browned. For the Mexican oregano, toast for approximately 45 seconds, then remove from pan, place in a small bowl, allow to cool, and then crush with your fingers for use. For the cumin, toast in the same pan for 45 seconds until the seeds crackle and begin to turn brown, remove from the pan, and set aside. For the coriander, toast for approximately 1 minute until the seeds begin to pop, remove from pan, and set aside.

Do not over-toast or the spices will taste burned. (Sometimes a small amount is difficult to do, so I toast 1 to 2 teaspoons of each at a time and reserve the additional ground spice for future use.) Grind the spice in a spice grinder or coffee grinder until it is a fine powder. Or you can use a mortar and pestle and grind them by hand.

In a saucepan, over medium to high heat, heat the sunflower oil until it is hot but not smoking. Add the onions and sauté for approximately 6 minutes, stirring occasionally, until they are caramelized. Reduce the heat to medium low, add the garlic, and cook for 1 minute. Add the water, which will bubble in the pan, and stir to deglaze the pan and release all the good flavor from the bottom of the pan. Add the Mexican oregano, cumin, coriander, chile powder, and salt, and stir. Add the beans and the bean juice. The bean juice should be just enough to cover the beans and spices. Bring to a boil over high heat, stirring to make sure all the spices are incorporated evenly, then reduce heat and simmer, uncovered, for 25 minutes. Stir the reducing bean mixture every couple of minutes to make sure it is not burning.

After the mixture has simmered for 25 minutes, turn off the heat. Taste and adjust seasoning if desired. Remove

approximately 2 cups of the cooked bean mixture and purée in a food processor until it is smooth. Add the purée back to the whole bean mixture in the sauté pan and stir them together. If you do not have a food processor, you can mash some of the beans in the pan using a potato masher or wooden mashing tool. Cook for an additional 5 minutes, stirring constantly, until the mixture is thick and you have the desired texture, which is thick but can still be spooned onto a plate.

Serve immediately or use as per the recipe instructions.

Note:
If you are using this recipe for enchiladas, allow the refried beans to cool for about 10 minutes so you don't burn yourself when handling them with the tortillas. The mixture will thicken a little more as it cools. If the beans become too thick, add a little hot water to loosen when making the enchiladas.

BLACK BEANS WITH CHOCOLATE & CHIPOTLE

Black beans are full bodied and rich in flavor as well as very nutritious. While you may think chocolate is the special ingredient, in this recipe it's actually epazote. Epazote is a leafy green medicinal and culinary herb indigenous to Mexico and South America. Raw, it has a resinous, medicinal pungency, similar to anise, fennel, or even tarragon, but stronger. Although it is traditionally used with black beans for flavor and its carminative properties (less gas), it is also sometimes used in other Mexican dishes as well. If epazote is unavailable in your area, it can be purchased dried online (see source guide) or omitted in the recipe.

This recipe makes a nice accompaniment to the Green Chile Herbed Rice (page 140) and the Mole Sauce (page 228) and even the Mole Enchiladas with Mushrooms & Potatoes (page 230), but it can also be used in tacos with freshly sliced ripe avocado and Lois's Pico de Gallo (page 164).

MAKES 4 TO 6 SERVINGS

1 tablespoon sunflower or olive oil

1 medium yellow onion, diced (approximately 1½ cups)

1 teaspoon garlic, finely chopped

½ teaspoon dried epazote, or 1 teaspoon fresh, chopped (optional)

2 ounces 72 percent dark chocolate, chopped (approximately ⅓ cup)

1 tablespoon plus 2 teaspoons chipotle en adobo, finely chopped, or to taste

1 teaspoon dried Mexican oregano, crumbled

2 bay leaves

5 cups cooked black beans, or 4 cans (15.5 ounces each)

1½ cups water or bean juice

1 teaspoon kosher salt, or to taste

Heat the sunflower oil in a large saucepan over medium to high heat until it is hot but not smoking. Add the onions and sauté until they are clear, approximately 4 minutes, stirring frequently to prevent burning. Add the garlic and cook for 1 more minute. Add the epazote, if using, chocolate, chipotle, Mexican oregano, and bay leaves and cook for 1 minute, stirring constantly to make sure the chocolate doesn't burn. Add the beans and water and bring to a boil. Reduce the heat and simmer for 10 minutes to let all the flavors blend. Season with the salt, taste, and adjust if necessary.

Serve hot as a side or as part of your favorite entrée.

Note:

Chipotle en adobo has a wonderful smoky flavor but has some spice to it. Add it in small increments if you have a less spicy palate. You can always add more until you reach the amount recommended in the recipe, but you cannot undo the heat once you have added it. My palate is medium spicy, so this recipe reflects that.

RED CHILE PINTO BEANS

Pinto beans are a Southwest staple. They are used as a main course, as a side, in tacos, in soups and stews, on salads, and as a part of almost every Pueblo Feast Day menu. Served on its own with White Corn Tortillas (page 27), No Fry Frybread (page 266), made into a burrito, or even just served with flour tortillas, this dish is a perfect way to enjoy flavorsome and nutritious beans. If you have a spicier palate, you can use a medium or hot ground New Mexico red chile, as well as increase the amount of red chile powder that you add to the beans. I prefer using freshly cooked beans in this dish, but you can certainly use canned beans.

MAKES 4 TO 6 SERVINGS

1 tablespoon sunflower oil or olive oil

1 medium yellow onion, diced (approximately 1½ cups)

1 tablespoon minced garlic

1 tablespoon New Mexico red chile powder, mild

2 teaspoons ground coriander

4 cups cooked pinto beans (see directions on page 74) (or about three 15.5-ounce cans)

2 cups water or bean juice (if using canned beans, I recommend using water as the juice is salted in canned beans)

1½ teaspoons kosher salt, or to taste

½ teaspoon epazote, dried, or 1 teaspoon fresh, finely chopped (optional)

Heat the sunflower oil in a large saucepan over medium to high heat until it is hot but not smoking. Add the onions and sauté until they are clear, for 5 to 6 minutes, stirring frequently to prevent burning. Add the garlic and cook for 1 more minute. Add the chile powder and coriander and cook for 1 more minute. Add the beans, water, salt, and epazote, if using. Bring to a boil. Reduce the heat and simmer for 10 minutes to let all the flavors blend.

Serve hot and immediately with your favorite tortilla or bread.

THREE SISTERS STEW

Chef Walter and I originally made this recipe on the Navajo Reservation in the town of Pinon, Arizona, where he grew up. It has been made for numerous family gatherings and Ceremonies. For this version, I've added zucchini instead of meat; the squash makes this hearty without being heavy. This recipe is great because you can make it to feed four to six people, or you can add to it and make enough to feed sixty to six hundred people. A satisfying meal by itself or a side to any feast, this recipe goes great with homemade White Corn Tortillas (page 27), Blue Corn No Fry Frybread (page 268), or No Fry Frybread (page 266).

2 teaspoons sunflower oil

½ large yellow onion, chopped
(approximately 1 cup)

½ green bell pepper, seeded and chopped
(approximately ½ cup)

1 zucchini, cut into small cubes
(approximately 1½ cups)

2 teaspoons blackened garlic (page 253)

1 can (14.5 ounces) diced tomatoes,
no salt added if possible

1½ cups cooked organic dark red kidney beans
(or one 15-ounce can)

1½ cups cooked organic pinto beans
(or one 15-ounce can)

1 cup corn kernels, fresh or frozen

1½ tablespoons New Mexico red chile powder,
mild

1 teaspoon New Mexico red chile powder,
medium (optional for a slightly
hotter stew)

1 teaspoon kosher salt, or to taste

¼ teaspoon black pepper, or to taste

¼ teaspoon dried thyme

¼ teaspoon dried oregano

4 cups water or bean juice

Preheat a cast-iron soup pot or heavy-bottomed metal soup pot over medium-high heat. Add the sunflower oil and heat until hot but not smoking. Add the onions, sauté for approximately 3 minutes until translucent, stirring to prevent burning. Add the bell pepper and sauté for another 3 minutes, stirring to prevent burning. Add the zucchini and sauté for another 3 minutes. You want the vegetables to caramelize and begin to turn brown. The bottom of the pan may begin to turn brown, but this is part of the caramelization process. Add the garlic and cook for another minute, stirring to prevent burning and to incorporate into the other ingredients.

Add the tomatoes. Cook for another 2 minutes, stirring constantly. Add the kidney beans, pinto beans, corn, mild chile powder, and medium chile powder (if you want a spicier stew), salt, black pepper, thyme, and oregano and mix well. Add the water, bring to a boil, then reduce heat and let simmer for 25 minutes, stirring occasionally. Taste, and adjust salt or other seasoning, if desired. Remove from heat and serve immediately.

Note:
Fresh thyme and fresh oregano can be used if available. Simply double the amount from ¼ teaspoon of each to ½ teaspoon of each. I usually buy herbs fresh if they are available, and if I have leftover herbs from whatever I am cooking, I dry them on a sheet tray in my pantry and then put them into glass jars for future use.

NAVAJO MINESTRONE SOUP

Former Navajo Nation president Jonathan Nez and former first lady Phefelia Nez have been vocal proponents of healthy eating. President Nez found that plant-based eating shortened his recovery time after long-distance runs and helped him maintain his weight loss. First Lady Nez provided us with one of her family-favorite soup recipes that we modified. We used the modified version for a course called Native Food for Life Online, offered through the American Indian Institute (Aii) and the Physicians Committee for Responsible Medicine (PCRM). "Minestrone" is its Italian name, but the ingredients in this soup originated in the Americas. Chef Walter Whitewater said that when growing up on the Navajo Nation, he used to harvest wild onions, carrots, garlic, and spinach. With the addition of frozen corn, canned beans, and zucchini, as well as the pasta—all foods that most community members have on hand or receive as part of the Food Distribution Program on Indian Reservations (FDPIR)—our version of this recipe is a favorite of Chef Walter. Serve with No Fry Frybread (page 266), Blue Corn No Fry Frybread (page 268), White Corn Tortillas (page 27), or Blue Corn Tortillas (page 28). This soup serves approximately 6 depending on your serving size.

MAKES APPROXIMATELY 2 QUARTS OF SOUP

1 cup mini farfalle (bow tie pasta) or other pasta, like penne or elbows (approximately 2 cups cooked)

1 tablespoon sunflower oil

1 small yellow onion, diced (approximately 1 cup)

3 carrots, peeled and cut into ⅛-inch thick half-moon slices (approximately 1 cup)

2 stalks celery, sliced (approximately 1 cup)

½ cup frozen yellow sweet corn kernels

1 tablespoon blackened garlic (page 253)

1 zucchini, cut into ½-inch cubes (approximately 1 cup)

1 can (14.5 ounces) diced tomatoes, organic and no salt added if possible

2 tablespoons tomato paste

1 cup spinach, fresh or frozen

5 cups water or vegetable broth (page 264)

1 can (15.5 ounces) dark red kidney beans, drained and rinsed (approximately 1½ cups)

1 can (15.5 ounces) pinto beans, drained and rinsed (approximately 1½ cups)

1 tablespoon finely chopped fresh basil

½ teaspoon finely chopped fresh oregano

½ teaspoon finely chopped fresh thyme

2 teaspoons New Mexico red chile powder, mild

1 tablespoon finely chopped flat-leaf parsley leaves

2 teaspoons kosher salt, or to taste

¼ teaspoon black pepper, or to taste (optional)

In a large cooking pot, boil water and cook the pasta until done following the directions on the package. Remove from heat, drain the hot water, and then rinse with cold water to stop the pasta from cooking and set aside.

In a separate soup pot, heat the sunflower oil over medium-high heat until hot but not smoking. Sauté the onion for approximately 4 minutes, stirring occasionally to prevent burning. Add the carrots and the celery and cook for an additional 5 to 6 minutes, stirring. Add the corn and cook for another 2 minutes, stirring once to prevent burning. Add the garlic and cook for another minute, stirring constantly to mix. The bottom of your pan will turn brown, and the vegetables should begin to caramelize. Add the zucchini and cook for another 3 minutes, stirring to prevent burning.

Add the tomatoes and tomato paste, stirring to completely mix and to deglaze the bottom of the pan. Add the spinach and water and bring to a boil. Then simmer, covered, for 10 minutes, stirring occasionally.

Add the kidney and pinto beans, stirring to blend, and then add the basil, oregano, thyme, chile powder, parsley, and salt. Bring back to a boil, then reduce the heat and let simmer for another 10 minutes.

Taste, season with additional salt and pepper, if desired. Add the cooked pasta, stir, and bring to a boil. Cook for an additional 1 to 2 minutes until the soup is completely hot. You do not want to cook the soup too long, as the pasta is already cooked and will become overcooked. Remove from heat. Serve immediately.

WHITE BEAN, BUTTERNUT SQUASH & KALE SOUP

This soup is a wonderful fall harvest meal. The white bean complements the butternut squash, making a rich, hearty soup with the coconut milk giving it a creamy consistency and the kale adding color and lots of nutrients. While the evolutionary origin of the coconut is disputed, according to some sources, there is evidence of a pre-Columbian introduction of the Pacific-domesticated coconuts to Panama from Austronesian sailors. Here, I use lacinato kale, also called dinosaur or Tuscan kale, since I find it to be more tender than curly kale, but you can use whichever is your favorite. Serve with No Fry Frybread (page 266), Blue Corn No Fry Frybread (page 268), or White Corn Tortillas (page 27).

MAKES APPROXIMATELY 3 QUARTS

1 tablespoon sunflower oil

1 large yellow onion, diced (approximately 2 cups)

2 tablespoons blackened garlic (page 253)

2 teaspoons New Mexico red chile powder, mild

2 teaspoons ground coriander

1 butternut squash (about 3 pounds), peeled and cut into 1-inch pieces (about 8 cups)

2 cans (15.5 ounces each) Great Northern beans, drained and rinsed well

1 can (13.5 ounces) unsweetened coconut milk

6 cups water

1 bunch lacinato kale, torn into bite-size pieces (approximately 6 cups)

3 teaspoons kosher salt, or to taste

¼ teaspoon black pepper

In a large soup pot over medium heat, add the sunflower oil. Heat until hot but not smoking, then add the onions and cook until they are translucent and begin to caramelize, for 8 to 10 minutes, stirring occasionally to prevent burning. Add the garlic, chile powder, and coriander and cook for another 2 minutes, stirring frequently. Add the squash, beans, coconut milk, and water. Bring the soup to a boil, then reduce the heat and cook until the squash is tender, approximately 30 minutes.

Turn off the heat and carefully blend 4 cups of the soup until smooth and then return it to the pot. Add the kale and cook for an additional 5 minutes. Season with the salt and pepper. Taste and adjust seasoning, if necessary. Ladle into large bowls. Serve immediately.

BEAN & SPINACH TACOS

For this recipe, fresh spinach greens are sautéed with cooked beans for an easy, tasty taco. You can be flexible with the beans: Anasazi beans are fairly easy to get, but this dish also tastes great with pinto beans that you can buy canned at your grocery store for a quick meal. I like to use either White Corn Tortillas (page 27) or the gordita-size store-bought flour tortillas. Top with freshly made Lois's Pico de Gallo (page 164) and My Favorite Guacamole (page 165).

MAKES 12 TACOS FILLED WITH 3 TABLESPOONS OF FILLING

12 White Corn Tortillas (page 27),
    or use store-bought
2 teaspoons sunflower oil
½ medium white onion, diced
    (approximately ⅔ cup)
2 teaspoons blackened garlic (page 253)
1 cup chopped Roma tomatoes
    (approximately 2 to 3)
3 cups packed fresh baby spinach,
    chopped (approximately 4 ounces)
1½ cups cooked Anasazi beans,
    pinto beans, or brown tepary beans,
    or 1 can (15.5 ounces) pinto beans
¾ teaspoon kosher salt
¼ teaspoon freshly ground black pepper

If you are making the White Corn Tortillas (page 27), prepare these first as per the recipe instructions. If you are serving with store-bought tortillas, heat tortillas over an open flame, wrap in a clean kitchen towel, and hold in a basket to keep them warm.

Preheat a medium cast-iron skillet over medium to high heat until it is hot but not smoking. Add the sunflower oil and onions and sauté for 4 to 6 minutes, stirring to prevent burning and to caramelize and brown the onions. Add the garlic and cook for an additional minute, stirring constantly. Add the tomatoes and cook for an additional 2 minutes. Add the spinach and cook for another minute, stirring constantly, then add the beans, salt, and pepper and cook for another minute, mixing all the ingredients. Taste and adjust seasoning, if desired.

Remove from heat. Serve immediately.

Opposite: *Bean & Spinach Tacos with My Favorite Guacamole (page 165) and Lois's Pico de Gallo Salsa (page 164) with Blackened Corn (page 252)*

HEALTHY INDIAN TACOS

Indian Tacos are made in almost every Indian community all over the United States. They are served at almost every fair, many powwows, some Pueblo Feasts, and at the annual Indian Market here in Santa Fe. This version uses either No Fry Frybread (page 266) or Blue Corn No Fry Frybread (page 268). Try the toppings below or some alternatives like arugula greens, daikon radish sprouts, cut purple daikon radishes, watermelon radishes, any kind of microgreens, and diced red bell pepper.

MAKES 8 TACOS AND SERVES 4 AS A MAIN COURSE OR 8 AS AN APPETIZER

8 No Fry Frybreads (page 266) or 8 Blue Corn No Fry Frybreads (page 268) (see directions)

For the Taco Filling:
About 4 New Mexico green chiles (will yield about 1 cup diced), or use frozen prepared chiles

1 tablespoon sunflower oil

½ medium to large yellow onion, diced (approximately 1 cup)

1 teaspoon blackened garlic (page 253)

2 ripe tomatoes, diced (approximately 1½ cups)

2 tablespoons New Mexico red chile powder, mild

2 teaspoons kosher salt, or to taste

5 cups cooked pinto beans (page 74)

1½ cups bean juice or water

Basic Taco Garnish:
½ white onion, finely diced (about 1 cup)

2 ripe tomatoes, diced (approximately 1½ cups)

½ head romaine or mixed baby lettuce, chopped (about 2 cups)

1 perfectly ripened avocado, sliced

3 radishes, cut into matchstick-size pieces (approximately ½ cup)

⅔ cup (a handful) sunflower sprouts (optional)

First prepare the No Fry Frybread (page 266) or Blue Corn No Fry Frybread (page 268).

Using the open flame method, roast the green chiles until completely charred. Place them in a glass or metal bowl and cover with plastic wrap to allow the chiles to sweat and cool down. Peel the charred skin off, remove the seeds, and chop them into dice-size pieces.

In a cast-iron pan, heat the sunflower oil on high heat until it is hot but not smoking. Add the onion and sauté for 4 to 5 minutes, stirring to prevent burning. Add the garlic and sauté for another minute, stirring constantly. Add the tomatoes and cook for another 3 minutes, stirring to prevent burning and ensure all the ingredients are evenly cooked. Add the green chile, red chile powder, and salt. Stir until the chile and chile powder are completely mixed into the other ingredients. Add the beans and the bean juice. Stir to make sure all the ingredients are completely mixed. Taste and adjust seasoning, if desired.

Bring the mixture to a boil, then reduce heat to medium low and cook for 5 minutes, stirring to prevent burning. Remove from heat and serve hot over either of the No Fry Frybread recipes and top with any number of garnishes.

Squash

Squash (*Cucurbita spp.*) is one of the most important Native American crops, along with corn and beans—the Three Sisters (and sometimes called the Native Trio or Indian Triad). It has always been a staple and a major part of the Native American diet. Native American agriculture was not only very different from the practices in other parts of the world prior to contact, but according to Peter Farb, "in many ways it was superior as well. Indians cultivated a wider variety of plants than did Europeans at the time of the discovery of North America, and they used horticultural techniques that were in many cases more advanced." Some scientists say that Native Peoples had made agricultural advances far beyond those in other parts of the world, and with the use of companion planting and natural fertilizing, Native American agriculture was producing a wide variety of crops, and the diet was as diverse as the agricultural techniques.

There are many different types of squash being grown today. Some varieties have woven their way into the fabric of other cultures after being introduced in the 1500s and 1600s.

Most types of squash are categorized into summer and winter squashes. Summer squashes are those varieties with edible skin like zucchini, yellow summer squash, yellow crookneck squash, pattypan squash, chayote squash, cousa squash, and green striped Mexican squash, to name a few. Winter squashes have a hard outer shell and include varieties such as acorn squash, butternut squash, Honeynut squash, Hubbard squash, spaghetti squash, kabocha squash, delicata squash, turban squash, red kuri squash (Hokkaido pumpkin), sugar pumpkin, buttercup squash, sweet dumpling squash, and other varieties. And while squash is often treated as a vegetable, it is actually a type of fruit, as it comes from a flower and contains seeds, which are also edible.

Considered a superfood, squashes are probably one of the most delicious and versatile foods now available and they pack some serious health and medicinal benefits. Full of fiber and antioxidants, they can help improve heart health and manage type 2 diabetes; and they can help normalize blood-pressure levels when eaten. Squash contain many vitamins and minerals, all providing health benefits such as eye, cardiovascular, and brain health. They aid in maintaining a healthy immune system and may help reduce the risk of depression. Basically, these fruits are essential to a whole-food healthy diet and should be eaten on a regular basis. The flowers from the squash plants can also be eaten and are considered a summer delicacy. Native American communities have been harvesting squash blossoms for millennia.

Many Native communities are reclaiming important varieties of squash for health and wellness in their own communities. The Mvskoke Food Sovereignty Initiative (MFSI) in the Muscogee (Creek) Nation in East Central Oklahoma is working on increasing production, availability of seeds, and consumption of two traditional Mvskoke tribal crops. One is the sofke (osafke) corn, and the other is the Indian Pumpkin. The Indian Pumpkin belongs to the gourd family and has been cultivated by ancestors of the Mvskokvlke for over four thousand years. Because it is endangered in terms of availability of seed, they have created an initiative to revitalize this particular variety of pumpkin because of its nutritional value and its cultural significance to the Muscogee Nation. The revitalization of the Indian Pumpkin is just one food that the MFSI is working hard to secure a future for in their community.[20]

The beauty about squashes is that they can be eaten in their savory form or in desserts with a sweeter flavor. The recipes that follow include both savory and sweet dishes. From summer fried squash blossoms to grilled summer squash, to a traditional New Mexican favorite called calabacitas as savory incarnations of this amazing fruit, to pumpkin pie with piñon pecan crust or the pumpkin piñon cake, there are lots of recipes in this chapter that truly celebrate this amazing fruit.

DELICATA SQUASH SALAD

Delicata is one of the lesser-known winter squashes, but with its sweet flavor and creamy flesh, it deserves top billing. Because delicata squash has a thinner, delicate skin, it is completely edible. However, be sure to wash the outside well before cooking it because oftentimes it will be coated with a wax, unless purchased from your local farmers' market or from a grocery where it is certified organic and doesn't have a wax coating. Roasting this squash makes for a lovely way to eat it, and this recipe pairs it perfectly with winter sprouts and/or microgreens. This is one of my favorite winter salads.

MAKES 4 SERVINGS

For the Squash:

3 small delicata squashes, washed, both ends trimmed, cut into 1-inch rings, then seeded (approximately 3 pounds total)

1 large red onion, sliced

¼ cup fresh sage leaves, finely sliced

2 tablespoons sunflower oil

1 teaspoon kosher salt, or to taste

¼ teaspoon freshly ground black pepper

For the Dressing:

1 Honeycrisp, Fuji, or Gala apple, peeled, cored, and finely diced or minced

2 tablespoons apple cider vinegar

2 tablespoons sunflower oil

1 tablespoon pure maple syrup

2 teaspoons smooth Dijon mustard

¼ teaspoon kosher salt, or to taste

For the Garnish:

2 ounces sprouts or microgreens (approximately 1 cup)

Preheat the oven to 425°F. Line a large sheet tray with parchment paper. In a large bowl, toss the squash, onion, sage, oil, salt, and pepper together. Transfer this mixture to the sheet tray and make sure the squash pieces are in a single layer so that they will caramelize while cooking. Roast in the oven for 45 minutes, or until the squash starts to crisp on the edges and is tender when pierced with a knife.

To make the vinaigrette, stir together the dressing ingredients.

To serve, arrange the warm roasted squash mixture on a large platter or individual plates. Stir the dressing right before serving to make sure the oil, vinegar, and apples are well combined and spoon a drizzle on top. Garnish with a generous amount (approximately ¼ cup) of sprouts and/or microgreens.

Note:

Some groceries, like Trader Joe's and Natural Grocers, sell mixed microgreens all year. I try to buy mine at my local Santa Fe Farmers' Market, but check to see what is available in your area or at your local farmers' market.

KABOCHA SQUASH SALAD

If you have never tried kabocha, you are in for a treat. It's similar to butternut, but I find it creamier and richer; it has flavorful smooth and sweet-tasting flesh. The best season for this squash is in late summer and early fall. This salad is a wonderful introduction to it; the sweetness of the dressing pairs wonderfully with the rich squash and bitter, peppery greens. The squash can be eaten whole, skin and flesh, once cooked, but many people, including myself, prefer to cut the skin off because they find it tough, even after cooking.

MAKES 4 SERVINGS

For the Roasted Squash:
1 small kabocha squash (around 2 pounds)
2 tablespoons sunflower oil
1 tablespoon maple syrup
2 teaspoons ground coriander
1 teaspoon New Mexico red chile powder, mild
½ teaspoon kosher salt
¼ teaspoon freshly ground black pepper

For the Vinaigrette:
Zest of 4 organic lemons (approximately 4 tablespoons)
4 tablespoons freshly squeezed lemon juice (juice from approximately 2 lemons)
6 tablespoons sunflower oil
4 teaspoons pure maple syrup
2 tablespoons minced fresh sage leaves
2 shallots, minced (approximately ¼ cup)
1 teaspoon kosher salt, or to taste
4 teaspoons whole-grain Dijon mustard

For the Salad:
1 head of radicchio, halved and sliced
4 cups arugula (approximately 4 ounces)
½ cup dried cranberries
½ teaspoon kosher salt, or to taste
⅛ teaspoon freshly ground black pepper, or to taste

Preheat the oven to 425°F. Line a large sheet tray with parchment paper. Trim the top and bottom off the squash. Cut in half down the center, remove seeds, and cut squash into ½-inch wedges. Place the squash in a large bowl and toss with the sunflower oil, maple syrup, coriander, chile powder, salt, and pepper. Transfer the squash to the sheet tray, making sure not to overcrowd, and bake until the squash is tender and the pieces are beginning to caramelize, approximately 20 minutes. When the squash is done cooking, let it cool enough so that you can handle it. If you are going to peel the outer skin of the squash off, now is the time to do that with a small paring knife.

While the squash is cooking, prepare the vinaigrette. In a small bowl, whisk together the dressing ingredients. To make the salad, in a large bowl toss the squash, radicchio, arugula, and cranberries with just enough vinaigrette to coat everything. Add salt or pepper as needed and to taste.

Place approximately ¼ of the radicchio and arugula onto a plate. Top with slices of the squash, then drizzle dressing around the edge of the plate and serve immediately.

SPAGHETTI SQUASH SLAW

Spaghetti squash looks like all other hard-shelled squashes on the outside and comes in a variety of colors ranging from light yellow to orange. The difference with this squash, however, is that when it is cooked, the flesh falls away from the skin into strands and pieces that resemble spaghetti, thus its name. It can be used as an alternative to spaghetti noodles and makes a delicious dish when prepared that way; here, I use the "spaghetti" as the basis for a chilled slaw, with chiles to enhance the flavor.

1 small spaghetti squash, around 3 pounds
    (approximately 8 x 5 inches)

For the Dressing:
1 New Mexico or Anaheim green or poblano
    chile, roasted, peeled, seeded, and diced
    (page 250)
2 tablespoons freshly squeezed lime juice
    (approximately 1 lime)
2 tablespoons sunflower oil
2 teaspoons agave sweetener
½ teaspoon kosher salt
½ teaspoon New Mexico red chile powder,
    mild

For the Salad:
½ cup golden raisins
1 red bell pepper, seeded and sliced into
    1-inch strips
1 small red onion, thinly sliced
    (approximately 1 cup)
½ cup roughly chopped flat-leaf parsley leaves
½ cup roughly chopped cilantro leaves

For the Garnish:
½ cup Toasted Pumpkin Seeds (page 261)

Bring a large pot of water to a boil. Wash squash thoroughly and trim both ends. Peel the squash, cut in half lengthwise, remove the seeds, and then cut in half again so that it is cut into quarters. Carefully place the squash quarters in the water and cook until the squash is just tender, for around 15 minutes. Drain the squash into a colander and let cool. With a large spoon or your hands, pull the squash and separate into strands. If the pieces are long, gather them all together and cut them in half so each strand is no longer than approximately 3 inches in length.

In a large salad bowl, whisk together the dressing ingredients. Add the golden raisins and let them sit in the vinaigrette for 5 minutes to soften and plump a little with the flavoring of the vinaigrette. Add the cooled squash, bell pepper, red onion, parsley, and cilantro.

Gently toss everything together. The squash can be made in advance and chilled. Just before you are ready to serve the salad, garnish with pumpkin seeds and then serve immediately. This way, the pumpkin seeds will retain their crunchiness and add a nice texture to the salad.

SUMMER FRIED SQUASH BLOSSOMS

Squash blossoms are a seasonal delicacy and one of my favorite things to eat during the summer months. For several weeks each year, they can be purchased at the Santa Fe Farmers' Market. Native American communities only use the male squash blossoms to cook with, which are the ones sold at the farmers' market. The male blossoms are used because they never bear fruit and they have a long narrow stem and stamen. The female blossoms become the fruit, and they will always have a tiny fruit under the flower. They are not harvested in the flower stage to allow them to produce the squash fruits. As long as some of the male blossoms are left in the squash patch for pollination, the bees will do the rest and the additional male blossoms can be harvested. The male blossoms are used widely throughout Mexico in a variety of dishes including quesadillas and soups; here in Northern New Mexico, they are primarily stuffed with cheese and batter-fried using cream. This recipe makes a crispy unique stuffed version of a dish that is traditionally not plant-based. Enjoy them while you can during their short summer season.

MAKES 4 SERVINGS

1 recipe Lois's Pico de Gallo (page 164)
12 to 16 male squash blossoms
    (depending on size)

For the Blossom Stuffing:
2 teaspoons sunflower oil
½ small yellow onion, finely chopped
    (approximately ¼ cup)
1 teaspoon blackened garlic (page 253)
1 Anaheim or New Mexico Green chile,
    roasted, seeded, peeled, and finely
    chopped (page 250)

1 vine-ripened tomato, seeded and finely
    chopped (approximately ½ cup)
1 teaspoon kosher salt, or to taste
½ can (15.5 ounces) organic Great Northern
    beans, puréed (approximately ⅔ cup)

For Frying and for the Batter:
1 liter (about 4 cups) sunflower oil, for frying
⅓ cup cornstarch
1 teaspoon baking powder
¼ cup plus 2 tablespoons white rice flour
½ cup sparkling water, cold

First prepare the pico de gallo recipe as per the instructions and set aside.

Preheat a medium cast-iron pan over medium heat until it is hot but not smoking. Add the sunflower oil and the onion and sauté for 3 to 4 minutes until the onions begin to caramelize. Add the garlic and chile and sauté for another minute, stirring to prevent burning. Add the tomato and continue to cook for an additional 3 minutes. Add the salt and stir. Remove from heat, taste, adjust seasoning if desired, and then place in a small bowl and allow to cool to room temperature.

While the mixture is cooling, prepare the bean purée. Place the beans in a food processor and process until smooth. Then fold the onion mixture into the bean purée. Your stuffing mixture is now ready to stuff inside the blossoms. Each blossom should have the stamen removed (the stamens are edible, but I think they taste bitter). I make a single cut lengthwise to each flower so that it is easier to get the stuffing into the flower.

Fill each blossom with approximately 1 tablespoon of stuffing mixture, then twist the flower at the top in a circular direction gently to seal in the filling. Set aside on a sheet tray.

Pour the oil into a deep saucepan or cast-iron Dutch oven that is at least 4 inches deep so that the oil doesn't splatter while frying. Because frying with oil can be dangerous, it's important to note that whatever pan you use, you need to make sure that there is plenty of room up the sides of the pan to prevent oil from bubbling over. Over medium to high heat, heat the oil until hot but not smoking. You can test a little batter once the oil is ready to make sure that it is hot enough. The batter will begin to cook immediately, bubbling in the oil, and turn brown shortly after being placed in the oil.

To prepare the batter, in a medium mixing bowl, mix all the dry ingredients and then add the cold sparkling water. Using a whisk, stir to make sure there are no lumps. Then, one at a time, dredge each stuffed squash blossom into the batter so that it is completely coated. Then gently place in the hot oil and cook until it turns brown, for approximately 3 to 4 minutes. I use a spoon or round mesh kitchen skimmer (also called a kitchen spider) to immerse the stuffed blossom completely into the oil, making sure that it cooks evenly. Then remove it from the oil, and place on a sheet tray covered with a piece of paper towel to absorb any excess oil that drains off. Cook all the blossoms and then turn off the heat.

Place 3 to 4 blossoms onto each plate and serve with Lois's Pico de Gallo (page 164). Serve immediately.

SAVORY PUMPKIN SPICED CRISPY CHICKPEAS

When you see "pumpkin spice," you may think of the more sweet autumnal flavor profile. Here, crispy chickpeas are coated with a savory blend of pumpkin seeds, chile, and garlic. Because I work long hours as a chef and teacher and sometimes skip a meal, this snack is the perfect way to keep my energy up. It's also perfect at a party and a great healthy snack for kids.

MAKES 2 CUPS

2 cans (15.5 ounces each) chickpeas, drained and rinsed thoroughly
1 tablespoon sunflower oil
1 teaspoon kosher salt
2 tablespoons Toasted Pumpkin Seeds (page 261)
1 teaspoon New Mexico red chile powder, mild
1 teaspoon garlic powder

Preheat the oven to 400°F. Line a large sheet tray with parchment paper. Dry the rinsed chickpeas very well on all sides with paper towels. Taking time to dry them thoroughly will ensure that they get crispy in the oven. Transfer them to a mixing bowl, and toss them with the sunflower oil and salt.

Transfer them to the parchment-lined sheet tray and roast in the oven until they are crispy, for approximately 50 minutes.

While the chickpeas are roasting, prepare the pumpkin seed spice blend. In a food processor, pulse together the pumpkin seeds, chile powder, and garlic powder. Reserve this mixture.

Once the chickpeas come out of the oven, let them cool for 10 minutes. Transfer them to a large bowl. Toss them with the pumpkin seed mixture and let cool completely.

They can be eaten right away or stored at room temperature in a container with the lid left ajar. This will help them stay crispy for a couple of days.

BUTTERNUT SQUASH SOUP WITH CHILE OIL

Butternut squash is one of the healthiest squashes you can eat. It has a sweet, nutty flavor, similar to that of pumpkin, and is considered to be a superfood by many health practitioners. This recipe makes an exquisite savory soup that is both delectable and nutritious. It makes a lot of soup, so I suggest you freeze the extra or have it for an encore meal the following day. We use coconut milk in this recipe for its rich, thick, smooth, silky texture and subtle flavor. The earthy flavor of the soup with the spiciness of the chile oil and crunchiness of the pumpkin seeds pairs perfectly with the tanginess of the lime if you choose to serve it this way.

MAKES 3 QUARTS

For the Soup:

1 medium-size butternut squash, ends trimmed, halved lengthwise, and seeds removed (2½ to 3 pounds)

2 tablespoons sunflower oil, divided

2¼ teaspoons kosher salt, divided

¼ teaspoon freshly ground black pepper, divided

1 large yellow onion, diced (approximately 2 cups)

1 medium-size sweet and firm apple, peeled, cored, and diced

2 garlic cloves, thinly sliced, or 2 teaspoons blackened garlic (page 253)

1 teaspoon ground turmeric

1 can (13.5 ounces) unsweetened coconut milk or coconut cream

6 cups water

½ recipe of chile garlic oil (page 254), for garnish

Toasted Pumpkin Seeds (page 261), for garnish

1 lime, cut into wedges and served on the side (optional)

Preheat the oven to 400°F and line a sheet tray with parchment paper. Rub both inside halves of the squash with 1 tablespoon of the sunflower oil, reserving the other tablespoon for later, and season with both ¼ teaspoon of the salt and ⅛ teaspoon of the pepper. Roast flesh side up for approximately 90 minutes, or until tender when pierced with a knife. Remove from the oven and let cool. Then remove the skin and cut into approximately 2-inch pieces and set aside.

While the squash is roasting, heat the remaining 1 tablespoon of sunflower oil in a heavy-bottomed soup pot over medium to high heat. Add the onions and apples and cook over medium-high heat until they start caramelizing, about 15 minutes, stirring occasionally to prevent burning. Add the garlic and turmeric and cook for another minute. Pour in the can of coconut milk and the water, then add the cooked squash pieces and the remaining salt and pepper and stir, being sure to scrape up any stuck bits from the bottom of the pot. Bring to a boil, then reduce the heat to low and let the soup simmer for 30 minutes. Stir occasionally to prevent the soup from burning.

Turn off the heat, and carefully working in batches, blend the soup in a blender until smooth. Return the blended soup back to a clean soup pot and heat on low until hot.

To serve, ladle soup into a bowl, drizzle a little of the chile garlic oil on top, garnish with the pumpkin seeds, and serve immediately with lime wedges, if using, on the side.

PUMPKIN CORN SOUP WITH GINGER LIME CREAM

This recipe was a staple from my James Beard Award–winning cookbook, *Foods of the Southwest Indian Nations*. Originally made with chicken stock and heavy cream, I have modified this all-time favorite to be made with water and the ginger lime cream with coconut milk. This simple recipe is easy to prepare and utilizes two very basic ingredients in southwestern cooking: pumpkin and corn. It is a luscious and rich-bodied soup, and the ginger lime cream adds a refreshing zest.

MAKES APPROXIMATELY 1½ QUARTS

For the Soup:

1 tablespoon sunflower oil

1 medium-size yellow onion, diced (approximately 1½ cups)

1 teaspoon blackened garlic (page 253)

3 cups white corn kernels (fresh if in season, otherwise use a 1-pound bag of organic frozen yellow sweet corn)

3 cups water, divided

1 teaspoon kosher salt

3 cups cooked pumpkin purée (page 260), or canned pumpkin purée

For the Ginger Lime Cream:

Zest of 2 large organic limes and the juice from the limes (approximately ¼ cup juice)

1 tablespoon peeled and grated fresh ginger

½ cup unsweetened coconut milk, solids (from a 13.5-ounce can of coconut milk)

¼ cup coconut milk, liquid (from the same can of coconut milk)

Place a soup pot over medium-high heat and add the sunflower oil. Heat the oil until it is hot but not smoking. Add the onion and cook for 3 to 4 minutes, stirring constantly to prevent burning. Add the garlic and cook for 1 additional minute, stirring to prevent burning. Add the corn, reduce the heat to medium low, and sauté until soft, about 10 minutes, stirring occasionally to prevent burning. Add 2 cups of the water and the salt and cook for another 5 minutes. Remove from heat.

In a blender, blend the cooked corn mixture until smooth, for about 2 minutes. Pass through a fine-mesh strainer, then discard the pulp, compost it, or store corn pulp in the freezer for future use. The corn pulp will yield approximately ½ cup of pulp, which can be frozen and saved. Chef Walter uses the pulp in some of his soups and stews or sometimes adds it to his Navajo Kneel Down Bread (page 45).

In a medium saucepan, combine the blended corn purée with the remaining 1 cup of water and heat it over medium high until it boils. Reduce the heat to low, add the cooked pumpkin purée, and stir until the pumpkin and corn are completely mixed. Allow to cook on low for an additional 10 minutes, stirring occasionally to prevent burning.

In another small saucepan, cook the lime juice and ginger for 2 minutes over medium to high heat. Remove from the heat and pour through a sieve to remove the ginger. In a mixing bowl combine the lime juice, the lime zest (save some for the garnish), coconut cream solids, and coconut milk. Whip with a whisk until the mixture is completely combined and set aside. You can put the ginger lime cream into a squirt bottle to paint onto the soup for a nice presentation, if you like.

Paint or spoon a dollop of the ginger lime cream into each bowl filled with soup, and garnish with the remaining lime zest. Serve immediately.

Note:
I recommend using an organic lime for the lime zest as then you can be sure that the lime skin is pesticide-free.

Kabocha Squash, also known as Japanese Pumpkins, are perfect for puréeing and would work nicely if you wanted to substitute them puréed in this recipe for the pumpkin purée.

CALABACITAS

This traditional Southwestern favorite dish featuring yellow summer squash and zucchini is served on almost every Pueblo and all throughout Northern New Mexico and on many of the Pueblo Feast Days. Calabacitas means "little squashes" in Spanish and refers to the squashes used in this dish. Everyone makes it slightly differently, and there is no right or wrong way to make it. You can cube the squash, cut it into half-moons, or julienne. It can be served as a vegetable side dish or a filling for a taco, but it is always a tasty dish that brightens any meal. In the summer months the Santa Fe Farmers' Market is bursting with fresh locally grown zucchini and yellow summer squash. I buy the squash from the market every week and prepare this dish often.

MAKES 4 TO 6 SERVINGS

1 to 2 mild New Mexico green chiles, roasted, peeled, seeded, and diced (see page 250) (approximately ¾ cup)

2 teaspoons sunflower oil

½ yellow onion, sliced (approximately 1 cup)

2 medium zucchini, cut into half-moons (approximately 2½ cups)

2 medium yellow summer squashes, cut into half-moons (approximately 2½ cups)

¾ teaspoon kosher salt, or to taste

2 teaspoons blackened garlic (page 253)

1 cup sweet yellow or white corn kernels, fresh or frozen

Roast the chiles and prepare as per the instructions on page 250.

In a cast iron-skillet or heavy-bottomed sauté pan, heat the sunflower oil on high until hot but not smoking. Add the onion and sauté until translucent for approximately 4 minutes. Turn the heat to medium and add both types of squash and the salt and sauté for another 3 minutes, stirring to prevent burning. Add the garlic, corn kernels, and chile and sauté for another 3 minutes, stirring to ensure all the vegetables cook evenly. Taste, and adjust salt, as needed. Serve immediately with your favorite main course.

GRILLED SUMMER SQUASH

Zucchini and yellow summer squash have traditionally always been eaten in the summer months when the squashes are young and tender. This recipe is easy to make and celebrates these squashes at their best. The fresh lemon herb dressing brings out the sweetness of each squash, marrying the two together perfectly. Grilling these vegetables adds a little smoky earthiness to this dish. This can be served as a main course, a side, or an accompaniment to a crisp summer salad.

MAKES 4 TO 6 SERVINGS

For the Summer Squash:
2 medium zucchini (approximately 8 inches long by 2 inches wide)
2 medium yellow summer squashes (approximately 8 inches long by 2 inches wide)

For the Lemon Herb Dressing:
⅓ cup freshly squeezed lemon juice (2 to 3 lemons)
1 tablespoon plus 1 teaspoon smooth Dijon mustard
1 tablespoon whole-grain Dijon mustard
1 tablespoon fresh garlic, finely minced
1 tablespoon finely chopped flat-leaf parsley leaves
1 tablespoon finely chopped fresh basil leaves
2 tablespoons finely chopped fresh chives
1 teaspoon agave sweetener
¼ teaspoon kosher salt
3 tablespoons cold water
2 tablespoons sunflower or olive oil

Prepare the zucchini and yellow summer squash by washing and drying each squash. Using a sharp chef's knife, slice each zucchini and yellow summer squash lengthwise into three to four slices approximately ½ inch wide in thickness, depending on the size of the squash. The squash I used for this recipe were between 7 to 8 inches long by 1½ inches to 2 inches wide.

In a medium mixing bowl, whisk together the lemon juice, both types of mustard, garlic, parsley, basil, chives, agave, salt, and water. While whisking slowly, add the sunflower oil until it is completed integrated. Set the dressing aside.

Brush each squash with about ½ teaspoon of dressing before placing it onto the grill, then grill with dressing side down for 2 to 3 minutes over a high to medium flame on a gas grill or once the charcoal embers have burned down on a charcoal grill. Flip the squash over and brush with another ½ teaspoon of dressing. Cook for another 2 to 3 minutes. Remove from heat and place onto a sheet pan or platter. Place slices of grilled squash onto each plate and drizzle a little of the extra dressing on top. Serve immediately.

GRILLED SQUASH & MUSHROOMS SKEWERS

These skewers are a perfect dish to make when summer squash is locally available at your farmers' market, and you can assemble these ahead of time and then put them on the grill. They make a great accompaniment to the Green Chile Herbed Rice (page 140) and the Red Chile Pinto Beans (page 77) or the Black Beans with Chocolate & Chipotle (page 76) to make a complete meal.

MAKES 14 TO 16 SKEWERS

For the Skewers:

2 medium zucchini (5 to 8 inches long by
    2 inches wide)
2 yellow summer squashes (5 to 8 inches long by
    2 inches wide)
½ pound cremini mushrooms, larger ones halved
    (approximately 12 mushrooms)
½ pound oyster mushrooms (approximately
    12 mushrooms)
16 skewers, soaked in water to prevent them
    from burning

For the Lime Sauce:

3 tablespoons water
⅓ cup freshly squeezed lime juice (2 to 3 limes)
⅓ cup sunflower or olive oil
½ teaspoon kosher salt, or to taste
1½ teaspoons fresh minced garlic
⅓ cup mint, chiffonade cut
1 tablespoon plus 1 teaspoon basil,
    chiffonade cut

First cut zucchini and yellow summer squash using a mandolin slicer or sharp knife. You will want to slice the squash lengthwise so that each slice is thin enough to ribbon yet thick enough to shape without breaking. I used slices that were between ⅛ and ¼ inch thick. Fold the zucchini slice by bending it so that it resembles a ribbon and skewer each piece of squash ribbon onto a skewer.

Cut the larger mushrooms in half and leave the smaller ones whole so that they don't break while cooking. Alternate each skewer first with a yellow summer squash ribbon, then a mushroom, then a zucchini ribbon and repeat the process two to three times for each skewer. Once all the ingredients are skewered, then set aside while you prepare the sauce.

Next combine the water, lime juice, sunflower oil, salt, garlic, mint, and basil. Place mixture in a blender and blend on low until mixed for approximately 15 seconds until mixed. Remove from the blender and place in a small bowl with a brush for brushing onto the skewers.

Place each prepared skewer on the grill, medium to high if using a gas grill or after the charcoal embers have burned down a little on a charcoal grill, and brush some of the lime sauce onto each skewer. Rotate each skewer about every minute until the edges get blackened on the vegetables, rotating about four times to cook each skewer. Each skewer should cook for 4 to 5 minutes to achieve perfection.

Remove from the grill and place on a platter or individual plates, then spoon a little of the extra lime sauce onto each skewer, and serve immediately.

ZUCCHINI, QUINOA & PIÑON NUT SALAD

Quinoa originated in the Andean regions of Peru and Bolivia in South America and gets its name from the Quechua word *kinuwa*. It is a rich source of protein, fiber, some B vitamins, and minerals including iron, zinc, and magnesium as well as manganese and phosphorus. I like to buy organic and Native-sourced quinoa, whenever possible, to support small independent Native-owned farms. Here the quinoa is combined with fresh zucchini, a little lemon, mint, arugula, and toasted piñon (pine) nuts, making a refreshing salad that is both nutritious and flavorsome. It is great as a cold salad, and equally tasty warm with wilted greens as a staple for both lunch and dinner.

MAKES 4 TO 6 SERVINGS

For the Cooked Quinoa:

1 cup dry white quinoa

2 cups water

½ teaspoon kosher salt

Zest of 2 organic lemons

For the Salad:

3 tablespoons sunflower oil, divided

3 shallots, thinly sliced (approximately ½ cup)

2 medium zucchini, diced (approximately 4 cups)

½ teaspoon kosher salt

½ teaspoon freshly ground black pepper

½ cup packed mint leaves, finely chopped

2 cups arugula, chopped

½ cup piñon nuts, toasted

2 lemons, juiced (approximately ¼ cup)

In a medium saucepan over medium heat, combine quinoa, water, salt, and lemon zest. Bring to a boil, then reduce heat to low and simmer, covered, for 12 to 15 minutes, or until quinoa is cooked and all the water is absorbed. Fluff with a fork and transfer to a big salad bowl.

In a large cast-iron skillet over medium heat, add 1 tablespoon of the sunflower oil and heat until hot but not smoking. After a minute, add the shallots and cook for approximately

5 minutes, stirring occasionally to prevent burning. Add the zucchini, salt, and pepper and cook for another 10 minutes or until squash is tender, again stirring occasionally to prevent burning but allowing the zucchini to begin to turn brown. Remove from the heat and transfer to the big salad bowl, along with the quinoa. Add the mint, arugula, piñon nuts, lemon juice, and remaining 2 tablespoons of sunflower oil. Gently toss and take a taste. Add more salt or pepper as needed. Serve warm, or allow to cool and serve cold.

Notes:

You can purchase piñon nuts that are already toasted; however, I find that the most flavor comes from raw piñon nuts that you toast yourself. To dry toast the nuts, heat a small, seasoned cast-iron pan over medium to high heat until hot but not smoking. Add the raw nuts and toss them in the pan with a wooden spoon until they begin to turn brown (approximately 3 minutes), then remove from pan, let cool, and use as per the recipe.

I recommend using an organic lemon for the lemon zest as then you can be sure that the lemon skin is pesticide-free.

BAKED ACORN SQUASH WITH MAPLE & PECANS

Acorn squash is easy to grow, yet also readily available and not too expensive, especially when in season. Its distinct dark green exterior with long ridges covers a bright yellow-orange flesh on the inside. It is well-known for having a rich, sweet flavor and wonderful smooth and somewhat creamy texture. In this simple recipe, the natural sweetness of the squash is enhanced by pure maple syrup with a lovely crunchiness of toasted pecans. It can be served on its own or as a side; it can also be combined with the Native American Wild Rice & Sweet Corn Sauté (Manoomin) (page 52) for a very hearty meal. This dish is a favorite of the students in the Indigenous Concepts of Native American Food class at the Institute of American Indian Arts (IAIA) and was recently a huge hit with the Hopi community in Arizona for a health and wellness class Chef Walter and I did there.

MAKES 4 SERVINGS

For the Baked Acorn Squash
2 acorn squashes, cut in half, seeds removed
1 cup water

For the Maple Pecan Topping
¾ cup pecans, toasted and roughly chopped
½ cup pure maple syrup

Preheat the oven to 425°F. Place halved acorn squash on a sheet pan or baking dish with the open side down, then pour water onto pan; make sure it is evenly spread over the entire area. Bake for approximately 1 hour, depending on their size, checking at 45 minutes to make sure there is still water on the tray and the doneness of the squash. If all the water has evaporated, add a little more. After about an hour, check with a small knife to make sure squash is soft and completely cooked.

While the squash is cooking, prepare the pecans. Preheat a small to medium seasoned cast-iron skillet over high heat. Add the nuts and toast until they begin to turn brown, approximately 3 to 4 minutes. Stir the nuts with a wooden spoon or toss them in the pan while cooking to ensure that they cook evenly and do not burn. Remove from the pan, chop into pieces, and set aside.

Once the squash is completely cooked and still hot, turn it over on the sheet tray and add 1 tablespoon of the maple syrup onto each squash, then return to the oven for approximately another 5 to 10 minutes until they begin to caramelize. Remove from oven, place on a plate or platter, top each squash with another tablespoon of maple syrup, then garnish with the toasted pecans. Serve immediately.

SPICE-ROASTED BUTTERNUT SQUASH

Butternut squash is a common winter hard-shelled squash that is filled with nutrients and flavor. Today, it is used all over the world, with roasting the most common way to prepare it. This recipe is a great side on its own, but the hollow of the squash could also be filled with the Native American Wild Rice & Sweet Corn Sauté (Manoomin) (page 52), the Red Mesa's Refried Pinto Beans (page 74), the Zucchini, Quinoa & Piñon Nut Salad (page 110), or even the Spaghetti Squash Slaw (page 95).

MAKES 4 TO 6 SERVINGS

1 whole butternut squash, peeled and
   cut in half, around 4 pounds
   (approximately 9 x 5 inches)
1 tablespoon sunflower oil
2 tablespoons pure maple syrup
1 teaspoon New Mexico red chile powder,
   mild
1 tablespoon minced fresh sage
¼ cup Toasted Pumpkin Seeds (page 261)

Preheat the oven to 425°F. Line a large sheet tray with parchment paper. Trim the top and bottom off the squash so it can sit safely on a cutting board. Carefully slice the squash down the center and remove the seeds with a spoon. Brush the flesh side of the squash with the sunflower oil and place the cut side down on the sheet tray. Bake for approximately 45 minutes (depending on how hot your oven is) or a little longer until the squash is tender when pierced with a small paring knife.

Whisk together the maple syrup, chile powder, and sage. Turn the squash halves over and brush the maple mixture all over the flesh side of both halves. Return to the oven and cook for another 10 minutes. Sprinkle pumpkin seeds over the top before serving. Cut into slices or into four to six pieces and serve immediately.

ROASTED KABOCHA SQUASH WITH GINGER

There are many ways to roast kabocha squash, but I think this recipe is the perfect way to eat it. While kabocha is packed with vitamins and minerals, the best reason to eat it is that, with its creamy, luscious flesh, it is simply delicious. Fresh ginger adds a little zing, maple adds a touch of sweetness—and the orange zest adds both. This is great on its own or the perfect accompaniment with any whole grain: serve with the Green Chile Herbed Rice (page 140) or use instead of the sweet potatoes in the Sweet Potato, Kale & Wild Rice Bowl (page 195).

MAKES 4 TO 6 SERVINGS

1 kabocha squash, skin left on, halved, seeded, and cut into 1-inch wedges (approximately a 3-pound squash, 7 x 7 inches)

4 tablespoons vegan butter

Zest of 1 organic orange (orange reserved for another use)

1 tablespoon freshly grated peeled ginger

2 tablespoons maple syrup

1 teaspoon New Mexico red chile powder, mild

1 teaspoon finely chopped fresh thyme leaves

1 teaspoon kosher salt, or to taste

Preheat the oven to 425°F. Line a large sheet tray with parchment paper. In a small saucepan over medium heat, add the butter, zest, ginger, maple syrup, chile powder, thyme, and salt. Bring to a simmer and then turn off the heat. Place the squash in a single layer on the sheet tray and pour the vegan butter mixture over the top, using a spoon to make sure each piece of squash is evenly coated. Roast in the oven for 20 minutes, or until the squash has browned on the edges and is tender when pierced with a knife.

BUTTERNUT SQUASH WITH ARUGULA PESTO & PASTA

Butternut squash pairs perfectly with peppery arugula and fresh mint pesto. Whip up a batch of Blue Corn Pasta (page 43) and you have an easy, healthy, filling dinner. The pesto part of this recipe can be made the day before, so all you have to do is cook the butternut squash and the pasta. The pesto was such a hit that I recommend you make twice the amount of the pesto so that you have enough to spread onto No Fry Frybread (page 266) or other toasted bread as a delectable first course.

MAKES 4 TO 6 SERVINGS

For the Butternut Squash:
½ butternut squash
2 tablespoons sunflower oil
2 teaspoons ground coriander
2 teaspoons ground New Mexico red chile powder, mild
1 teaspoon kosher salt
¼ teaspoon freshly ground black pepper

For the Pesto:
2 cups packed fresh arugula leaves
¼ cup packed fresh mint leaves
½ cup piñon (pine) nuts, raw
1 tablespoon blackened garlic (page 253)
Zest of 2 organic lemons (lemons reserved for another use)
⅓ cup sunflower oil
½ teaspoon kosher salt, or to taste
½ teaspoon freshly ground black pepper, or to taste

1 recipe of Blue Corn Pasta (page 43) or 1 pound dried pasta, any shape

Preheat the oven to 350°F and line a large sheet tray with parchment paper.

Next prepare the butternut squash. Cut the bottom end of the squash off and then the top end. Cut the squash in half lengthwise. Peel the squash with a vegetable peeler and scoop out the seeds to save for planting in the spring if it is an organic squash, or toast them like the pumpkin seeds (page 261) for a healthy snack. Cut the half squash into ½-inch cubes (about 4 cups) and reserve.

Combine the sunflower oil, coriander, chile powder, salt, and pepper in a large bowl and whisk together. Add the butternut squash cubes and toss together until the squash cubes are evenly coated. Transfer the coated butternut squash cubes to the sheet tray and roast until the squash pieces are tender and crispy, around 30 minutes.

To make the pesto, place all the pesto ingredients into a food processor. Process until it is smooth and creamy in texture. Taste and adjust seasoning if desired. Transfer to a bowl until ready to use. You can make the pesto in advance as it will last for 1 to 2 days in the refrigerator.

Bring a large pot of salted water to a boil. Cook the pasta until tender and drain, transferring the noodles to a large bowl. Mix in the pesto and spoon into bowls, topping with the roasted butternut squash.

Serve immediately.

PUMPKIN & GINGER SCONES

Pumpkin and ginger are considered superfoods now, but both have impressive histories. Pumpkin has long been used in a variety of ways by many Native communities. Here I pair this Native staple with ginger, one of the healthiest roots known today. Together they make a scone that has just the right amount of sweetness with a little zing from the ginger. Chef Walter and Chef Marianne love the zing of ginger, but I tend to be a little more conservative with my ginger palate. If you love ginger, feel free to increase the amount for these scones, which is why the amount called for says "or to taste." Enjoy them for breakfast, as an afternoon snack, or anytime.

MAKES 8 SCONES

For the Scones:

2 cups all-purpose flour

2 teaspoons pumpkin pie spice

2 teaspoons baking powder

½ teaspoon kosher salt

6 tablespoons vegan butter, cold and diced

½ cup cooked pumpkin purée (page 260) or canned pumpkin purée

½ cup brown sugar, packed

2 teaspoons vanilla extract or vanilla bean paste

2 tablespoons freshly grated ginger, or to taste

For the Glaze:

½ cup powdered sugar

½ teaspoon cinnamon

1 tablespoon almond or oat milk

Preheat the oven to 400°F. Line a large sheet tray, or two smaller ones, with parchment paper or a Silpat baking mat.

In a large bowl, mix together the flour, pumpkin pie spice, baking powder, and salt. Add the butter and crumble together with your fingers until the mixture resembles small peas. Add the pumpkin purée, brown sugar, vanilla, and

ginger and stir with a wooden spoon until a dough forms. If it's too sticky, sprinkle in a little more flour. It it's too dry, add a splash of almond milk.

Transfer the dough to a clean, well-floured work surface and gently knead it a few times until it comes together. Form the dough into a round and gently press until it is approximately 1 inch thick. The key to tender and flaky scones is not to overwork the dough. Using a knife, slice the dough in half, then again the other way to quarter it. Then slice each quarter in half so that you have eight triangle-shaped scones. Transfer scones to your prepared sheet tray and bake for approximately 15 minutes, until they are golden brown and firm to the touch. Remove from oven and let cool.

To make the glaze, whisk together the powdered sugar, cinnamon, and almond milk. Drizzle the glaze on top of the cool scones. Serve immediately or store the scones at room temperature until served. Scones will last 1 to 2 days in a sealed container but are best the day you bake them.

SPICED PUMPKIN BUTTER

In the fall, food makes a wonderful harvest gift. This recipe is a great way to use up some of the pumpkins from your garden and share the bounty with friends and family. If you don't grow a garden or make your own pumpkin purée, this can easily be made with canned pumpkin. The pumpkin butter is the perfect morning accompaniment to a piece of toasted bread, or it can be used on a peanut butter and jelly sandwich instead of jelly. If you are making this to gift, this recipe makes four 8-ounce jars, but I recommend keeping at least one jar for yourself.

MAKES APPROXIMATELY 3½ CUPS

4 cups pumpkin purée (page 260) or 2 cans
   (15 ounces each) pumpkin purée
½ cup agave sweetener
¼ cup packed brown sugar
½ cup apple cider or unfiltered apple juice
2 tablespoons lemon juice (approximately 1 lemon)
2 teaspoons pumpkin pie spice
½ teaspoon kosher salt

In a large, heavy-bottomed pot or saucepan over medium heat, whisk together all the ingredients. Bring the mixture to a boil, then reduce the heat to low and simmer, stirring frequently until the pumpkin butter has reduced, for approximately 60 minutes. The mixture will be very thick as the apple cider reduces, so it is important to stir frequently to make sure it doesn't burn. Remove from the heat, let cool to room temperature, then transfer to four 8-ounce jars.

The pumpkin butter can be stored in the fridge for 2 weeks or in a freezer-safe container in the freezer for up to 3 months.

PUMPKIN PIE WITH PIÑON PECAN CRUST

Pumpkin pie is a holiday classic. This recipe gives it a twist from the Ancestral past by using piñon (pine) nuts and pecans for the crust. Both piñon nuts and pecans are packed with protein and fat; in the Native Ancestral past, when there was no wild game, or a hunt was unsuccessful, both of these nuts provided protein, calories, and good plant-based fats and played a very important role in the Ancestral diet.

For the Crust:

1 cup piñon nuts, raw

1 cup pecan pieces, raw

1 teaspoon ground cinnamon

½ teaspoon kosher salt

¼ cup unbleached sugar (organic if possible)

3 tablespoons sunflower oil

For the Filling:

1 can (15 ounces) of unsweetened pumpkin purée, or 2 cups cooked pumpkin purée (page 260)

2 teaspoons pumpkin pie spice

4 tablespoons arrowroot powder

⅔ cup packed brown sugar

¾ cup full-fat canned coconut milk (unsweetened)

For the Topping:

1 recipe coconut whipped cream (page 273)

1 teaspoon ground cinnamon

Preheat the oven to 350°F and line the bottom of a 9-inch springform pan with a round of parchment paper that sits neatly in the bottom. You can also use a pie dish as well, in which case, spray it with a nonstick spray or lightly rub it with a thin coating of sunflower oil.

First prepare the crust. Combine the piñon nuts, pecans, cinnamon, salt, and sugar in a food processor. Pulse for approximately 30 seconds until the mixture resembles small wet pebbles. Add the sunflower oil and then pulse again. Transfer this mixture to the bottom of your pie dish and press with your hands so the crust is flat across the entire bottom and comes up around the side. Use a flat-bottomed cup or a ramekin to finish pressing against the bottom and sides until everything looks flat and firm. Bake for 15 minutes. Remove crust from the oven and let cool on a cooling rack for 15 minutes before filling.

While the crust is cooling, prepare the filling: In a large bowl, whisk together the pumpkin purée, pumpkin pie spice, arrowroot powder, brown sugar, and coconut milk. Mix well until there are no lumps.

Pour this mixture on top of the baked crust. Place the pie back in the oven for 45 minutes, or until the filling is set and no longer wobbles. Remove from oven, and let cool to room temperature and then at least 2 hours in the fridge before slicing.

To make the coconut whipped cream, use the recipe on page 273. After you have added the agave and vanilla as per recipe, add the cinnamon, which we are using for this recipe version. Whisk for another 10 seconds until completely combined.

Serve a dollop of the whipped cream on top of a slice of pumpkin pie.

PUMPKIN PIÑON NUT CAKE

This recipe is a new incarnation from a recipe that first appeared in my James Beard Award–winning cookbook, *Foods of the Southwest Indian Nations*. The original recipe made two loaves as a quick bread and contained both eggs and milk. Here, it is served as a single cake with a pumpkin sauce and a dollop of the coconut whipped cream (page 273). The pumpkin sauce complements the cake perfectly as does the whipped cream. This is a lovely dessert that can be served at any time of the year but is especially good during the fall harvest months. I use vanilla bean paste, which is a little more expensive than vanilla bean extract but worth the extra cost because of the flavor. However, if you cannot get vanilla bean paste or it is too expensive, then the vanilla bean extract will work fine here.

For the Cake:

1 cup all-purpose flour

1 teaspoon baking powder

½ teaspoon baking soda

¼ teaspoon kosher salt

¾ cup organic unbleached sugar

¾ teaspoon ground cinnamon

¾ cup oat milk

¼ cup sunflower oil

1 teaspoon vanilla bean paste

1 cup cooked pumpkin purée (page 260),
    or canned pumpkin purée

½ cup piñon (pine) nuts, toasted (see Notes)

For the Pumpkin Sauce:

½ cup cooked pumpkin purée (page 260),
    or canned pumpkin purée

½ cup organic coconut milk

1 teaspoon vanilla bean paste

2 tablespoons pure maple syrup

1 recipe coconut whipped cream (page 273)

To make the pumpkin cake, preheat the oven to 350°F. Combine the flour, baking powder, baking soda, salt, sugar, and cinnamon, mixing with a slotted spoon. In a separate bowl, whisk together the oat milk, sunflower oil, and vanilla. Add the pumpkin purée and whisk until the mixture is completely combined. Pour the dry ingredients slowly into the wet, whisking them together until the mixture is completely smooth and there are no lumps. Fold in the piñon nuts.

Pour the batter into a greased 9-inch cake pan and bake for 55 minutes, until the cake springs back when touched and a toothpick pushed into the center comes out clean. The sides of the cake will start to separate from the outer edge of the cake pan.

While the cake is cooking, prepare the pumpkin sauce. Combine all the ingredients in a bowl and whisk together, then set aside. This sauce can be served chilled or at room temperature. Next prepare the whipped cream as per the recipe instructions. Place in the refrigerator until ready to use.

Remove the cake from the oven, place on a cooling rack, and allow to cool before cutting. Serve with a little of the pumpkin sauce on each plate, then place a cut slice of the cake on top and add a dollop of coconut whipped cream.

Notes:

To toast the piñon nuts, place them in a seasoned dry frying pan over medium to high heat and stir constantly so that they brown evenly, for 3 to 5 minutes. No oil is needed because the nuts contain natural oils.

If you are using canned pumpkin for this recipe, a 15-ounce can will be the perfect amount for the cake and the sauce as one can yields 1½ cups of cooked pumpkin.

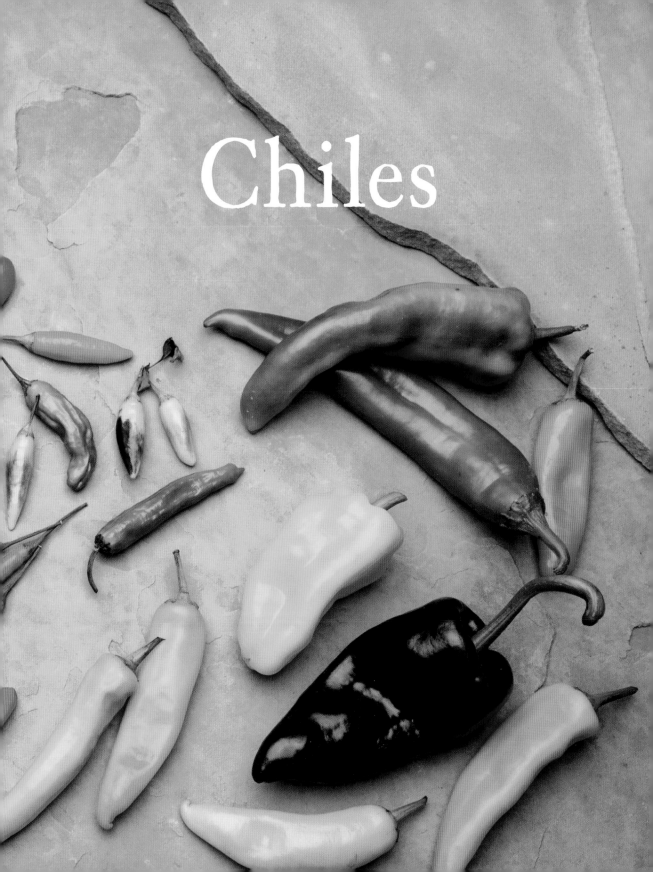

Chiles

Chiles have always been the spice of life to me—and to many others. Chiles have become one of the most important spices in the world, with most people not even knowing the story of their origin, their importance to the Indigenous Peoples who first cultivated them, or that they are not a "pepper" at all but a pungent fruit with spice. They were first called peppers by Columbus, actually probably something along the lines of "pimento de chile," which later translated to chile pepper. Columbus, who was in search of black pepper, which ethnobotanically speaking is not even closely related to a chile, found these spicy fruits instead. However, when the Queen thought that Columbus had found a new "pepper" spice that would revolutionize the world, Columbus was sent back and more varieties of chiles made their way into other regions of the world. It is a five-hundred-year-old inaccuracy, one that probably won't be corrected anytime soon. Most people call chiles "peppers," not even knowing that they aren't in fact a pepper at all.

Chiles play a major role in Southwestern cuisine and are now intricately woven into cuisines all over the world since their introduction over five hundred years ago. They are characteristic of several Asian cuisine styles, including Szechuan Chinese, Korean, and Thai. They add heat to East Indian curries, are a part of African cuisine, and are used in Cajun and Creole cuisine. Chiles are intricately used in Mexican cuisine, Central and South American cuisine, and Caribbean cuisine and play an integral part in many dishes from the cuisines of the Americas, where they first originated.

Chiles, both hot and sweet, were most likely first cultivated by the Aztecs sometime between 7200 B.C.E. and 5200 B.C.E.,[21] making them one of the oldest crops in the Americas, alongside beans, corn, and squash. While originating in Bolivia, chiles were first cultivated in southern and central Mexico as well as Central America, and the term we now use to describe these prized flavorful and pungent fruits comes from the Nahuatl word *chilli*. I use the Spanish spelling, *chile*, which is the most commonly used spelling here in New Mexico, throughout these recipes.

There is a wide variety of chiles available today, from tabasco chiles, which are used to make the famous Tabasco sauce, to Scotch bonnet and the habanero chiles. Bell peppers, jalapeños, serrano chiles, New Mexico chiles, poblano chiles, shishito peppers, peter peppers, and cayenne peppers are just a few of the most common chiles today.

Chiles have varied heat, as calibrated by the Scoville scale, a measurement of pungency, spiciness, or "heat," and recorded in Scoville heat units (SHU). For instance, the bell pepper has 0 Scoville units; the poblano, 1,000 to 2,000 units; the jalapeño has 2,500 to 8,000 units; and the Trinidad Scorpion chile (sometimes referred to as the Trinidad Moruga scorpion chile pepper) and the ghost pepper have over 1,000,000 Scoville heat units.

According to many health professionals and online medical resources, chiles have some powerful health benefits. The capsaicin in chiles contributes to gut health; contrary to the belief that chiles upset your stomach, they can actually be an anti-irritant and can soothe digestive issues including upset stomachs, intestinal gas, cramps, and diarrhea, and they may even treat stomach ulcers.

These fruits may reduce the risk of certain cancers, can alleviate migraines, fight inflammation, decrease the risk of type 2 diabetes, help with cardiovascular health, promote red blood cell growth, may improve cognitive function, and may improve eyesight, clear a runny nose, and help to keep your hair and skin healthy. They are chock-full of vitamins and minerals, and they also release endorphins in the body, the neurotransmitters that reduce pain and increase euphoria in the body. I call this the feel-good mechanism from chiles.

Health benefits aside, chiles were a basis for Ancestral dishes. The Spanish friar Bernardino de Sahagún reported on some of the dishes that were being prepared by the Aztecs, which included what we now know of as mole, sauces with chiles and tomatoes, and powdered chiles being used with cacao as a highly regarded drink.[22] There are many savory dishes featuring chiles, and, as mentioned, it's a common ingredient in Southwestern cuisine.

One of the most famous chile farmers in Northern New Mexico is Matt Romero of Romero Farms. He and his wife, Emily, grow a number of varieties of chiles in addition to several other vegetables. He won Best Farmer in the Edible New Mexico "Local Hero Awards" in 2018, which recognizes individuals for their work to create healthy, sustainable food systems in New Mexico. During the peak of the chile season, when Matt sells tons of chiles at the Santa Fe Farmers' market, I roast, stuff, chop, make into sauce, freeze, and make dishes featuring chiles at their best. The recipes in this chapter feature some of my most favorite chile sauces, salads, sides, stews, enchiladas, and desserts that feature the wonderful flavor of different kinds of chiles.

Whether chiles were cooked, roasted and peeled, eaten fresh, dried and ground into powder, or used as a seasoning, this indigenous American fruit was and still is an important part of the Native American diet and Native American Cuisine. Chiles truly are the spice of life.

RED CHILE SAUCE

Red chiles are iconic symbols in Santa Fe. Many homes display *ristras*, strands of red chiles strung together. Ristras are always dried for later consumption and are believed to bring good health to those who hang them in their homes. This sauce will bring good health and good flavor to your home; use it in the Red Chile Potato Stew (page 143), the Red Chile Potato Casserole (page 144), the Pinto Bean & Mushroom Rolled Enchiladas (page 148), or top onto any recipe for a little extra zing. Keep a batch on hand in the freezer; it's a staple for any Southwest pantry.

MAKES APPROXIMATELY 3½ CUPS

8 cups water

8 to 10, depending on size, New Mexico red chile pods, mild, rinsed, dried, and then stemmed and seeded

2 teaspoons sunflower oil

1 medium to large yellow onion, diced (approximately 2 cups)

1 tablespoon blackened garlic (page 253), finely chopped

2 tablespoons water

2 cups warm water

1½ teaspoons kosher salt, or to taste

1 to 2 teaspoons agave sweetener, or to taste (optional)

In a medium saucepan, heat the water until it boils. Place the cleaned chile pods into boiling water for 3 minutes, stirring frequently to make sure that they stay immersed in the water and reconstitute. Turn off the heat and let the chile pods sit until soft, approximately 5 minutes, making sure they are immersed in the water. Sometimes I put a small plate on top of them to hold them down. They will change color from a dark red to a lighter red, indicating that they are ready and fully reconstituted. Drain the chiles in a colander and discard the chile water.

In a medium, heavy-bottomed skillet or pot, over medium to high heat, heat the sunflower oil until hot but not smoking. Add the onions and sauté for approximately 6 to 7 minutes, stirring occasionally, until they have caramelized. Add the garlic and cook for 1 additional minute, stirring to prevent burning. Add the 2 tablespoons of water and continue to stir until absorbed. This deglazes all the good flavor from the pan. Place the rehydrated red chiles in the pan, stir, and turn off the heat. Reserve.

Place the chiles mixture, garlic, the 2 cups of warm water, and salt in a blender. Cover and blend for 3 to 5 minutes until completely smooth. Taste, and if your sauce is a little bitter, add a small amount of agave (about 1 teaspoon, if using) and taste again. If it needs more agave, add the second teaspoon. The fresher the dried chiles, the less bitter they will be. I find that they tend to get bitter over time.

I use a high-powered blender, so I rarely have to strain my sauces; however, if your sauce is not completely smooth, you may want to strain it to remove any seeds or chile skin that has not been fully blended.

Serve immediately or let cool. This chile sauce may be stored in the refrigerator for approximately 3 days or frozen in an airtight container for later use.

GREEN CHILE SAUCE

Homemade green chile sauce is one of my favorite sauces in the world, and I love to use it in a lot of different ways. The official New Mexico state question is "Red or green?" What you are really being asked is, "Red chile sauce or green chile sauce?" This savory mild green chile sauce can be used with almost any dish and even eaten on its own like a salsa, with chips, or with warm White Corn Tortillas (page 27). I like to double or even triple the recipe and freeze it so I have it on hand to use in soups, stews, enchiladas, and in any dish where I can pour the sauce on top.

MAKES APPROXIMATELY 4 CUPS

About 10, depending on their size, fresh New Mexico green chiles or Anaheim green chiles, mild (2 cups chopped chiles), or 2 cups frozen chopped green chiles, mild

2 teaspoons sunflower oil

1 medium to large white onion, diced (approximately 2 cups)

2 teaspoons garlic, finely chopped

1 can (14.5 ounces) chopped tomatoes, organic and no salt added if possible

1 cup water or juice from frozen chiles (See Notes)

1½ teaspoons kosher salt, or to taste

Roast the chiles (page 250), then peel, seed, and chop them.

In a medium saucepan, heat the sunflower oil until hot but not smoking. Sauté the onion over medium to high heat until it begins to brown, approximately 4 to 5 minutes. Add the garlic and sauté for another minute, then reduce the heat. Add the tomatoes, chiles, water, and salt. Simmer for approximately 10 minutes, stirring to prevent burning.

Remove from heat. Taste and adjust seasoning with additional salt, as needed.

In a blender, put in half the sauce and blend on high for approximately 1 minute until completely smooth. Return the blended mixture to the saucepan with the unblended sauce. Serve immediately, or let it cool, refrigerate, and then use with your favorite recipe. This chile sauce may be stored in the refrigerator for approximately 3 days or frozen in an airtight container for later use.

Notes:
If you are using frozen roasted, peeled, and chopped green chiles, I highly recommend you use mild chiles for this sauce and not the hot ones—they will be too spicy. A 1 pound container will yield a little more than 2 cups with just over 1 cup of chile water, so you will not need to add additional water; you should use the chile water from the frozen chile container.

If you are using this sauce to make enchiladas, you may want a slightly thinner sauce. Just add water to get your desired consistency and adjust the salt to taste. You can also completely blend all the sauce to make a smoother sauce, especially for enchiladas, which I do all the time.

GUAJILLO CHILE SAUCE

Guajillo chiles have an incredible earthy flavor. Next to the New Mexico red chile, they are one of my favorite dried chiles. Here they are combined with pumpkin seeds, which are sometimes called pepitas. I buy the green hulled pumpkin seeds, which are available in most supermarkets. This sauce can be used on its own with many recipes. My favorite way to use this sauce is with the Chile Empañaditas (page 137), where it perfectly pairs with the flavor of the mushrooms and carrots. This sauce would also make a great enchilada sauce by adding just a little more water to thin it out, which I like to serve with Pinto Bean & Mushroom Rolled Enchiladas (page 148).

The best thing about this sauce is that it freezes well for later use. You can also cut the recipe in half to make less sauce, but when I tested the recipe cut in half, I still used the "plus ⅓ cup" of water to rinse out the blender and make the sauce the right consistency. Everything else cut in half perfectly fine, but always adjust the salt and lime to match and fit your own palate.

MAKES APPROXIMATELY 5 CUPS

12 guajillo chiles
11 cups water plus ⅓ cup water, divided
1 cup pumpkin seeds, toasted and salted
2 tablespoons freshly squeezed lime juice
    (1 to 2 limes), or to taste
1½ teaspoons kosher salt, or to taste

Preheat the oven to 350°F. Place the guajillo chiles on a baking sheet, and toast them for approximately 3 minutes. Do not over-toast the chiles as they will burn—we want to lightly toast the chiles without burning them, as burned chiles will make the sauce taste bitter. Remove from oven and allow to cool. Remove the stem and seeds and break them into small pieces.

In a medium saucepan, heat 8 cups of water until it boils. Place the cleaned toasted chile pods into boiling water for 3 minutes, stirring frequently to make sure that they stay immersed in the water and reconstitute. Turn off the heat and let the chile pods sit until soft,

approximately 5 minutes, making sure they are immersed in the water. Sometimes I put a small plate on top of them to hold them down. Drain the chiles in a colander and discard the chile water.

Place the chiles, pumpkin seeds, and 3 cups water in a high-powered blender and blend on high for 2 to 3 minutes, or until completely smooth. Add the lime juice and salt, blend again, and then taste. Adjust lime and salt as needed.

Pass through a fine strainer to remove any unblended chiles and/or seeds. Pour the remaining ⅓ cup of water into the blender, swirl around to remove the remaining sauce, and pass through the strainer. I have found that there is about 1 tablespoon of the chile and pumpkin seed paste left in the strainer.

Serve immediately or allow to cool and then place in containers for freezing.

APPLE, RAISIN & PECAN SALAD

This refreshing salad combines the sweetness of apples and golden raisins with the tartness of lime dressing and the crunchiness of the toasted pecans. Apples and raisins are foods that are a part of the Food Distribution Program on Indian Reservations (FDPIR), so they are found in many Native households and are very healthy to eat, which is why we chose to add these ingredients to the salad. Pecans are an indigenous nut (with its origin coming from the Algonquin word *pakani*, which evolved into the American French word *pacane*, referring to a nut that required a stone to crack and one that the crows could break open) and are native to areas in the southern part of the United States, with New Mexico now being the largest nut-producing state in the nation. It was in fact the crows, as well as squirrels and other animals, that helped the pecan migrate westward by dispersing the nuts.

MAKES 4 SERVINGS

For the Salad:

6 cups baby salad greens or 1 bag (5 ounces) of baby salad greens

⅔ cup dark or golden raisins

2 medium Fuji, Pink Lady, Gala, Honeycrisp, or Braeburn apples, finely sliced

1 cup sprouts (sunflower sprouts, radish sprouts, or microgreens, i.e., broccoli, cabbage, amaranth, etc.) (optional)

¾ cup pecans, toasted and coarsely chopped

For the Dressing:

6 tablespoons agave sweetener

3 teaspoons New Mexico red chile powder, mild

½ cup freshly squeezed lime juice (approximately 6 small limes)

2 tablespoons plus 1 teaspoon smooth Dijon mustard

½ teaspoon kosher salt

⅛ teaspoon freshly ground black pepper, or to taste

In a medium salad bowl, add the salad greens, raisins, apples, and half of the sprouts and gently toss together.

In a separate mixing bowl, combine the agave, chile powder, lime juice, mustard, salt, and pepper. Whisk until all the ingredients are completely mixed. Pour half of the salad dressing over the salad greens. Divide the salad into four equal portions and plate on individual salad plates or plate the entire salad if you want to serve it family style. Top the salad with the chopped pecan nuts and the remainder of the sprouts and/or microgreens, if using. Drizzle a little of the leftover salad dressing around the greens and serve immediately, or serve family style in a large bowl.

TRI-COLOR COLESLAW

I've been making this recipe for Native communities for years now as a wonderful alternative to coleslaws that use mayonnaise. This nutritious slaw has a rainbow of colors, making it a beautiful addition to any meal. The secret ingredient here is raspberry jam, which adds sweetness to the shredded cabbage and kale. This coleslaw can be made in advance as it holds well in the summer months. Just wait to add the dressing until right before serving. This recipe is perfect at any family gathering, Ceremonial event, or family meal. It makes a great side or is a delicious salad on its own.

MAKES APPROXIMATELY 8 SERVINGS

For the Coleslaw:
2 cups packed, thinly shredded red cabbage
2 cups packed, thinly shredded white cabbage
2 cups packed, thinly shredded lacinato kale
2 cups matchstick carrots (I buy these already cut)
1 tablespoon apple cider vinegar
½ teaspoon kosher salt

For the Dressing:
3 tablespoons low-sugar raspberry jam (organic if possible)
1½ tablespoons smooth Dijon mustard
3 tablespoons balsamic vinegar
1 teaspoon New Mexico red chile powder, mild (or more for a spicier slaw)
¼ teaspoon kosher salt, or to taste
⅛ teaspoon freshly ground black pepper
7 tablespoons water

For the Garnish:
½ cup Toasted Pumpkin Seeds (page 261)

In a large bowl toss together the red cabbage, white cabbage, kale, carrots, apple cider vinegar, and salt. Let sit for approximately 7 to 10 minutes. This helps begin to break down the cabbage, making it softer and easier to eat without losing its crunchiness.

To make the dressing, in a medium bowl, whisk together the raspberry jam, mustard, vinegar, chile powder, salt, pepper, and water. Pour half of the dressing over the slaw and toss together. Plate the slaw in the middle of the plate, drizzle a little of the extra dressing around the coleslaw, and then sprinkle the pumpkin seeds on top of the slaw and around the plate. Serve immediately or refrigerate until needed.

CHILE EMPAÑADITAS

Turnovers are a dough filled with a variety of savory or sweet ingredients that are either baked or fried. In some parts of the Southwest and on many of the Pueblos of New Mexico where the Spanish influence is strong, these turnovers are called *empañadas*, meaning "wrapped in bread." These smaller ones that I like to make, I call *empañaditas*.

These savory turnovers taste best hot from the oven and served with a Guajillo Chile Sauce (page 132), Green Chile Sauce (page 131), or Red Chile Sauce (page 129). They can be made in advance; they freeze well and are a nice appetizer to have on hand for family gatherings.

MAKES APPROXIMATELY 42 EMPAÑADITAS

For the Dough:

4 cups all-purpose flour, plus more for rolling out the dough

½ teaspoon kosher salt

3 tablespoons baking powder

1 cup all-vegetable shortening, nonhydrogenated (organic if possible) (see Notes), or vegan butter

1½ cups unsweetened oat milk

For the Filling:

1 tablespoon sunflower or olive oil

1 medium to large yellow onion, diced (approximately 2 cups)

1 tablespoon blackened garlic (page 253)

2 large carrots, finely diced (approximately 1 cup)

2 cups finely diced brown cremini mushrooms (about 12 mushrooms or one 8-ounce package)

2 cups finely diced shiitake mushrooms (9 to 10 mushrooms or two 3.5-ounce packages)

2 cups finely diced oyster mushrooms (8 ounces)

3 green New Mexico or Anaheim chiles, roasted, peeled, and diced (approximately ¾ cup) (page 250)

1 tablespoon plus 1 teaspoon dried New Mexico red chile powder, mild

2 teaspoons kosher salt, or to taste

1 tablespoon very finely chopped fresh tarragon

¼ teaspoon dried thyme

4 tablespoons water

For the Plant-Based Egg Wash (See Notes):

6 tablespoons aquafaba (garbanzo bean juice)

2 tablespoons unsweetened oat milk

In a bowl, mix the flour, salt, and baking powder. Add the shortening and work it into the dry ingredients with your hands. Add the oat milk and mix until the dough is soft and pliable, being careful not to overwork it. If the dough feels too moist, add a little of the additional flour. If you overwork it, it will get tough and be harder to roll out. Replace the dough back into the bowl and cover with plastic wrap, or place in a sealable heavy-duty plastic bag and let the dough sit at room temperature for approximately an hour.

While the dough is resting, prepare the chiles.

In a large cast-iron skillet or heavy-bottomed sauté pan (I use a 15-inch cast-iron skillet), heat the sunflower oil until hot but not smoking, then add the onions. Cook for approximately 5 minutes, stirring to prevent burning. Add the garlic and cook for another minute, stirring to prevent from burning. Stir in the carrots, cooking for another 3 minutes. Add the mushrooms, reduce the heat to medium, and sauté for 10 minutes, stirring every couple of minutes to make sure they caramelize. Now add the chiles, stir, and cook for another minute. Add the chile powder, salt, tarragon, and thyme. Mix completely. Add the water and stir to remove anything that has stuck to the bottom of the pan. Remove from the heat, taste, adjust seasoning if necessary, place into a small bowl, and set aside.

In a small bowl make the vegan egg wash by whisking together the aquafaba and oat milk. Reserve. Preheat the oven to 400°F.

Cut the dough in half and sprinkle flour on a work surface. Roll out the dough. The dough should be no thicker than ⅛ inch. Make sure that it is completely and evenly rolled out. Using a 3½-inch diameter circular cookie cutter, cut approximately twenty-one circles per half batch of dough. Remove excess dough and discard.

Place 1 tablespoon of the filling onto one-half of each dough circle. I place the cooked mushroom mixture on one side of the circle so it is easy to fold over. Brush a little of the vegan egg wash around the outer edges of the circle and fold the dough over, sealing the edges, first with your finger and then with a fork to secure the edges and make sure that they are sealed. You will now have a half-circle dough turnover filled with the mushroom mixture. Using the cookie cutter, trim the edges so that the turnover is smooth and round and place on a sheet tray lined with parchment paper. Next use the remaining half of the dough until you

have all forty-two empañaditas completed. If you are going to freeze some for future use, now is the time to do that. I put the whole tray into the freezer, and then once the empañaditas have frozen, place them in a freezer storage bag marked with the date I made them.

To cook the empañaditas, brush the top of each empañadita with the remaining plant-based egg wash. Bake for 7 minutes, remove from the oven, and brush again with the vegan egg wash. Return to the oven and bake again for another 7 minutes; remove from oven and brush again with the plant-based egg wash. Do this a total of five times so that you have a nice golden-brown color on the empañaditas. You will cook the turnovers for a total of 35 minutes, depending on your oven, brushing them each time you remove them from the oven.

Remove from the oven and serve hot with the guajillo chile sauce (page 132) or any of the other sauces mentioned above. You can serve four to six as a part of an entrée, or two as an appetizer.

Notes:
To make the plant-based vegan egg wash, I use the juice from a can of garbanzo beans. One can of garbanzo beans will yield ¾ cup bean juice or aquafaba and 1⅔ cups beans. I usually drain and wash canned beans but, in this instance, I use the juice drained right from the can for the wash and reserve the beans for a later use.

For the all-vegetable shortening, I use Spectrum culinary brand. It is Rainforest Alliance Certified, Fair Trade Certified, certified sustainable palm oil, non-GMO Project Verified, USDA organic, and available in most supermarkets.

GREEN CHILE HERBED RICE

This rice makes a great accompaniment to many dishes. I like it the most with the Mole Sauce (page 228) and the Black Beans with Chocolate & Chipotle (page 76) as a meal, but it is also delicious with the Guajillo Chile Sauce (page 132) and Chile Empañaditas (page 137).

MAKES 4 TO 6 SERVINGS

2 teaspoons sunflower or olive oil

1 small yellow onion, small dice
(approximately 1 cup)

1 teaspoon blackened garlic (page 253)

1 cup uncooked long-grain white rice
(basmati works great for this recipe)

1 New Mexico or Anaheim green chile, roasted,
peeled, seeded, and chopped (about ½ cup)
(page 250)

2 green onions, chopped (approximately ¼ cup)

½ cup tightly packed cilantro, leaves chopped
(approximately ½ bunch)

1 teaspoon kosher salt

2½ cups water, divided

In a large saucepan over medium-high heat, heat the sunflower oil until hot but not smoking. Add the onions and stir occasionally for approximately 5 minutes, until they begin to caramelize. Add the garlic and continue to cook for another minute. Add the rice and toast with the onions and garlic for an additional 3 minutes, mixing completely. Stir constantly to prevent the rice from burning.

In a blender, combine the green chile, green onions, cilantro, salt, and 2 cups of the water. Blend until smooth.

Pour mixture into the pan with the rice, add the remaining ½ cup of water and mix completely. Bring to a boil, then reduce the heat and simmer, covered, for approximately 20 minutes for basmati rice, longer for brown rice, or until the rice has absorbed the liquid and is tender.

Remove from heat. Using a spatula or two forks, gently fluff the rice and serve immediately. Makes a great side or accompaniment to many dishes.

POBLANO STUFFED CHILES

The fresh poblano chile is one of the most popular chiles in both Mexico and the United States, originating in the state of Pueblo in Mexico. Poblanos are the perfect chile for making stuffed chiles (rellenos) not only because of their size and sturdy structure but because of the smoky, earthy flavor they have when roasted.

I like to serve this with the Heirloom Tomato Sauce recipe (page 171), which I can into jars every year using heirloom tomatoes that I buy from farmer José Gonzalez at Gonzalez Farm. If you cannot get heirloom tomatoes, you can use any tomato sauce for this recipe or try it with the Guajillo Chile Sauce (page 132) for a spicier sauce to accompany the stuffed chile. If you can purchase organic or Native-sourced quinoa, I recommend that you do so.

For the Chile Stuffing:

¾ cup uncooked quinoa

1 tablespoon sunflower oil

½ medium to large yellow onion, diced
    (approximately 1 cup)

8 ounces shiitake mushrooms, halved and
    thinly sliced (about 2 cups)

4 ounces cremini mushrooms, halved and
    thinly sliced (about 1 cup)

1 tablespoon blackened garlic (page 253)

½ cup corn kernels, frozen or fresh

¾ teaspoon kosher salt, or to taste

2 cups fresh baby spinach, washed and cleaned

For the Stuffed Chiles:

4 whole fresh poblano chiles

4 tablespoons water

1 pint Heirloom Tomato Sauce (page 171)
    or other canned tomato sauce

First make the quinoa. Rinse quinoa in a
fine-mesh strainer and transfer to a medium
saucepan with 1½ cups water. Bring to a boil,
reduce heat to a simmer, cover, and cook for
approximately 12 to 15 minutes or until all the
water is absorbed. The cooking ratio for this
grain is always two parts water to one part
quinoa. Remove from heat and set aside.

To make the stuffed chiles, roast and peel the
chiles (see directions on page 250). Then slice
the chiles lengthwise (making sure that you have
a little bit of unsliced chile on the bottom and
that the stem stays intact so the chile will hold
together once you stuff it) and spread open on a
work surface. Remove any seeds and set aside.

Heat a large cast-iron skillet over medium to
high heat, add the sunflower oil and the onions,
and sauté for 2 to 3 minutes, until the onions
are translucent. Add the mushrooms and sauté
for another 8 to 9 minutes, stirring to prevent
burning, until they are caramelized. Add the
garlic and sauté for another 2 minutes. Add
the corn and salt and cook for another minute.
Add the spinach, stir, and cook for another
minute or until the spinach starts to wilt. Add
the cooked quinoa and mix well, ensuring that
all the ingredients are completely combined.
Taste, and adjust seasoning, as needed. Remove
the filling from the heat and set aside.

If you plan on baking the chiles immediately,
preheat the oven to 350°F (see Note).
Generously stuff each chile with the quinoa
mixture. Place the stuffed chiles on a lightly
oiled baking pan, to prevent them from
sticking, with the open (stuffed) side up.
Add 2 tablespoons of water to the bottom of
the pan. Bake for 15 minutes. Remove from
the oven, add the remaining 2 tablespoons
of water to the bottom of the pan, and cook
for an additional 10 minutes or until they are
hot all the way through.

Remove from oven. Spoon some of the tomato
sauce onto each plate, and then top with the
cooked stuffed chile and serve immediately.

Note:

*You can make this dish a day ahead, place on
a sheet tray, wrap with plastic wrap to cover,
and refrigerate overnight. The next day you can
remove the plastic wrap and then reheat in a
350°F oven for approximately 25 to 30 minutes
until hot, right before serving.*

RED CHILE POTATO STEW

Every Pueblo in New Mexico has a recipe for a red chile stew. It's a staple of Pueblo cuisine and made in a multitude of ways, the most common way, with potatoes, red chile, and some kind of meat or wild game. I was originally taught the traditional Picuris Pueblo way to make this stew many years ago by Margaret Archuleta, who has since passed, of Picuris Pueblo when her brother Richard Mermejo was governor of the Pueblo. I've made it many times over the years and have changed it slightly each time depending on whom I was cooking it for and what ingredients were available at the time. For this version, I added onion, carrots, celery, and mushrooms, packing this stew with vegetables in addition to just the potatoes, and I've added some coconut milk to give a creamy thick rich texture to the stew and to make it more filling. The constant for me has always been the Red Chile Sauce recipe (page 129). This is my new contemporary favorite from a traditional Pueblo staple.

MAKES 4 TO 6 SERVINGS

2 tablespoons sunflower oil

1 large yellow onion, diced (approximately 2 cups)

2 large carrots, diced (approximately 2 cups)

2 stalks of celery, diced (approximately 2 cups)

8 ounces cremini mushrooms, diced (approximately 2 cups)

2 cloves garlic, minced (approximately 1 teaspoon)

2 teaspoons ground coriander

1 can (13.5 ounces) unsweetened coconut milk

2 to 3 large Yukon gold or russet potatoes, cubed in ½-inch cubes (approximately 5 cups weighing about 1½ pounds)

1 recipe Red Chile Sauce (page 129)

2 cups water

1 teaspoon kosher salt, or to taste

⅛ teaspoon freshly ground black pepper, or to taste

1 bunch of chives, minced, for garnish

In a heavy-bottomed soup pot over medium-high heat, add the sunflower oil. After a minute, add the onion, carrots, celery, and mushrooms. Cook for approximately 10 minutes, stirring occasionally until the vegetables have released their water and are just starting to caramelize. Add the garlic and cook for an additional 1 to 2 minutes, stirring to prevent burning.

Add the coriander and coconut milk, scraping any bits from the bottom of the pot with a wooden spoon. Next add the potatoes, Red Chile Sauce, and water and bring to a boil. Reduce the heat to low and let simmer for approximately 45 minutes, or until the potatoes are tender. Season with the salt and pepper to taste. Garnish with chives. Serve immediately.

RED CHILE POTATO CASSEROLE

A stacked enchilada is a common dish made throughout Northern New Mexico and many Native communities in the Southwest. These stacked enchiladas are primarily made with red chile, cheese, meat, and tortillas that are stacked and layered together. Instead of corn tortillas, this version uses Yukon gold potatoes for their rich and creamy flavor. They are very thinly sliced like a corn tortilla and then layered together. I've changed the traditional red chile sauce by adding a modern twist to it. I've added additional spices and coconut milk in this version, yet the flavors are perfectly layered together and still keep the delicious and rich flavors of the region.

MAKES 6 TO 8 SERVINGS

1 tablespoon plus 1 teaspoon of sunflower oil, divided

1 large yellow onion, thinly sliced into slivers (approximately 3 cups)

2 teaspoons kosher salt

1 tablespoon minced garlic (approximately 4 cloves)

1 teaspoon dried Mexican oregano

1 teaspoon dried thyme

1 teaspoon dried rosemary, finely chopped

1 can (13.5 ounces) unsweetened coconut milk

1½ cups Red Chile Sauce (page 129)

2 pounds Yukon gold potatoes, thinly sliced (⅛ inch thick and approximately 6 cups, about 2 large potatoes)

1 tablespoon minced fresh chives, for garnish

Preheat the oven to 350°F. In a large, heavy-bottomed skillet or pot, over medium to high heat, add 1 tablespoon of the sunflower oil. Heat until it is hot but not smoking. Add the onion and salt and cook for approximately 10 minutes, stirring to prevent burning, until the onions are caramelized.

Stir in the garlic, Mexican oregano, thyme, and rosemary and cook for another minute. Add the coconut milk and Red Chile Sauce to deglaze the cooked onions and spices and scrape the bottom of the skillet to incorporate all the flavor into the sauce.

Bring mixture to a boil, reduce the heat to low and let simmer for 5 minutes, stirring occasionally to prevent burning. Turn off the heat and set aside. This should yield approximately 4 cups of sauce.

Rub 1 teaspoon of sunflower oil on the bottom and sides of a baking dish that is approximately 9 x 12 inches. Layer evenly as follows: first spread ¾ cup sauce evenly over the bottom of the casserole dish, then cover with 3 cups of the thinly sliced potatoes (we fanned them in a circle and then another circle inside that one), then top with another ¾ cup sauce and a second layer of 3 cups of the thinly sliced potatoes, then finish with remaining ½ cup sauce evenly spread over the entire top.

Gently cover the baking dish with aluminum foil or an ovenproof lid and bake for 40 minutes. Remove foil, and bake uncovered for an additional 20 minutes, or until the potatoes are tender when pierced with a paring knife. Garnish with the minced chives and serve immediately.

GREEN CHILE ENCHILADA LASAGNA

New Mexico is known for its stacked chile enchiladas. Instead of rolling ingredients inside a corn tortilla and then covering each one in sauce, layers of vegetables and a variety of other fillings are stacked in between corn tortillas that are layered together flat in a baking pan, which is then baked and served like a lasagna. These stacked enchiladas are always layered together with either a red chile or green chile sauce.

This recipe takes some time to make, but it is worth it. With its blend of vegetables, this is a wonderful and healthy alternative to cheese or chicken enchiladas. Serve it with the Red Chile Pinto Beans (page 77), Posole with Red Chile (page 37), or a simple salad.

MAKES 4 TO 6 SERVINGS

18 White Corn Tortillas (page 27),
　or use store-bought
2 batches of Green Chile Sauce (page 131),
　plus 1 cup water or vegetable stock (page 265)
　mixed in to make the sauce a little thinner
　for the enchiladas

For the Mushrooms:

2 tablespoons sunflower oil
8 ounces cremini mushrooms, washed, dried,
　and sliced (approximately 3 cups)
8 ounces white mushrooms, washed, dried,
　and sliced (approximately 3 cups)
½ teaspoon kosher salt, or to taste
1 tablespoon blackened garlic (page 253)
2 tablespoons water
6 ounces fresh baby spinach leaves
　(approximately 6 cups packed)

For the Zucchini:

1 tablespoon sunflower oil
3 small zucchini, thinly sliced
　(approximately 8 inches long
　by 1½ inches wide and sliced about
　⅛ inch thick) (approximately 5 cups)
½ teaspoon kosher salt, or to taste

In a large, seasoned cast-iron skillet or on a cast-iron stove-top cooking grill (see Pantry Staples, page 249), over high heat, cook the tortillas one at a time or however many can fit in the skillet without touching for approximately 1 minute on each side, or until each one gets lightly blistered. Once each tortilla is cooked, transfer it to a basket or bowl lined with a clean kitchen towel to keep warm. Drape the towel over the top of the basket or bowl to keep the cooked tortillas clean, moist, and warm.

Warm the Green Chile Sauce over low to medium heat.

Add the 2 tablespoons of sunflower oil to the large hot skillet. Add both varieties of mushrooms and salt. Reduce heat to medium and cook for approximately 10 minutes, or until all the water from the mushrooms has evaporated and they are caramelized. Add the garlic and cook another minute. Add 2 tablespoons of water to deglaze the pan. Cook for 3 to 4 minutes until the water has evaporated and all the flavor from the bottom of the pan releases. Add the baby spinach and stir, cooking until the spinach wilts into the mushrooms. Remove from heat. Transfer the mixture to a bowl and reserve.

In the same cast-iron pan, over high heat, add 1 tablespoon of sunflower oil. Add the zucchini and salt, making sure the pieces of zucchini are separated and not in clumps. Cover, turn down the heat to medium, and cook for approximately 10 minutes, until the water cooks out of the zucchini. Stir occasionally to make sure the zucchini cooks evenly and is completely cooked. Remove from heat and transfer to a bowl.

Now it's time to build the stacked enchilada lasagna. Preheat the oven to 350°F. Make sure the Green Chile Sauce is heated and you have added the additional water to thin out the original sauce recipe.

You will spread each layer below evenly across the bottom of a 9 x 13-inch (or similar size) baking dish. When placing tortillas on each layer, it is okay if the corn tortillas overlap a little as you build your enchilada lasagna. Repeat in the order below until you have built the stacked enchilada lasagna and then bake in the oven.

Build in This Order:
1 cup Green Chile Sauce to cover the bottom
   of the pan
6 cooked warm corn tortillas
1½ cups Green Chile Sauce
½ of the cooked zucchini, layered evenly over
   the sauce
½ of the cooked mushroom mixture, spread
   evenly over the zucchini
⅛ teaspoon kosher salt sprinkled over the top
   of this layer

6 cooked warm corn tortillas
1½ cups Green Chile Sauce
Remaining cooked zucchini, layered evenly
   over the sauce
Remaining cooked mushroom mixture,
   spread evenly over the zucchini
⅛ teaspoon kosher salt sprinkled over the top
   of this layer
6 cooked corn tortillas
1½ cups Green Chile Sauce

Cover with foil and bake for 60 minutes. You will have some leftover Green Chile Sauce from the two batches of sauce, which I reheat once the enchilada is cooked to serve it on the side since I love sauce and it is delicious with the cooked enchilada.

Remove from oven and serve with your favorite side dishes or a simple salad. Ladle some of the remaining Green Chile Sauce over each cut slice of the enchilada lasagna on the plate and serve immediately.

Note:
To prepare in advance: make the zucchini mixture and the mushroom mixture, keeping them separate, and wait to build the enchilada lasagna until right before cooking to preserve the structure of the tortillas and to ensure that they don't get soggy.

PINTO BEAN & MUSHROOM ROLLED ENCHILADAS

Enchiladas are a wonderful way to make a hearty meal that is both nutritious and flavorful. This recipe uses the Red Mesa's Refried Pinto Beans recipe (page 74), blackened corn recipe (page 252), and the Red Chile Sauce recipe (page 129). The mushrooms give this an earthy, rich flavor profile that will please any palate. It is a great dish to serve individually plated or family style right from the oven in the baking dish, with the additional Red Chile Sauce on the side.

MAKES 4 TO 6 SERVINGS OR 12 ENCHILADAS

1 batch Red Mesa's Refried Pinto Beans (page 74)
1 batch Red Chile Sauce (page 129), warmed

For the Mushrooms:
2 teaspoons sunflower or olive oil
8 ounces cremini mushrooms, thinly sliced
    (approximately 2 cups)
8 ounces white mushrooms, thinly sliced
    (approximately 2 cups)
3.5 ounces shiitake mushrooms, cut in half and
    then thinly sliced (approximately 1 cup)
1 teaspoon kosher salt, or to taste
¼ teaspoon freshly ground black pepper,
    or to taste
1 cup blackened corn (page 252)
1 tablespoon water

For the Enchiladas:
12 corn tortillas, heated (store-bought)
¼ teaspoon kosher salt
2 green onions, thinly sliced on a bias
    (approximately ¼ cup), for garnish
2 tablespoons finely chopped cilantro,
    for garnish

First make the Red Mesa's Refried Pinto Beans as per the recipe and set aside. Then make the Red Chile Sauce as per the recipe, set aside, and keep warm.

Preheat a medium cast-iron pan or heavy-bottomed skillet over medium to high heat until it is hot but not smoking. Add the sunflower oil, mushrooms, salt, and pepper and sauté for 7 minutes, stirring to prevent burning so that the mushrooms begin to turn golden brown and caramelize. Add the corn, stir. Add the water and cook for an additional 2 minutes to deglaze the pan, stirring to incorporate all the ingredients. Remove from the heat and transfer the cooked mushrooms and corn to a bowl and reserve.

Heat the tortillas using an open flame on a grill or in a very hot, seasoned cast-iron pan. Cook each tortilla for about 30 seconds on each side. Place in a basket lined with a clean kitchen towel to hold and keep warm. Repeat until all the tortillas have been heated as you prepare the enchiladas.

Preheat the oven to 350°F. To assemble the enchiladas, place a warmed open tortilla on a flat work surface. Spoon approximately 2 tablespoons of the cooked mushroom mixture onto each corn tortilla, then top with 2 heaping tablespoons of the savory refried pinto bean mixture. Spread the bean mixture evenly across the center portion of the tortillas. Roll each side of the tortilla toward the center, turn it over, and place open side down onto a lightly oiled baking dish or sheet tray approximately 8½ x 12 inches.

Spoon 2 cups of the prepared Red Chile Sauce over the entire baking dish of rolled enchiladas, place in the oven, and heat until hot. Cook for approximately 20 to 25 minutes, or until they are hot all the way through. Sprinkle ¼ teaspoon of salt across the top, then garnish with the green onions and cilantro.

When plating the enchiladas, add a little of the additional Red Chile Sauce onto the plate and place the cooked enchilada on top. If serving family style, place the remaining warmed Red Chile Sauce in a bowl and let each person spoon a little of the sauce onto their own plates. Serve immediately.

Note:
Sometimes I end up with just a little bit of the refried bean mixture left over. I don't like to waste anything, so I take the leftover refried bean mixture, add a little water to it, and blend it into a sauce, which I ladle on top of the Red Chile Sauce and the enchiladas before I garnish and serve them. It is a great way to use up all the bean mixture and adds additional flavor to your dish.

PUMPKIN SEED TRAIL MIX

Trail mix is an easy and healthy way to have a snack that is not only nutritious but also very flavorful. The seeds, dried fruits, and chocolate may be what you expect; the red chile powder adds a unique spicy kick that complements the sweetness of the fruit and chocolate.

MAKES 4 CUPS

1 cup hulled and raw sunflower seeds
1 cup hulled and raw pumpkin seeds
½ teaspoon sunflower oil
½ teaspoon kosher salt
2 teaspoons New Mexico red chile powder, mild
¾ cup dried tart cherries
¾ cup dried apricots, quartered
½ cup dark chocolate chips

In a large bowl, toss together the sunflower seeds, pumpkin seeds, sunflower oil, and kosher salt. In a large cast-iron or heavy-bottomed skillet over medium heat, toast the seeds, stirring frequently until they are golden brown and crispy, for around 15 minutes, stirring to ensure that they cook evenly and don't burn.

Transfer seeds back to the large bowl and allow to cool completely at room temperature.

Gently stir in the red chile powder, cherries, apricots, and chocolate chips. Store in an airtight container in the refrigerator for up to 1 month.

POBLANO CORN BREAD

Corn bread is a Native American Southwest staple. This recipe adds a little spice from the poblano chiles and some little bursts of sweetness from the fresh corn kernels. Another key component of this moist, delicious corn bread is ground chia seeds. Chia is an ancient grain indigenous to the Americas. Scientists believe that chia dates back to approximately 3500 B.C. Considered a superfood, chia seeds have many health benefits including promoting digestive health, aiding in skin health, improving heart health, boosting energy, balancing blood sugar, building strong bones, fighting cancer growth, and enhancing oral health as well as providing omega-3 fatty acids.

For the Dry Mix:

1¼ cups finely ground yellow cornmeal

1¼ cups all-purpose flour

1 teaspoon kosher salt

¼ cup organic unbleached sugar

1 teaspoon baking soda

For the Wet Mix:

3 tablespoons ground chia seeds

1¼ cups oat milk

2 teaspoons apple cider vinegar

¼ cup sunflower oil

¼ cup unsweetened applesauce

1 large poblano chile, roasted, peeled, and
   chopped (page 250) (approximately ½ cup)

1 cup corn kernels, fresh or frozen

Preheat the oven to 425°F. Grease an approximately 8 x 8-inch baking pan, a round cast-iron skillet, or cast-iron corncob pans with baking spray.

In a large bowl, mix the cornmeal, flour, salt, sugar, and baking soda. In a separate bowl, whisk together the chia, oat milk, vinegar, sunflower oil, and applesauce. Let this mixture sit for 10 minutes. Then add the wet ingredients to the dry and fold together with a rubber spatula until a wet batter is formed. Fold in the chiles and the corn.

Transfer the batter to the prepared baking dish or cast-iron pan, and bake for approximately 35 to 40 minutes, or until a paring knife or toothpick pushed into the center comes out clean. If you are making the bread in the corncob pans, cook for approximately 15 to 20 minutes until done. The bread should be golden brown and spring back when touched. Let rest for 10 minutes before slicing. This corn bread can be cooked ahead of time and reheated slightly right before serving. I prefer to eat it warm.

Notes:

You can also use blue or white cornmeal for this recipe as well.

According to Sarah Klemn, RDN, CD, LDN, in her article from Eat Right *in the Academy of Nutrition and Dietetics, chia seeds came from the desert plant* Salvia hispanica, *a member of the mint family, which was a staple in the Ancestral Aztec diet, and the seeds of a related plant,* Salvia columbariae *(golden chia), were used by Native Americans in the southwestern United States.*

CHILE PECANS

Pecans are the only major nut tree indigenous to North America and a close relative of the hickory nut. Native Americans in southern Mississippi are thought to have been the first people to add the pecan to their diet, according to Barbara Bryant and Betsy Fentress in their book *Pecans*. Coming from an Algonquian word meaning "nut requiring a stone to crack," it was in fact the crows that helped it migrate westward by dispersing the seeds while flying. Throughout history, these nuts provided an important source of protein to many Native American tribes using them for nourishment, as medicine, and as a form of barter. When wild game was scarce, the nuts, which could be eaten both raw and cooked, provided an important source of both calories and unsaturated fats. I also love to use these on salads with any kind of greens from my local farmers' market.

MAKES 2 CUPS CHILE PECANS

For the Chile Coating:
2 tablespoons New Mexico red chile powder, mild
1 teaspoon kosher salt
¼ cup organic unbleached sugar

For the Pecans:
¼ cup maple syrup
1 tablespoon water
2 cups raw pecans (½ pound)

Preheat the oven to 350°F. Line a large sheet tray with parchment paper or a silicone baking mat. In a large bowl, mix the chile powder, salt, and sugar, making sure there are no lumps, and reserve.

In a medium to large heavy-bottomed sauté pan, bring the maple syrup and water to a boil over medium heat. Add the pecans and cook for 4 to 5 minutes, stirring constantly until the liquid is evaporated. The pecan nuts should still be moist for dredging in the chile mixture but the liquid evaporated. Remove from heat and transfer pecans to the bowl with the chile mixture, stirring or tossing gently to evenly coat all the nuts.

Gently pour the coated nuts onto the prepared tray and bake for 10 minutes in the oven. Remove from oven and let cool.

Place nuts in a glass jar or airtight plastic container and store for several weeks if they last that long. Mine always disappear shortly after they are made.

ZUCCHINI BREAD WITH CHILE & CHOCOLATE

My childhood memories include my mother growing a garden every year. One of the vegetables she grew was zucchini. There was always lots of it. We would set up a small stand and try to sell some of it, but the zucchini never sold as quickly as we wanted them to. So I turned them into small quick-bread loaves that I sold to the local health food store. There they sold very quickly; I think it was at this point in my life—I was maybe eleven or twelve—that I realized my passion and love for cooking and my desire to become a chef when I grew up. Here is an evolved version of that small zucchini quick-bread loaf that may have started my career.

MAKES 1 LOAF

1 medium zucchini (about 8 inches long by 2 inches wide), shredded (approximately 2 cups)

1 teaspoon kosher salt

1½ cups all-purpose flour

1 teaspoon baking powder

½ teaspoon baking soda

2 teaspoons pumpkin pie spice

3 teaspoons New Mexico red chile powder, mild

¾ cup dark brown sugar

½ cup unsweetened applesauce

¼ cup sunflower oil

¼ cup unsweetened almond or oat milk

2 teaspoons vanilla bean paste or extract

½ cup 72 percent dark chocolate chips

Preheat the oven to 350°F. Spray a standard-size loaf pan with a nonstick spray or rub sunflower oil on the inside of the pan.

In a medium bowl, toss together the zucchini and salt. Let this sit for 15 minutes while you prepare the rest of the batter.

In a large bowl, mix together the flour, baking powder, baking soda, pumpkin pie spice, and red chile powder. Make a well in the center of the bowl and add the brown sugar, applesauce, sunflower oil, almond milk, and vanilla. Using a wooden spoon or rubber spatula, stir it all together until completely combined.

Finish preparing the zucchini. Strain the zucchini through a colander, then transfer it to a clean kitchen towel, two layers of paper towel, or a nut bag. Working over a bowl, twist and squeeze the towel or bag to remove as much additional liquid as possible. This should yield around 1 heaping cup of shredded and strained zucchini.

Add the zucchini and chocolate to the batter and gently stir to combine. Pour this mixture into the prepared loaf pan and bake for 60 minutes, or until a paring knife or toothpick inserted into the center comes out clean. Let cool for 30 minutes before slicing.

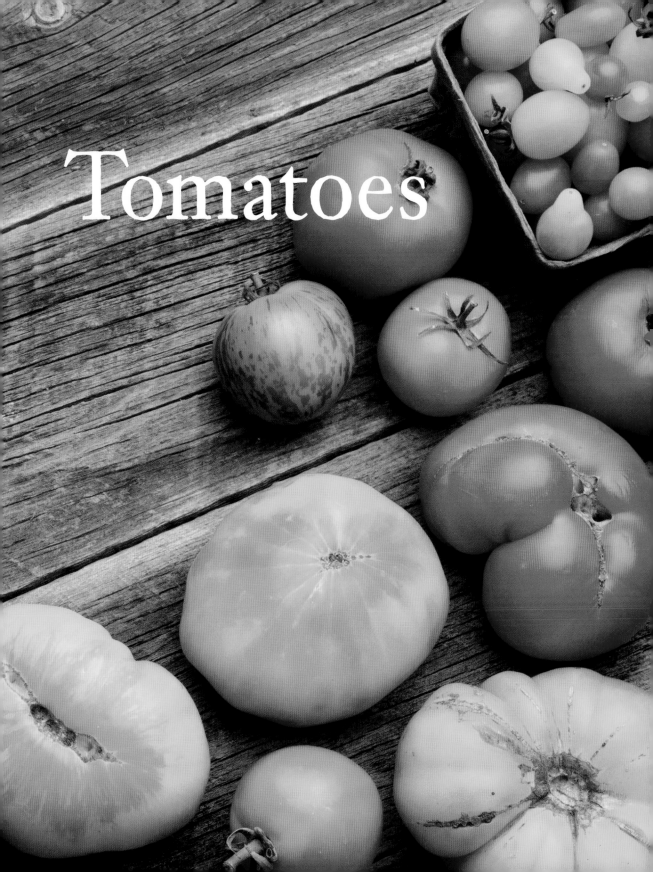

Tomatoes

The tomato originated in the Americas, with its domestication and cultivated use most likely originating with the Aztec Peoples of Mexico. The Nahuatl word *tomatl* is the root of the Spanish word *tomate*, which ultimately became the English word *tomato*. According to Friar Bernardino de Sahagún, the Aztecs used the tomatoes in cooked sauces along with chiles. They were some of the fresh foods that he witnessed at the great marketplace at Tenochtitlán, the Aztec capital in the 1500s.[23] During the Columbian exchange, the plant and its fruits were brought to Europe, where it, like some of the other Magic Eight foods— corn, beans, squash, chiles, potatoes, vanilla, and cacao—became woven into the cuisines of the cultures that were exposed to it. Some researchers credit the Spanish conquistador Hernán Cortés as the first to introduce the seeds to Europe. There is evidence that the tomato was being grown in Spain in the mid-1500s, where it was referred to as *tomate*, and that cooks there were already using it in culinary dishes like gazpacho.[24]

But the tomato was not as widely accepted as other foods of the Americas; in fact, it was viewed with suspicion and feared as being poisonous. It was referred to as the forbidden fruit and considered an exotic food in many places where people were wary to use it. And yet, regardless of its history of being feared and distrusted, the tomato today is widely used in almost every country in the world. They are on almost all supermarket shelves and grown in almost every backyard garden in the United States. They are made into cans of whole tomatoes, chopped tomatoes, stewed tomatoes, tomato paste, tomato sauce, tomato purée, and tomato juice, and they are dried and used fresh.

Like others in the nightshade family, tomatoes are packed with vitamins and nutrients including vitamin C, vitamin K, potassium, folate, and fiber. Tomatoes contain lycopene, which is an antioxidant that has many health benefits on its own. Tomatoes are good for the heart, eyes, and lungs; they ease inflammation, boost the immune system, lower cholesterol levels, and may help keep blood clots from forming, all factors that can help with the prevention of strokes. Lycopene, the nutrient in tomatoes, has a higher concentration in cooked—including canned—tomatoes; however, the heat used to make canned tomatoes lowers the amount of vitamin C, so many health professionals recommend eating both fresh and canned tomato products.

Heirloom tomatoes are my favorites. An heirloom tomato is a variety of tomato that has been passed down through generations— sometimes for hundreds of years and for many generations. According to the Gardener's Path, some of the best heirloom tomato varieties include the Yellow Pear, Chocolate Stripe, Cherokee Purple, Brandywine, Black Cherry, Green Zebra or Cherokee Green, Amish Paste, Bonny Best, Hillbilly, and Kellogg's Breakfast. But there are many kinds of heirloom tomatoes available, and there are more than three thousand varieties in active cultivation. And many people would argue that heirloom tomatoes are more flavorful, which I tend to agree.

Every year, I work with farmer José Gonzalez of Gonzalez Farm. José and his family sell produce every week at the Santa Fe Farmers' Market and have sold there since 2006. In 2015 the Gonzalezes received the Santa Fe Farmers' Market Institute's "Farmer All Star" award. José grows some of the best tomatoes I've ever tasted and runs an amazing family operation. I buy hundreds of pounds of José's heirloom tomatoes, which I make into an heirloom tomato sauce, and I also buy tomatoes from farmer Matt Romero of Romero Farms. I can

the sauce for my catering company, Red Mesa Cuisine, and use it throughout the year.

Everyone who has tried my sauce says it is the best tomato sauce that they have ever tasted, and I'm sharing my Heirloom Tomato Sauce recipe with all of you on page 171. You'll also sample recipes for some of the most delicious salads I've ever eaten, as well as some savory dishes, soups, and recipes that will make your mouth water, all of which celebrate tomatoes and their amazing flavor, texture, color, shape, and nutrients.

HEIRLOOM TOMATO SALAD

Heirloom tomatoes are an Ancestral variety that have been passed down from generation to generation. They are usually open-pollinated, meaning that they are pollinated by the bees, insects, birds, or by hand. The seeds are viable and can be saved and used the following year. Heirloom tomatoes are often oddly shaped, have a large water content, a sweet flavor, and come in yellow, orange, green, red, and purple varietals. This salad marries an Ancestral Native tomato with introduced ingredients from Europe for an appetizing starter to any meal.

MAKES 4 SERVINGS

2¼ cups balsamic vinegar or 1 bottle
    (16.9 ounces)
4 medium-size heirloom tomatoes,
    sliced about ¼ inch thick
    (yellow, orange, red, striped, etc.)
1 cucumber (approximately 7 inches long
    by 2 inches wide), sliced about ⅛ of an
    inch thick
10 basil leaves (approximately ¼ cup),
    chiffonade or sliced very thinly
½ teaspoon kosher salt, or to taste
¼ teaspoon freshly ground black pepper

In a medium-size saucepan over medium to high heat, bring the balsamic vinegar to a boil, then reduce the heat and simmer for approximately 45 minutes, or until you see a coating on the back of a spoon. If you tilt the saucepan toward yourself gently, the balsamic will bubble and you will notice that the coating will be apparent on the bottom of the pan.

Turn the heat off, let cool to room temperature, and transfer to bottle or jar for using in this recipe and the future. This reduction should yield approximately ½ cup and will last for several weeks refrigerated or approximately 1 week unrefrigerated if it is covered tightly. I let it warm to room temperature before use if it has been refrigerated.

Carefully wash and dry each heirloom tomato. They are delicate and can bruise easily, so baby them a little. Cut the rough skin off each tomato, if there is any, and then cut into slices, discarding the top, or what I call the hat of the tomato. Place sliced tomatoes and cucumbers on a plate, alternating between the two. Drizzle some of the balsamic reduction on top and then garnish with the fresh basil, salt, and pepper. Serve immediately.

TOMATO QUINOA SALAD

This salad can be made at any time of the year, but it is a great salad in the summer when baby tomatoes are in season and full of their sweet, succulent flavor. It makes a wonderful dish on its own or can be eaten as a side to any meal. It features heirloom baby tomatoes and the ancient grain quinoa. Quinoa comes from the Quechua word *kinwa* and is indigenous to the Americas, specifically the Andean region of northwestern South America in what is now the Lake Titicaca basin of Peru and in Bolivia. Fresh mint and onion round out this simple yet flavorful dish. We make this dish often at the food service culinary teachings I teach for senior centers throughout New Mexico for the New Mexico Department of Health. It is great as a warm side dish or served cold as a salad.

MAKES 4 TO 6 SERVINGS

For the Salad:
1 cup dried white quinoa
½ red onion, finely chopped
      (approximately 1 cup)
1 cup heirloom, baby tomatoes, sliced in half,
      unless large and then quartered
2 tablespoons finely chopped fresh mint

For the Salad Dressing:
3 tablespoons low-sugar raspberry jam
      (organic if possible)
1 tablespoon plus 1 teaspoon balsamic vinegar
1 tablespoon smooth Dijon mustard
½ teaspoon kosher salt, or to taste
⅛ teaspoon freshly ground black pepper,
      or to taste
4 tablespoons water, or as needed

First make the quinoa. Rinse the grain in a fine-mesh strainer and transfer to a medium saucepan with 2 cups water. Bring to a boil, reduce heat to a simmer, cover, and cook for 12 to 15 minutes, or until all the water is absorbed. The cooking ratio for this grain is always two parts water to one part dried quinoa. Remove it from the heat and place in a bowl to cool. Once cool, combine with the onion, tomatoes, and mint. Mix well.

For the salad dressing, combine the jam, vinegar, mustard, salt, and pepper. Whisk together until it becomes thick and creamy. Slowly add the water, 1 tablespoon at a time, whisking it into the other ingredients until you have the desired texture for a creamy salad dressing. Once you have a nice texture, stop adding water. Set aside.

In a large salad or mixing bowl, place the quinoa salad and pour the dressing on top, mixing it well with a large spoon. Serve immediately or place in the refrigerator and chill until serving.

Note:
If you want to make this salad the day before, keep the dressing on the side and dress the salad right before serving.

CHERRY TOMATO & ARUGULA SALAD

Tomatoes are a part of summer for me. I grow a variety of yellow, orange, and red cherry tomatoes, and this salad highlights their delightful, delicate flavor. They are easy to grow and so sweet and flavorful that they are worth the effort. While you can usually get arugula from your regular grocery store, I recommend getting it from your local farmers' market if you can, as it will have a much more pungent flavor than store-bought arugula. The sunflower sprouts, which I purchase at my local Santa Fe Farmers' Market, are also sold in some specialty supermarkets including Whole Foods, and at the local co-op here, and they pair perfectly with the piñon nuts, which enhance the flavors of the greens and tomatoes. While you can make this salad at any time throughout the year, for me, summer is the perfect season for this salad.

MAKES 4 TO 8 SERVINGS, DEPENDING ON THE SERVING SIZE

For the Salad Dressing:
6 tablespoons whole-grain Dijon mustard

2 tablespoons smooth Dijon mustard

6 tablespoons agave sweetener

4 teaspoons freshly squeezed lemon juice
   (approximately 1 small lemon)

2 teaspoons finely chopped garlic

4 tablespoons water

1 teaspoon kosher salt, or to taste

¼ teaspoon freshly ground black pepper,
   or to taste

For the Salad:
8 cups arugula, packed, washed and dried,
   tough stem bottoms (if any) removed

Pinch of kosher salt

Pinch of freshly ground black pepper

For Topping:
2 cups cherry tomatoes, cut in half
   (approximately thirty 1-inch cherry
   tomatoes)

½ cup sunflower sprouts, cut in half

½ cup piñon nuts, toasted

In a small mixing bowl, combine the ingredients for the salad dressing and whisk together. Season the greens in a salad bowl with a little pinch of both salt and pepper. Add ½ cup of the salad dressing to dress the greens and then toss. Serve family style on a large platter or divide into four portions for an entrée salad or eight portions as an appetizer, and put onto each of the plates.

Top with the tomatoes, sprouts, and piñon nuts. Drizzle the remaining salad dressing on the salad.

Serve immediately.

LOIS'S PICO DE GALLO

I love fresh salsa. It is one of my favorite things to eat with almost everything. It adds a nice zest of flavor to lots of recipes, and while I think every chef and home cook has a version of how to make this kitchen staple, this version is mine and I make it all the time. Top it on almost anything or try it with Red Mesa's Refried Pinto Beans (page 74), Bean & Spinach Tacos (page 85), Healthy Indian Tacos (page 86), Summer Fried Squash Blossoms (page 97), or Perfect Baked Potato with All the Fixings (page 194).

MAKES APPROXIMATELY 3 CUPS

2 vine-ripened tomatoes or 4 ripened Roma tomatoes, small dice (approximately 2 cups)
½ red onion, finely diced or minced (approximately ½ cup)
1 jalapeño, minced (approximately 2 tablespoons)
1 tablespoon blackened garlic (page 253)
¼ cup finely chopped fresh cilantro
1 tablespoon plus 1 teaspoon freshly squeezed lime juice (approximately 1 small lime)
½ teaspoon kosher salt, or to taste

In a medium-size mixing bowl, combine all the ingredients and gently stir together. Serve immediately or refrigerate for later use.

Note:
The longer this salsa sits, the hotter it will get due to the chile. For a spicier salsa, you can increase the amount of jalapeño from one to two or add one finely chopped serrano chile for a much spicier salsa.

MY FAVORITE GUACAMOLE

While this recipe is in the tomato chapter, guacamole is the perfectly paired complement to Lois's Pico de Gallo salsa; I serve them together. With its creamy texture, guacamole makes a lovely accompaniment to Perfect Baked Potato with All the Fixings (page 194), Potato & Bean Burrito (page 189), and the Bean & Spinach Tacos (page 85). This recipe is easy to make. The secret, however, is to plan your menu far enough in advance to have perfectly ripened tomatoes and avocados. Unripe avocados are hard and flavorless as are tomatoes, while overripe avocados do not taste fresh and can quickly become discolored, and overripe tomatoes are mushy. I find that store-bought unripe avocados and tomatoes usually take two to three days to ripen, so you must plan for them to be perfectly ripe on the day you want to use them. That's my secret to making my favorite guacamole.

MAKES APPROXIMATELY 4 CUPS

5 small Hass avocados or 2 large avocados, roughly chopped (approximately 2 cups)

1 small red onion, finely diced (approximately 1 cup)

4 ripe fresh Roma or other tomatoes, diced (approximately 2 cups)

2 fresh jalapeños, seeds and stems removed and minced (approximately 6 tablespoons) (see Note)

2 teaspoons blackened garlic (page 253)

2 tablespoons finely chopped fresh cilantro leaves (stems removed)

3 tablespoons freshly squeezed lime juice (approximately 2 small limes)

¾ teaspoon kosher salt, or to taste

Peel the avocados, remove the pits, and cut into approximately 1-inch pieces. Mash lightly in a medium-size bowl with a fork or potato masher. Add all the remaining ingredients to the bowl and stir to mix thoroughly, leaving some of the avocado chunky. Serve immediately or cover with plastic wrap and chill for later use.

Note:

The longer this guacamole sits, the hotter it will get due to the chile. For a spicier guacamole, you can increase the jalapeño from one or two to three or add one finely chopped serrano chile for a much spicier guacamole.

HEARTY TOMATO SOUP

I grew up eating tomato soup from a can like many of you may have. It was an easy-to-make meal and good on a cold wintry day. And until I was old enough to prepare tomato soup from fresh tomatoes, I really had no idea what a difference they make in this classic American soup and what I had been missing for so many years. Now I know, and for me, there is nothing like a good bowl of fresh tomato soup made from fresh tomatoes. This soup is savory, filling, nutritious, and delicious. It is perfect when topped with the croutons.

MAKES 2 QUARTS

2 tablespoons sunflower or olive oil
1 yellow onion, diced (approximately 2 cups)
1 tablespoon blackened garlic (page 253)
10 medium ripened tomatoes, diced
    (approximately 8 cups)
1 teaspoon dried thyme
1 teaspoon dried oregano
3 fresh basil leaves
1 tablespoon agave sweetener
2 cups water
2 teaspoons kosher salt, or to taste
¼ teaspoon freshly ground black pepper
¼ cup minced chives, for garnish

For the Croutons:

3 tablespoons sunflower or olive oil
2 cups diced baguette bread
    (about ⅔-inch square)
1 tablespoon blackened garlic (page 253)
½ teaspoon kosher salt

In a medium soup pot over medium to high heat, heat the sunflower oil until hot but not smoking. Add the onions and cook until the onions are translucent, approximately 4 minutes. Add the garlic and cook for 1 minute, stirring to prevent burning. Add the tomatoes, thyme, oregano, basil, agave, water, salt, and pepper. Bring to a simmer, cover, and let cook over low heat for 30 minutes. Remove from heat.

While the soup is cooking, make the croutons. Over medium heat, add the oil. Once you see ripples in the pan, add the diced bread. Stirring frequently, cook until croutons are golden on all sides, around 5 minutes. Reduce the heat to low. Add the garlic and salt and cook for 1 more minute, stirring to make sure all the croutons have flavor from the garlic and salt. Transfer croutons to a bowl and store at room temperature until ready to serve.

Once the soup has cooked, carefully blend it until completely smooth. Transfer it to a saucepan and heat until hot. Garnish with the croutons and minced chives.

Serve immediately.

FOUR DIRECTIONS

This dish features freshly baked zucchini topped with Heirloom Tomato Sauce that is garnished with toasted pumpkin seed powder and *chííłchin*, which is the berry from the wild edible three-leaf sumac bush (*Rhus trilobata*) that grows all over the Southwest. Chef Walter and I serve this dish as an appetizer for many of our dinners at Red Mesa Cuisine. The heart of what we do is to combine Indigenous cuisine with cultural education to give all our guests a unique and rich culinary experience as well as educate them. We honor the four sacred directions, thus the recipe's name "Four Directions" and their corresponding colors. We plate this dish with the four pieces of zucchini, topped with heirloom tomatoes, toasted pumpkin seed powder, and a little chííłchin that we grind into a powder. If you cannot get or harvest your own chííłchin, then you can substitute with sumac powder available from your grocers or you can omit it.

MAKES 4 SERVINGS

4 medium-size zucchini (7 to 8 inches long by 1½ to 2 inches wide)

1 teaspoon sunflower oil

½ teaspoon kosher salt

1 cup Heirloom Tomato Sauce, heated (page 171)

¼ cup pumpkin seeds, toasted and ground into a powder

Pinch of kosher salt, for garnish

½ teaspoon ground chííłchin (three-leaf sumac berries), or other ground sumac (optional)

¼ ounce of radish or other sprouts (approximately 1 tablespoon)

Preheat the oven to 425°F. Wash, dry, and cut zucchini. First cut the end and top off each zucchini. Then cut each zucchini in half crosswise, and then in half again, this time lengthwise. You should have four pieces for each serving.

Preheat a seasoned cast-iron frying pan over high heat until hot but not smoking. Place the cut zucchini cut side down, and blacken for 3 to 4 minutes. Turn over and cook with the skin side down for another 3 to 4 minutes. Remove from the pan and place on a sheet tray lightly greased with a little of the sunflower oil.

Season both sides of the seared zucchini with the kosher salt and place in the oven, with the flat (seared) side of the zucchini down, and roast for 15 minutes. Carefully turn over each piece of the zucchini and cook for another 10 minutes, or until they are completely cooked and soft when pierced with a small knife.

Place four pieces of zucchini onto a small plate, arranging them in each of the four directions. Top with 1 tablespoon of the heated Heirloom Tomato Sauce, spooned onto each piece of cooked zucchini. Sprinkle a little of the ground pumpkin seed powder on top of the tomato sauce and top the pumpkin seed with a small amount of the kosher salt. Finally, sprinkle a little of the ground sumac around the edge of the plate. Garnish with a small amount of the sprouts in the center.

Serve immediately.

HEIRLOOM TOMATO SAUCE

I started canning local heirloom tomato seconds, as a way to use the tomatoes that may be dented or too soft for a farmer to sell at full price. Tomato seconds are perfect for folks who make sauce or want to cook their tomatoes. Canning seems to be a lost art, but every year, for about four weeks, I can approximately three hundred to six hundred pounds of heirloom tomatoes in batches, and these are the tomatoes we use at Red Mesa Cuisine throughout the year. You don't have to can this sauce to enjoy its amazing flavor. Heirloom tomatoes are seasonal, and I encourage you to make this sauce when the tomatoes are available in your area (or try canning so that you, too, can have them to use all year round). If you don't want to can your tomato sauce, it freezes well, and this is a perfect way to have the sauce made for future use.

MAKES 1½ PINTS OR APPROXIMATELY 3 CUPS SAUCE

1 tablespoon sunflower oil

1 medium to large yellow onion, diced
(approximately 2 cups)

1 tablespoon blackened garlic (page 253)

10 cups heirloom tomatoes, cut into a large dice
about 1 inch in size (6 to 8 large tomatoes
or 10 to 12 medium-size tomatoes)

2 teaspoons kosher salt, or to taste

¼ teaspoon freshly ground black pepper

2 tablespoons agave sweetener
(optional, see Notes)

1 tablespoon fresh lemon juice
(about ½ lemon squeezed)
(optional, see Notes)

3 tablespoons chiffonade or very finely chopped
fresh basil

In a large saucepan, heat the sunflower oil until hot but not smoking. Sauté the onion over medium heat until it begins to brown, approximately 4 to 5 minutes. Add the garlic and sauté for another 1 to 2 minutes, stirring to prevent burning. Add the tomatoes, bring to a boil, reduce heat, and simmer for 60 minutes, uncovered. Stir occasionally to prevent burning, about every 10 minutes or so.

Then add the salt, pepper, agave (if using), lemon (if using), and basil, bring to a boil, then reduce the heat to the lowest setting, and simmer, for another 15 minutes uncovered.

Remove from the heat and use as per recipe, or you can use a hot-water-bath canning method and put the sauce into pint jars for future use. Can as per instructions in your favorite canning cookbook.

Notes:

If you cannot get local seasonal heirloom tomatoes, you can make this sauce with organic canned tomatoes.

If you want to can heirloom tomatoes, I recommend making two times this recipe for the sauce. Follow canning instructions for tomatoes. For me, two times this recipe yields 6 pints.

I only use the agave and the lemon when canning to bring up the acid level of the tomatoes to ensure that the jars seal properly. If just making the tomato sauce with perfectly ripened heirloom tomatoes, you don't need to add the agave or the lemon.

TOMATO & MUSHROOM MEDLEY

Two of my most favorite ingredients in the world are fresh tomatoes and mushrooms. I love not only the texture of mushrooms but also their flavor—and health benefits (they are loaded with vitamins, fiber, protein, and antioxidants).

In the higher elevations of New Mexico, mushrooms grow wild and have been harvested for millennia. The most common mushrooms harvested here include porcini, oyster, morels, and chanterelles. However, whenever harvesting wild mushrooms, be sure you know which mushrooms are edible, or go with an expert. Joining a mushroom society is a good way to learn about what mushrooms grow wild in your area.

You can use any mushrooms you like in this recipe; the most readily available include white button mushrooms, cremini brown mushrooms, portobello mushrooms, shiitake mushrooms, and oyster mushrooms. Whichever you choose will add a meaty texture and earthy, delicate flavor. Serve with fresh pasta, cooked quinoa, polenta, or over oven-roasted potatoes as an entrée, or serve as a side. I enjoy this dish alone, as its own course, because it is so flavorsome, and because I love mushrooms so much.

MAKES 4 TO 6 SERVINGS

1 tablespoon sunflower or olive oil

1 medium yellow onion, diced (approximately 2 cups)

1 tablespoon blackened garlic (page 253)

12 ounces oyster mushrooms, cut into large pieces (14 to 16 mushrooms depending on size or 3 cups)

12 ounces cremini brown mushrooms, cut into quarters or in half depending on their size (16 to 18 mushrooms depending on size or 3 cups)

10.5 ounces shiitake mushrooms, cut into large slices or in half depending on size (12 to 14 mushrooms depending on size or 3 cups)

2 teaspoons kosher salt, or to taste

1 pint Heirloom Tomato Sauce (page 171)

1 tablespoon chiffonade or thinly sliced fresh basil (optional)

In a large cast-iron pan or heavy-bottomed saucepan over medium to high heat, heat the oil until hot but not smoking. Add the onion and sauté until it begins to brown, about 4 to 5 minutes, stirring to prevent burning. Add the garlic and sauté for another 1 to 2 minutes, stirring to prevent burning. Reduce the heat to medium and add all the mushrooms and salt. Cook for 25 to 30 minutes, stirring occasionally to prevent burning. Cook until the mushrooms caramelize and turn brown.

Deglaze the cooked mushrooms by adding the tomato sauce and stirring into the mushrooms to make sure you get all the good flavor from the bottom of the pan. Add the basil, if using, and stir to completely mix it in.

Serve immediately as a side or as an entrée.

Note:
Mushrooms have different amounts of water. If you are using only cremini and shiitake, the cooking time will be less than if you use oyster mushrooms as oyster mushrooms have more water.

SUMMER VEGETABLE CASSEROLE

This is my Southwest version of a dish my grandma Elizabeth (Liz) Frank (my father's mother) used to make. While not one of the magic eight ingredients, eggplant is used by many cultures and was found a lot in the Sephardic Jewish cooking that my grandmother used to prepare. She would bake eggplant and sautéed tomatoes into a delicious casserole. Using eggplant, tomato, and zucchini in my version of this dish melds Ancestral Native ingredients with an ingredient my Jewish grandmother used often, fused into one. I purchase these ingredients from the Santa Fe Farmers' Market to make a delicious casserole that I hope you will enjoy as much as I do.

MAKES 4 SERVINGS

2 teaspoons sunflower oil

1 small yellow onion, diced (approximately 1 cup)

1 tablespoon blackened garlic (page 253)

2 cups Heirloom Tomato Sauce (page 171), divided

2 medium zucchini (about 8 inches long by 1½ inches wide), cut on a bias, approximately ¼ inch thick

2 medium yellow summer squashes (about 8 inches long by 1½ inches wide), cut on a bias, approximately ¼ inch thick

2 medium Japanese eggplant (about 9 inches long by 1½ inches wide), cut on a bias, approximately ¼ inch thick

1 teaspoon kosher salt, or to taste, divided

Preheat the oven to 400°F.

In a sauté pan over medium to high heat, heat the sunflower oil until hot but not smoking. Add the onion and sauté for 4 minutes, stirring to prevent burning. Add the garlic and cook for an additional 2 minutes, stirring constantly to prevent burning. Remove from the heat and set aside.

In an oval baking dish approximately 6 x 10 inches in size, place 1 cup of the Heirloom Tomato Sauce on the bottom and spread evenly. Layer the zucchini, yellow summer squash, and eggplant by placing them on top of the sauce, alternating until you have one layer of the mixed vegetables complete. Sprinkle half of the sautéed onion and garlic on top of the vegetables and then sprinkle ½ teaspoon of salt evenly over this layer.

Add ½ cup of tomato sauce on top of the first layer of vegetables, followed by the second layer of vegetables, again alternating. Add the remaining sautéed onion and garlic mixture and sprinkle the remaining ½ teaspoon of salt. Top with the remaining ½ cup of tomato sauce, spreading it evenly over the casserole.

Bake for 60 minutes or until the vegetables are tender when pierced with a knife. Serve immediately on its own for a main course, or alongside your favorite side dish.

CHERRY TOMATO TARTE

This is a modern version of a dish using Ancestral ingredients. It features small flavorful cherry tomatoes that are in abundance here in the summer months. I grow tomatoes and this is a great dish to use them in, but our local farmers' market is always bursting with fresh tomatoes throughout the growing season that are sweet and delicious. It's an exceptional dish, and my favorite way to make it is in a cast-iron frying pan that I can put directly into the oven and then serve it as soon as is ready.

MAKES APPROXIMATELY 4 TO 6 SERVINGS

For the Crust:

2 cups all-purpose flour

1 cup finely ground blue cornmeal

2 teaspoons kosher salt

½ cup sunflower oil

½ cup ice water

For the Tart:

4 teaspoons sunflower oil, divided

1 medium to large yellow onion, thinly sliced
    (approximately 2 cups)

1 tablespoon blackened garlic (page 253)

4 cups cherry tomatoes (different colors),
    cut in half

2 New Mexico or Anaheim green chiles,
    roasted, peeled, stemmed, seeds removed,
    and diced (page 250)

1 teaspoon kosher salt, divided

¼ teaspoon freshly ground black pepper,
    divided

To make the crust, combine the flour, blue cornmeal, and salt in a medium bowl. Add the sunflower oil and the ice water, a little bit at a time, until a dough forms, kneading on a lightly floured work surface with your hands until you have a moist dough that it is soft and pliable. If the dough feels dry, add a little more water, 1 teaspoon at a time.

Using a rolling pin, roll the dough out on a flat, lightly floured surface into a circle approximately 13 inches across. Transfer the circle of dough to line a large cast-iron skillet, which is approximately 11 inches in diameter, completely covering the bottom of the pan and up the sides.

Preheat the oven to 350°F. For the tart part of this recipe, in a sauté pan, heat 2 teaspoons of the oil until hot but not smoking. Sauté the onions over medium heat and slowly cook until they begin to brown, approximately 10 minutes, stirring occasionally. Add the garlic and sauté for another 3 minutes, stirring to prevent burning. Remove from the heat, transfer the onion mixture to a small bowl, and set aside.

In the same pan, heat the remaining 2 teaspoons of sunflower oil over high heat until almost smoking. Add the cherry tomatoes and stir. Add ½ teaspoon of salt and ⅛ teaspoon of black pepper and cook for 3 minutes, tossing gently to prevent the tomatoes from breaking all the way down. Turn off heat.

Fill the dough, first with the sautéed onions, spreading them evenly over the bottom. Then spread the diced chile evenly over the onions. Finally top with the tomatoes.

Fold the edges of the dough around the circle, making a fold every 2 inches. Sprinkle the top of the tart with the remaining ½ teaspoon of salt and ⅛ teaspoon of pepper. Bake for 1 hour. Remove from the oven, allow to rest for 10 minutes, then cut and serve immediately.

Potatoes

Potatoes are considered to be a buried treasure of sorts, in terms of a food and a food source. Potatoes are a starchy tuber of the plant *Solanum tuberosum* and a prized root vegetable. Along with its nightshade cousins chile and tomato, it originated in the Americas and was introduced in the second half of the sixteenth century to Europe and other parts of the world by the Spanish, where it has spread to become one of the world's most important crops.

The potato's origin begins in the high mountainous slopes of the Andes region in Peru and northwestern Bolivia where they were first cultivated, dating back from approximately seven thousand to ten thousand years ago, similar to that of corn. There were thousands of varieties of potatoes upon first contact ranging in all kinds of shapes, and ranging from the size of a pecan to larger than a small pumpkin. By the time the Inca arrived on the scene in approximately the 1400s, potatoes were being cultivated by Native farmers who raised other crops as well, in terraces that were carved out of the mountainous slopes.

According to Sylvia A. Johnson in her book *Tomatoes, Potatoes, Corn, and Beans*, by the time Hernán Cortés reached Mexico in 1519 and toured the outdoor market in Tenochitlán, the Aztec capital, he along with others witnessed corn, chiles, cacao, tomatoes, and beans. And he was already eating corn tortillas seasoned with chiles and drinking the Aztec cacao drink, *cacaoatl*, with foods that were initially found growing on the island of Hispaniola. What was missing from the market in Tenochitlán was the potato. At this

time in history, it could only be found in South America, growing in the Andes Mountains.

By the time the Spanish arrived in South America in 1532, they witnessed Inca miners eating *chuñu*, a kind of potato flour[25] traditionally made by the Quechua and Aymara communities. As the potato spread throughout the world, more and more cultures began to incorporate this new tuber into their diets and their cuisines. Sir Walter Raleigh introduced the potato to Ireland in the 1600s after the suppression of the Desmond Rebellions, where he planted the potato on the forty thousand acres he received from the seizure of land following the rebellion. The potato at this time had already been introduced to Spain, England, Ireland, Italy, and Germany. By the 1620s, potatoes were introduced to the colony of Virginia, by the governor of the Bahamas, who sent a gift box containing potatoes to the governor of Virginia.

Today, some of the most popular varieties include russet, red potatoes, white potatoes, yellow potatoes, purple potatoes (including the Peruvian blue and Russian blue), Yukon Gold potatoes, fingerlings, and petite potatoes. But even these potatoes are missing the vast varieties and hundreds of kinds that were originally found in the Andes, grown by the Incas, who domesticated and grew more root crops than any other culture in the world, and only recently have they begun to receive agronomic recognition.[26]

The sweet potato is only distantly related to the potato, but both varieties are native to the Americas. To make things a bit complicated, yams and sweet potatoes are not the same.

Yams are tubers related to both lilies and grasses. The majority of yams are grown in Africa and Asia; they are starchier and a drier root vegetable than sweet potatoes. However, what you typically find today in the grocery store, even if the label says "yam" is actually a sweet potato, native to the Americas.

Both the potato and the sweet potato are not only delicious but nutritional powerhouses more energy-packed than any other popular vegetable. For instance, the potato contains approximately 30 percent of the daily value of vitamin C. Potatoes are a nutrient-dense complex carbohydrate, making them a perfect food to eat with their skins on to provide healthy proteins, fiber, and potassium. The sweet potato is a great source of vitamin A, vitamin B6, and vitamin C.

Both types of potatoes contain beneficial plant compounds, and sweet potatoes are rich in antioxidants that help to fight cell damage in the body caused by free radicals. According to many medical sources, sweet potatoes contain health benefits that improve digestion, treat inflammation, boost the immune system, relieve asthma, treat bronchitis, reduce arthritis pain, aid in curing stomach ulcers, prevent dehydration by controlling water balance in the body, help to prevent cancer, and help to control diabetes. Wow. These nutrient-packed root vegetables are a delicious and healthy part of any diet. In the pages that follow, you'll find lots of ways to use these root vegetables as buried treasures to create amazing, delightful, and savory dishes.

HERB ROASTED POTATOES

This recipe makes the best roasted potatoes I've ever had. The garlic, rosemary, and thyme make them full of flavor—and a wonderful complement to any dish. I buy my potatoes at the Santa Fe Farmers' Market from José Gonzales of Gonzalez Farm or from Matt Romero of Romero Farms. See if your local farmers' market sells potatoes, or purchase small potatoes from your local grocers. I use potatoes that are approximately 1½ inches by 2 inches in size, cut in half, or quartered if they are larger potatoes.

You can also use fingerling potatoes, Dutch potatoes, small red fingerlings, Peruvian blue potatoes, or any other heirloom variety.

MAKES 4 TO 6 SERVINGS

2 tablespoons sunflower oil

1 tablespoon blackened garlic (page 253)

1 teaspoon kosher or sea salt

¼ teaspoon freshly ground black pepper

1 teaspoon finely chopped fresh thyme

2 teaspoons finely chopped fresh rosemary

2 cups small red potatoes, halved or quartered, depending on their size

2 cups small white potatoes, halved or quartered, depending on their size

2 cups small blue potatoes, halved or quartered, depending on their size

¼ cup finely chopped chives, for garnish (optional)

Preheat the oven to 425°F. In a large mixing bowl, combine the sunflower oil, garlic, salt, pepper, thyme, and rosemary. Add the potatoes and toss until completely coated with the herb mixture.

Transfer to a sheet tray and roast in the oven for approximately 15 minutes. Remove from the oven, turn the potatoes over, and return to the oven for an additional 15 minutes or until the potatoes are completely tender when pierced with a small knife.

The roasted potatoes should be a golden brown with a little crispness on the outside. If you like your potatoes very crisp, cook for an additional 5 minutes or so, until they are nice and crispy and your desired doneness.

Garnish with the chopped chives, if using, and serve immediately.

SWEET POTATO MASH

This all-around comfort food is a wonderful dish in the winter months. It is tasty on its own, though I also love to serve it with roasted whole portobello mushrooms as a main course or with the Black Beans with Chocolate & Chipotle (page 76) or the Red Chile Pinto Beans (page 77). These sweet potatoes can be mashed using the paddle of a stand mixer, by hand using a potato masher (Chef Walter's and my favorite way to do this at Red Mesa Cuisine), or for a finer and smoother mash, try a food mill or potato ricer. Canned chipotle en adobo can be purchased at most grocery stores. (Once you open the can, you'll need to decant the chiles and put them in a glass jar or container as they are acidic and will oxidize in the can.) If you have a spicier palate, feel free to add more chipotle en adobo to match your own palate.

MAKES 4 TO 6 SERVINGS

2 pounds sweet potatoes (2 to 3 potatoes), washed thoroughly

2 tablespoons diced chipotle en adobo, or to taste

Zest of 1 lime

1 tablespoon freshly squeezed lime juice (approximately ½ lime)

½ teaspoon kosher salt, or to taste

½ cup fresh cilantro leaves, minced

Preheat the oven to 400°F. Line a sheet tray with parchment paper and poke holes all over the potatoes with a fork. Roast the potatoes until they are completely tender when pierced with a knife, anywhere from 50 to 60 minutes, depending on their size. Once they are cool enough to handle, remove their peels and transfer the potatoes to the bowl of a stand mixer with the paddle attachment. Add the chipotle en adobo, lime zest, lime juice, and salt. Beat for around a minute, until the potatoes are mashed. Garnish with fresh cilantro.

Note:
I recommend using an organic lime for the lime zest as then you can be sure that the lime skin is pesticide-free.

ROASTED SWEET POTATO TWO WAYS

Sweet potatoes are a great source of vitamins, minerals, and fiber. They are an Ancestral Native food that is an important part of a healthy diet. This recipe features two different ways to make the roasted sweet potatoes: one with a mustard dressing that has a little spiciness from the mustard and the other, Chef Walter's favorite, and the other with a maple, red chile, and lime dressing that is sweet and a little sour in its flavor, which is my favorite and pictured here. These are wonderful served with Native American Wild Rice & Sweet Corn Sauté (Manoomin) (page 52) as a main course, or you can double the recipe and make it both ways.

MAKES 4 SERVINGS

For the Sweet Potatoes:
2 medium to large sweet potatoes,
    washed and cut in half lengthwise
2 cups water, divided

For the Mustard Version:
2 tablespoons smooth Dijon mustard
2 tablespoons whole-grain Dijon mustard
2 tablespoons pure maple syrup
1 teaspoon New Mexico red chile powder, mild
1 tablespoon freshly squeezed lime juice
    (approximately ½ lime)
1 tablespoon water
¼ teaspoon kosher salt, or to taste

For the Maple-Chile-Lime Version:
⅔ cup pure maple syrup
2 teaspoons New Mexico red chile powder, mild
2 tablespoons freshly squeezed lime juice
    (approximately 1 lime)

Preheat the oven to 400°F. Place the halved sweet potatoes, cut side down, on a sheet pan or baking dish and add 1 cup of the water. Cook for 20 minutes. Remove from the oven and add the remaining 1 cup of water to the pan. Return the potatoes to the oven for another 20 minutes (depending on their size) or until they are fully cooked through and soft when pierced with a small knife.

While the potatoes are cooking, in a small bowl, whisk together the dressing ingredients for the version you are making.

Remove the potatoes from the oven and turn them over so that the cut side is facing up. Using a sharp small knife, score the flesh of each sweet potato at a diagonal 4 to 5 times. Score them all the way down to the skin, but do not pierce the skin on the bottom of the sweet potato. Then score again 4 to 5 times in the other direction to make a crisscross design on each potato. Take approximately 1½ tablespoons of the dressing mixture if you are using the mustard version and a little more if you are using the maple-chile-lime version and drizzle completely over each sweet potato half. Allow the mixture to soak into the sweet potato. Return the pan to the oven and bake for another 5 minutes.

Remove the pan from the oven and place a sweet potato onto each plate. Sprinkle a pinch of the kosher salt on top and then drizzle a little of the remaining dressing mixture around the outside of each roasted sweet potato on each of the plates. Serve immediately or top with the Native American Wild Rice & Sweet Corn Sauté (Manoomin) (page 52) as a main course.

POTATO & GREEN CHILE TACOS

Tacos are my go-to meal when I don't want to spend a lot of time cooking because they are easy to make and full of flavor. Homemade tortillas taste best, but this recipe works wonderfully with store-bought tortillas as well. One taco is never enough, so this recipe makes eight tacos, allowing each person to have two. Chef Walter makes this using the matchstick-cut potatoes, and I love them cut this way as opposed to just diced. I recommend eating these tacos with My Favorite Guacamole (page 165), and they can be served with Tri-Colored Slaw (page 136) or Spaghetti Squash Slaw (page 95)—or just eaten on their own.

MAKES 4 SERVINGS, 2 TACOS PER SERVING

For the Taco Filling:

3 teaspoons sunflower oil, divided

1 small to medium yellow onion, thinly sliced
   (approximately 1 cup)

4 ounces cremini mushrooms, sliced
   (approximately 1 cup)

4 ounces white mushrooms, sliced
   (approximately 1 cup)

2 medium to large purple potatoes, cut into
   matchsticks (approximately 4 cups), soaked
   in water for 5 minutes, and then strained

½ teaspoon kosher salt, or to taste

1 tablespoon warm water

For the Tacos:

8 White Corn Tortillas (page 27),
   or use store-bought

4 New Mexico or Anaheim green chiles, roasted,
   peeled, and diced (page 250) (approximately
   1 cup)

2 to 3 Roma tomatoes, diced (approximately 1 cup)

2 limes, cut into wedges, for garnish

1 recipe My Favorite Guacamole (page 165)

In a large cast-iron skillet over medium to high heat, heat 2 teaspoons of the sunflower oil until it is hot but not smoking. Add the onions and cook until they are lightly caramelized, for 4 to 5 minutes, stirring to prevent burning. Remove the onions from the pan and transfer to a bowl to reserve. Add the mushrooms to the same hot skillet. Cook until they start to caramelize, around 10 minutes, stirring to prevent burning, then remove them from the pan and transfer them to the bowl with the onions. Add the remaining teaspoon of sunflower oil to the hot pan and add the potatoes with the salt. Sauté for approximately 8 minutes. Add the warm water, stir to prevent sticking, reduce the heat to medium, and cover. Cook for an additional 10 minutes, stirring once or twice, until the potatoes are both cooked all the way through and slightly golden brown. Add the onions and mushrooms back to the skillet with the potatoes. Turn off the heat and cover until ready to serve.

Heat the tortillas over an open flame, on a very hot, seasoned cast-iron skillet, or on a Cast Iron Cooking Grill (see source guide). Cook each tortilla for approximately 30 seconds, then turn it over and cook for another 30 seconds on the other side. Place in a basket lined with a clean kitchen towel to keep them warm.

To serve, fill tortillas with the potato mixture. Top with the chiles and tomatoes.

Serve immediately with the lime wedges and guacamole on the side.

POTATO & BEAN BURRITO

This makes a great burrito at any time of the day and is perfect for lunch or dinner. I happen to like breakfast burritos, so I make this dish on a weekend for brunch. The key is to have the Green Chile Sauce and pinto beans made in advance so you just must make the savory pinto bean recipe, the herbed rice, and the potatoes to compile the burritos. They are worth the effort, and I've even frozen them for quick, easy meals that I can enjoy during the week. It's also a flexible recipe: try just herbed rice and savory refried beans topped with the Green Chile Sauce, or potatoes and savory refried beans topped with the Green Chile Sauce, or potatoes, herbed rice, and savory refried beans topped with the Green Chile Sauce. Not a green chile sauce person? Make the Red Chile Sauce (page 129) instead or in addition to the Green Chile Sauce and serve the burrito with both sauces.

MAKES 4 SERVINGS

1 batch Green Chile Sauce (page 131)

For the Potatoes:
3 large Yukon gold potatoes, washed, dried, and diced into ½-inch pieces (2 pounds of potatoes will yield approximately 5 cups diced)
1 tablespoon sunflower oil
2 teaspoons ground coriander
2 teaspoons New Mexico red chile powder, mild
1 teaspoon kosher salt, or to taste
¼ teaspoon freshly ground black pepper, or to taste

For the Burritos:
1 batch of Green Chile Herbed Rice (page 140)
1 batch Red Mesa's Refried Pinto Beans (page 74)
4 large flour tortillas or 8 smaller-size flour tortillas
4 green onions or scallions, sliced on a bias, for garnish

Make the Green Chile Sauce and set aside.

Preheat the oven to 400°F. Line a large sheet tray with parchment paper. In a large bowl, toss together the potatoes, sunflower oil, coriander, chile powder, salt, and pepper. Place on a sheet tray and roast for 30 minutes or until the potatoes are tender inside and crispy on the outside.

While the potatoes are cooking, make the herbed rice and the savory refried pinto beans. Warm the Green Chile Sauce over low heat, until ready to serve.

Warm the tortillas on a dry skillet over medium heat for a minute on each side, or on an open flame for approximately 15 seconds on each side, and place in a basket lined with a kitchen towel to keep them warm.

Fill each tortilla with a spoonful of crispy potatoes, a spoonful of rice, and a spoonful of the savory refried beans. Use a little less of each filling if using smaller flour tortillas. Fold in both sides and roll snugly.

Spoon warm Green Chile Sauce over the top and garnish with the green onions.

Serve immediately.

SWEET POTATO & CARROT SOUP

This vibrantly colored, slightly sweet and creamy soup reminds Chef Walter of the wild carrots he used to harvest when he was a small child. Chef Walter and Chef Marianne Sundquist love the robust flavor of ginger, so they add a full tablespoon instead of the 2 teaspoons that I prefer. If you like ginger, use more of it, or if you prefer a milder flavor profile, add just the 2 teaspoons I have listed below. For the garnish, I use wild edible desert onion flowers when they are in season, as they grow all over and in my garden. They add a little burst of onion flavor and are quite nice as a garnish. However, if you don't grow onions or have access to the flowers, you can omit this ingredient. As with most soups, it makes quite a bit, so you can have it as a ready-to-eat meal the following day—or freeze it for later.

MAKES 3½ QUARTS

2 teaspoons sunflower oil
1 medium to large yellow onion, diced
    (approximately 2 cups)
2 teaspoons finely chopped garlic
8 large carrots, peeled and sliced
    (approximately 2 pounds)
2 large sweet potatoes, peeled and diced
    (approximately 2 pounds)
2 teaspoons finely grated fresh ginger,
    or to taste
¼ cup golden raisins
1 teaspoon kosher salt, or to taste
⅛ teaspoon freshly ground black pepper,
    or to taste
9 cups water or vegetable broth (page 264)
1 tablespoon chopped fresh chives, for garnish
2 teaspoons finely chopped fresh dill, for garnish
Edible onion flowers (optional), for garnish

In a large soup pot, heat the sunflower oil over medium heat until hot but not smoking. Add the onion and cook for approximately 4 to 5 minutes until translucent. Add the garlic and cook for an additional minute. Add the carrots, potatoes, ginger, raisins, salt, and pepper, stirring occasionally, for approximately 10 minutes, until the carrots begin to tenderize.

Stir in the water, scraping any stuck bits from the bottom of the pot. Bring the soup to a boil, then reduce heat, letting the soup simmer until the potatoes and carrots are tender, for approximately 30 minutes.

Working in batches, carefully blend the soup until completely smooth. Return to a large soup pot, taste, and add more salt and pepper as needed.

Serve hot, garnished with the chives, dill, or the wild onion flowers, if using.

POTATO & GREEN CHILE STEW

Potatoes and green chiles are New Mexico staples. In the later summer months and early fall, the Santa Fe Farmers' Market is bursting with locally grown potatoes and green chiles. This recipe is a plant-based version of a traditional Native green chile stew made with meat.

We made this recently at one of our hands-on health and wellness trainings for the New Mexico Department of Health's Obesity, Nutrition, and Physical Activity Program (ONAPA) and the Aging and Long-Term Service Department (ALTSD). The cooks used a medium spicy chile for this stew, which made it quite spicy, but everyone who ate it loved it. If your palate is spicy, use a spicier green chile. This stew is delicious, hearty, and perfect for a filling meal. Because it freezes so well, I sometimes double the recipe so I can freeze some for later use. I like to serve it with No Fry Frybread (page 266), Blue Corn No Fry Frybread (page 268) or White Corn Tortillas (page 27) for a complete meal.

MAKES APPROXIMATELY 2½ QUARTS

1 tablespoon sunflower oil

1 medium to large yellow onion, diced (approximately 2 cups)

1 tablespoon blackened garlic (page 253)

1 can (14.5 ounces) chopped tomatoes, no salt added if possible, or 2 cups Heirloom Tomato Sauce (page 171)

8 New Mexico or Anaheim green chiles, mild, roasted, peeled, seeded, and chopped (approximately 2 cups) (page 250)

6 cups water, plus ½ cup for blending

1½ pounds small Dutch or yellow potatoes, washed and diced with skins on (about 20 small potatoes approximately 1½ inches wide by 2 inches long)

1 cup corn kernels, fresh or frozen

1 teaspoon kosher salt, or to taste

4 scallions, sliced on a bias, for garnish

3 tablespoons chopped fresh cilantro, for garnish

1 lime, cut into wedges, for garnish

In a large soup pot or heavy-bottomed saucepan over medium to high heat, heat the sunflower oil until hot but not smoking. Sauté the onion until it begins to brown, for approximately 4 to 5 minutes, stirring to prevent burning. Add the garlic and sauté for another minute. Add the tomatoes and sauté for another 4 minutes. Add the chiles and sauté for another 3 minutes. Add the 6 cups of water and the potatoes and bring to a boil.

Reduce the heat and simmer for approximately 10 minutes, uncovered, stirring to prevent burning. Add the corn kernels, bring back to a boil, then reduce heat and cover. Simmer, covered, for 25 minutes, until the potatoes are soft. Stir every 5 minutes or so to prevent the stew from burning. Add the salt and stir to completely mix. Remove from heat.

In a blender, add 3 cups of the stew with the additional ½ cup of water and blend on high for several minutes until completely smooth. Return the blended mixture to the soup pot or saucepan with the unblended ingredients.

Taste and adjust the seasoning as needed. Serve immediately garnished with the scallions, cilantro, and a wedge of lime.

PERFECT BAKED POTATO WITH ALL THE FIXINGS

A perfect baked potato with all the fixings is one of my favorite meals. You can bake any kind of potato for this recipe; I have used russet potatoes, red potatoes, and white sweet potatoes, with Yukon gold potatoes being my favorite because they are rich and creamy without being dry after baking. Have some fun and be creative with the toppings. There is no right or wrong way to do this. I topped my baked potato with heated, plain canned black beans, sliced green onions, Lois's Pico de Gallo salsa (page 164), and My Favorite Guacamole (page 165) for one meal, and with Black Beans with Chocolate & Chipotlé (page 76), sliced green onions, Green Chile Sauce (page 131), and Red Chile Sauce (page 129) for another. Get creative with your own toppings!

MAKES 4 SERVINGS

4 medium Yukon gold or other potato, washed well

2 teaspoons sunflower oil

½ teaspoon kosher salt, or to taste

¼ teaspoon freshly ground black pepper, or to taste

Suggested Toppings:

1 cup cooked black beans (canned is fine)

½ cup sliced green onions (3 to 4)

Lois's Pico de Gallo (page 164)

My Favorite Guacamole (page 165)

Black Beans with Chocolate & Chipotle (page 76)

Red Chile Sauce (page 129)

Green Chile Sauce (page 131)

Ginger Lime Cream (page 103)

Preheat the oven to 450°F. Line a sheet tray with parchment paper. Poke the potatoes all over with the tip of a sharp paring knife, being careful to not poke your fingers.

Place the potatoes in a bowl and rub them all over with the sunflower oil, salt, and pepper. Transfer them to the prepared sheet tray and bake for approximately 45 minutes to 1 hour, depending on their size. Test to see if the potatoes are done by piercing them with a small knife. If the knife goes in easily, the potato is done.

Remove from the oven, slice in half, and serve two halves on a plate with all your favorite toppings. Makes a wonderful meal on its own or serve with Walter's Fresh Corn Salad (page 51), Spaghetti Squash Slaw (page 95), Tri-Color Coleslaw (page 136), Tomato Quinoa Salad (page 161), or Cherry Tomato & Arugula Salad (page 163) for a fulfilling meal.

Note:

Yukon gold potatoes tend to be a little smaller than russet potatoes or sweet potatoes. I recommend that you check them after 45 minutes to see if they are done as you don't want to overcook the potatoes.

SWEET POTATO, KALE & WILD RICE BOWL

The nice thing about this bowl is that you can easily prepare the components in advance, so you have meals throughout the week for multiple lunches or dinners. You can eat it hot or cold. I like to keep the wild rice, sweet potato, and kale mixtures in separate containers, bringing them together when I am ready to assemble a complete bowl. Additionally, you can add all kinds of other toppings. I recommend sliced green onions, freshly sliced avocado, any kind of sprouts or microgreens (sunflower, radish, broccoli, cabbage, amaranth, or alfalfa), sliced fresh jalapeños, Red Chile Sauce (page 129) or Green Chile Sauce (page 131), toasted piñon nuts, or toasted pecans.

MAKES 4 TO 6 SERVINGS

For the Sweet Potatoes:
2 large sweet potatoes, washed and cut into
 ½-inch square pieces (approximately 6 cups)
2 tablespoons sunflower oil
1 tablespoon coriander seed, toasted and crushed
 (I use a mortar and pestle for crushing
 the coriander, but you can also use a spice
 grinder)
2 teaspoons New Mexico red chile powder, mild
1 teaspoon kosher salt, or to taste
¼ teaspoon freshly ground black pepper,
 or to taste

For the Wild Rice:
1 cup hand-harvested wild, uncooked rice,
 rinsed thoroughly (see source guide)
3 cups water or vegetable broth (page 264)
1 teaspoon kosher salt

For the Kale:
1 tablespoon sunflower oil
1 medium yellow onion, diced
 (approximately 1½ cups)
1 tablespoon blackened garlic (page 253)
1 bunch of lacinato kale, washed, leaves removed
 from stems, and sliced or torn into pieces
 (approximately 3 cups)

Zest of 1 organic lime
2 tablespoons lime juice, or to taste
 (approximately 1 lime)
½ teaspoon kosher salt, or to taste
¼ teaspoon freshly ground black pepper,
 or to taste
1 lime, cut into wedges for garnish

First prepare the sweet potatoes. Preheat the oven to 375°F and line a large sheet tray with parchment paper. Combine the sweet potatoes, sunflower oil, coriander, chile powder, salt, and pepper in a large bowl until the potatoes are evenly coated. Transfer them to the sheet tray and bake until the potatoes are tender and crispy, approximately 1 hour. Test one piece of the sweet potatoes to make sure they are done and then remove from the oven and reserve.

While the potatoes are in the oven, cook the wild rice. Place the rice, water, and salt in a medium saucepan and bring to a boil. Reduce the heat to low, cover with a lid, and cook for approximately 40 minutes or as per the instructions on the package, until the rice has absorbed all the water and is tender. Turn the heat off, keep covered, let the rice rest for

5 minutes, and then fluff with a fork. Drain off any excess water if there is any.

Right before serving, cook the kale. In a large sauté pan over medium heat, add the sunflower oil and heat until hot but not smoking. After approximately 1 minute, add the onion and cook for 4 to 5 minutes until the onions become translucent and tender, stirring occasionally until they start to caramelize. Add the garlic and cook for 1 minute. Then add the kale, lime zest, lime juice, salt, and pepper. Stir and combine all the ingredients. Reduce the heat to low, and continue to cook until the kale wilts, for 3 to 4 minutes.

To serve, place the cooked wild rice in the bottom of the bowl. Top with about a quarter of the kale mixture if you are serving four or a little less if you are serving six (the kale mixture will yield approximately 2 cups, so I put on about ½ cup of the mixture for four servings). Then top with approximately a quarter of the crispy seasoned sweet potatoes.

Serve immediately with a slice of the fresh lime.

POTATO & BLUE CORN GNOCCHI

Gnocchi is the Italian word for a dumpling that is often made with potato. This recipe is basically a blue corn version of a Native American Navajo dumpling. Walter's grandmother, Susie Whitewater Begay, used to make a dumpling similar to this one, which she called Inishpeezhi (spelled phonetically as I couldn't find a Navajo spelling for this word), and hers was the first Native dumpling similar to a gnocchi I tried many years ago. Native communities all over the Southwest make versions of cornmeal dumplings in a variety of ways.

This is my version of a traditional dumpling that is both Native American and Italian. It can be added to any soup or stew; however, I like to serve it on its own with Guajillo Chile Sauce (page 132), Red Chile Sauce (page 129), or even Green Chile Sauce (page 131). My favorite way to eat these dumplings is with Heirloom Tomato Sauce (page 171).

1½ pounds Yukon gold potatoes, washed
   thoroughly (around 3 large potatoes)
   (approximately 1 pound once mashed
   equals 3 cups)
½ cup finely ground blue corn flour,
   plus a little more for dusting
½ cup all-purpose flour
1 teaspoon kosher salt
2 tablespoons finely chopped chives,
   or green onions, for garnish

Bring a large pot of water to a boil. Peel potatoes, quarter them, and boil until they are tender when pierced with a knife, approximately 20 minutes. Strain them and pass through a food mill or mash by hand. You want a total of 1 pound of mashed potatoes, which is 3 cups.

To the mashed potatoes, add the blue corn flour, all-purpose flour, and salt. Knead this mixture with your hands until a smooth ball of dough has formed. If for any reason the dough seems too dry and the potatoes have not absorbed all the dry ingredients, add a small splash of water to make it come together. Cover the dough with a clean kitchen towel and allow to rest for 30 minutes.

Prepare a large sheet tray lined with parchment paper and sprinkle lightly with blue corn flour. Cut off a quarter of the gnocchi ball to work with first. Gently roll it out into a log or rope shape with your hands on a lightly floured work surface, until it is about ½ inch in diameter. Cut 1-inch pieces and transfer them to the floured sheet tray. Repeat three more times with the

remaining dough until all gnocchi dumplings are formed.

At this point, you can boil them in a large pot of salted water for approximately 2 minutes if using them fresh or approximately 4 minutes if using them frozen. They will rise to the surface of the water when done. Once you have boiled them, you will need to serve them immediately. Remove the gnocchi dumplings from the boiling water and serve on a plate or in a bowl with your favorite sauce. Garnish with some chopped chives or green onions.

I recommend serving them fresh, as they hold together better; however, if you want to serve them later, place the sheet tray lined with parchment paper with the prepared gnocchi dumplings in the freezer until the gnocchi freezes completely, for at least an hour, and then transfer them to a freezer bag or airtight container to keep frozen with the date on them. These will last in the freezer for 2 to 3 weeks.

Notes:

I love to use everything when I cook, so I save the potato skins after peeling the potatoes to make a crispy treat. Drizzle the skins with a little sunflower oil, sprinkle with kosher salt, and roast in a 350°F oven for 20 minutes. These make a wonderful potato chip–like snack.

To learn more about Italian Gnocchi see Gnocchi Solo Gnocchi, *self-published by Christine Y. Hickman (2018) whom we consulted with for this recipe.*

SWEET POTATO TAMALE MASA

This sweet potato masa was created from my work with diabetes educators, community health workers, and community health representatives, and doctors practicing in Native communities who asked me to create a tamale masa that didn't use any vegetable shortening or other plant-based fat to bind the corn masa together. By using sweet potatoes, we created a no-fat tamale masa that is both nutritious and flavorful.

I tested this recipe with both the Japanese sweet potato (where the creamy white flesh turns yellow after cooking) and a Jewel sweet potato (where the flesh is orange), and it worked well with both, but I found that the Jewel sweet potato was a little easier to get and less expensive. Sweet potatoes also come in other colors, but I did not test those for this recipe. Use this with Sweet Potato & Black Bean Tamale (page 201), the Dried Fruit & Vanilla Dessert Tamales (page 218), or get creative and make your own new filling to go with this masa. The possibilities are endless.

MAKES ABOUT 4 CUPS OF MASA, WHICH WILL YIELD APPROXIMATELY 28 TAMALES

1 large sweet potato (approximately 7½ inches long by 3 inches wide) or 2 medium-size sweet potatoes (to yield 1½ cups sweet potato purée) or 1 can (15 ounces) sweet potato purée using 1½ cups from the can

4 cups dry white corn masa harina flour

2 teaspoons baking powder

2 teaspoons kosher salt

2 cups warm water

Preheat the oven to 375°F. Poke holes in the sweet potato(es) with a fork and place in a baking dish with ¼ inch of water. Cover the baking dish with foil. Bake for 1 hour or until tender when pierced with a sharp knife in the widest part. When the potatoes are cool enough to handle, peel them and process in a food processor until they form a smooth purée.

In a stand mixer with the paddle attachment or in a medium mixing bowl with a hand mixer, whip the sweet potato purée for 1 minute.

Scrape down the sides with a rubber spatula and whip for another minute to add air into the purée.

In a separate bowl, combine the masa harina, baking powder, and salt. With the mixer on low, add 1 cup of the dried masa mixture at a time to the sweet potatoes, alternating with about ½ cup of water. You will do this a total of four times to combine all the sweet potatoes, masa, and water. Scrape down the sides with the spatula as you go to ensure all the ingredients are completely mixed.

The goal is to form as moist a dough as possible without it sticking to the sides of the mixing bowl yet dry enough to form a cohesive ball that comes off the sides of the mixing bowl.

Because masa dries out quickly, it can be used immediately or placed in a plastic freezer bag and stored in the refrigerator for 1 to 2 days or in the freezer for up to 1 month.

Note:
I prefer to use King Arthur Baking Company's organic Masa Harina flour that is 100 percent American-grown and milled. This brand is 100 percent employee-owned and a certified B Corporation (see source guide).

SWEET POTATO & BLACK BEAN TAMALE

Featuring black beans and New Mexico red chile, this tamale is made with Sweet Potato Tamale Masa (page 199). I serve it with the Red Chile Sauce (page 129) or the Green Chile Sauce (page 131) as I love a good robust red or green chile sauce with my tamales to complement the black bean filling. Try a New Mexican tradition and serve it with both.

Making tamales has multiple steps but don't let this deter you; it is one of the most fun things to do when you have the time. Traditionally, women would get together to make dozens and dozens of tamales at the same time, with each person getting to take home several dozen. With a group of people making them, it is not only more fun to do, as you can catch up on the lives of each person cooking, but it also speeds up the process. The tradition is to make many all at once, some to eat immediately and some to freeze to enjoy later. So you may want to spend a day of preparing tamales and have a freezer full to enjoy for a while!

MAKES APPROXIMATELY 28 TAMALES

1 recipe Red Chile Sauce (page 129)
1 recipe Sweet Potato Tamale Masa (page 199)
32 dried corn husks
28 dried corn husk ties (see directions)

For the Tamale Filling:
⅔ cups black bean juice, divided (reserved from the cans or from cooking the beans)
1 medium yellow onion, diced (approximately 1½ cups)
2 teaspoons blackened garlic (page 253)
3 cups cooked black beans, or 2 cans (15.5 ounces each), rinsed with bean juice reserved first
1 cup blackened corn (page 252)
1½ teaspoons kosher salt, or to taste
1 tablespoon New Mexico red chile powder, mild
½ teaspoon dried Mexican oregano
½ teaspoon chipotle chile powder (use ¼ teaspoon if your palate requires mild heat)

Add ½ cup of Red Chile Sauce to your batch of masa while mixing it together and set aside. This will add flavor and make the masa a beautiful color. Because the masa dries out quickly, place it in a plastic freezer bag or airtight containers to keep it moist before setting it aside.

Soak the corn husks in hot water until soft, for approximately 10 minutes. I place a dinner plate on top of the soaking husks to keep them immersed in the hot water. Then remove them from the warm water and place in a mixing bowl.

To make the ties, tear a few corn husks into long strips, approximately 8 inches long by about ¼ inch wide.

To prepare the filling, heat a cast-iron skillet over high heat. Add 3 tablespoons of the bean juice, then the onion and sauté until the onions are translucent, for about 3 minutes. Add an additional 3 tablespoons of bean juice and the garlic and cook for 3 more minutes, stirring to prevent burning. Add the beans, blackened corn, salt, red chile powder, Mexican oregano, and chipotle chile powder.

Turn the heat down to medium and cook for another 10 minutes over medium heat. Stir every couple of minutes to prevent burning. After approximately 8 minutes, add the final 4 tablespoons of bean juice to deglaze the pan. Taste, adjusting the seasoning as needed. Remove from heat. Transfer to a small bowl and set aside. Place a piece of plastic snugly on top of the surface of the beans to keep them from drying out; if they do become dry, add a tablespoon or two of water and then stir to moisten.

Open a corn husk lengthwise, spread about 2 tablespoons of the masa on the bottom part of it and press evenly over the bottom side (wide side) of the husk, leaving at least 1 inch of husk on each side (left and right side) uncovered and several inches or approximately half on the top so that you can fold over the remaining corn husk to make the tamale. Spoon approximately 1 heaping tablespoon of the filling on the center of the pressed-down masa and then fold each side of the corn husk over the filling, rolling it together so that the masa wraps around the filling. Holding and bringing up both sides of the husk, gently press the masa up and around the filling as much as possible. Fold the left side, then the right side of the corn husk covering the masa so that the tamale is sealed inside the corn husk and fully wrapped. Fold down the remaining corn husk on the top without the filling in it, in half over the filled portion of the tamale with the bottom part still open.

Tie corn husk ties around each tamale into a knot and trim any excess corn husk that is hanging out from the piece that is tucked in. I use pieces of corn husks that are not large enough for wrapping to make my ties. Repeat the process with the rest of the ingredients until all the tamales are filled and tied.

Next, using a pasta pot with a strainer insert or a large pot with a steamer basket, add water and fill to the bottom of the insert or steamer basket. Bring to a boil, then place the tied tamales with the open side up into the insert or steamer basket and line with the completed tamales. Run hot water over a clean kitchen towel, then wring it out and lay it over the top of the tamales. Cover with a lid and steam for 45 minutes for frozen tamales or 35 minutes for fresh tamales. Turn off the heat and let rest for 5 minutes. Remove the towel and then the tamales and serve plated, like in the photo, with the Red Chile Sauce or place in a bowl and serve family style with the sauce on the side or serve plated. Serve immediately.

This recipe makes approximately twenty-eight tamales, which you can serve all at once, or steam only the ones you want to serve and freeze the additional tamales in a plastic freezer bag for future use.

Notes:
When you are first starting out making tamales, it may be easier to do one at a time until you get the hang of it. Once you have made tamales several times, and mastered the technique, it can be helpful to build five or six tamales at a time in a production line, or whatever your work area will allow, to speed up the process.

We have been able to make approximately three hundred or more tamales in a day using the production line with two or three people making them.

Vanilla

In the region of Papantla, in the state of Veracruz, of the Mexican republic, where the Totonaca people live, this prized spice was and is revered and worshipped as a gift given to them by the gods. The Totonacs learned how to process its long, slender seedpods to produce this fragrant spice. In Totanac *zacanatanuxanath* means ripe and black vanilla. The Aztecs acquired vanilla in the fifteenth century from the Totonacs. Today, vanilla and its sweet sister cacao are commonly used together, but each adds its own unique flavor to some of the most delectable, decadent, sensual, and rich-tasting desserts on the planet. And both are considered to be foods of the gods by the Ancestral Native communities that first cultivated them. Vanilla, with its sweet, delicate, aromatic scent, is one of the most widely used flavors in the world.

One of the students in my Indigenous Concepts of Native American Food class at IAIA reported on a story the Totonac people had about vanilla. He researched vanilla for his final paper and shared this story that the vanilla orchid was gifted to the People to remember, symbolize, and embody the forbidden love of Xanat, the young daughter of the Mexican fertility goddess, who fell in love with a Totanac youth. She was forbidden to marry him due to her divine nature, so she transformed herself into a plant that would provide pleasure and happiness. The sweetness, innocence, and deep richness of their love poured out onto the earth, and this essence became vanilla. The tribe celebrates this goddess with a festival to this day.

Vanilla doesn't grow like other plants. Its stem needs to be supported by a tree or other support system that it can grow up onto and out from. The leaves grow to be larger than its flowers with its fruit, the vanilla pod, and this is where the famous vanilla seeds are held. It is the only fruit-bearing member of the orchid species *Vanilla planifolia*. The flowers of this species are hermaphroditic, containing both the male (anther with the pollen) and the female (stigma), which are separated by a membrane that keeps them from self-pollinating. Vanilla is pollinated by a bee called the Melipona bee (a stingless bee) that is indigenous only to Mexico and is the only insect aware of how to extract the pollen from the vanilla flower and able to do so during the short window of time in which the flower blooms. If it is not pollinated during this short window of time, the flower wilts, dies, and drops to the ground.[27] The flower that produces vanilla only lasts for twenty-four hours, and the beans are hand-picked after pollination.

Once the pods are harvested, they are wrapped (usually in a blanket) and taken to a location to dry for three days. This process, called the sweating process, ultimately gives vanilla its subtle, fragrant, and beautiful aroma. The pods are then sun-dried to prevent them from molding. This second process lasts approximately a month and allows the outside skin of the vanilla pod to become like a soft pliable leather and turn black. During this stage, vanilla processors must keep a constant watch so that the pods aren't destroyed by rain, wind, or too much sun. The final stage for the pods is to store them in a cool, dark, dry place from where they are exported and/or sold. Total processing time for all of this is four to six months, which explains why vanilla beans are so expensive.

The seeds of this pod are the smallest seeds in the world; they contain hundreds of different flavor and fragrance components. These little black seeds are readily recognizable by the black specs you can see in the pods themselves once sliced open, in vanilla bean paste and in desserts like vanilla ice cream made from real vanilla.

Today, vanilla is grown in tropical regions around the globe with the most well-known sites being Madagascar, Mexico, and Tahiti. Vanilla is also now made synthetically because it takes a long time to mature, is hard to grow, must be hand-pollinated outside of its native environment, and is therefore very expensive to buy in its natural form.

Vanilla was completely unknown in other parts of the world, and some academics credit Hernán Cortés as first introducing it to Western Europe, along with other American imports. Upon its introduction, it was first thought of as an additive to chocolate until the early seventeenth century, when it was introduced to Queen Elizabeth I, in the form of chocolate-free all-vanilla-flavored sweetmeats.[28] Since that time, Europeans took to vanilla and have used it in everything, and not just with chocolate as it was originally used.

You can find synthetic vanilla, but I recommend the purest form for cooking and baking with either a whole pod or bean paste. I primarily buy pure vanilla bean paste (and while the paste is expensive, it is one of the ingredients, like chocolate, that I don't compromise on). I find that the flavor is so much better in the whole pods and the vanilla bean paste that it is worth every extra penny. But whatever you have, it will work in these recipes that celebrate this universally beloved flavor—another gift from the Indigenous Peoples of the Americas to the world.

VANILLA GRILLED PEACHES

For me fresh peaches represent a special part of summer. Peaches were introduced to New Mexico by the Spanish in the sixteenth century and are now grown on many farms and on many of the Pueblos. Paired with vanilla they make a simple summer dessert that celebrates both of these wonderful flavors, vanilla, with its aromatic delectable essence and peaches with their juicy, sweet texture and flavor. Look to see if you have fresh peaches from your own farmers' market or get them seasonally when they are available in your supermarket. Top this with Chokecherry Syrup (page 271) or use a store-bought variety (see source guide).

MAKES 4 SERVINGS

2 teaspoons vanilla bean paste

½ cup plus 2 teaspoons water

2 teaspoons sunflower oil

4 peaches, perfectly ripened (but not overripe), cut in half, and pit removed

½ cup piñon (pine) nuts, toasted

¼ cup chokecherry syrup (page 271)

In a small bowl mix the vanilla, 2 teaspoons of the water, and sunflower oil. Brush the open side of each peach with a little of the mixture. Using a cast-iron pan or grill over very high heat, place the peach halves, cut side down. Grill for approximately 4 minutes, then rebrush a little more of the vanilla mixture onto the peach and turn at a diagonal, rotating once for cross marks, and grill for another 4 minutes so that each peach has a crisscross pattern on it.

Once they are all grilled, and the peach is soft to the touch but not mushy, turn the peach over so that it is skin side down, add ½ cup water to the pan or place in a glass or metal bowl if using a grill, and cover. Turn off the heat and let sit covered for 3 minutes.

To toast the piñon nuts, heat a seasoned cast-iron pan over medium to high heat until hot but not smoking. Place the piñons in the dry pan and toast until they start to turn brown, approximately 3 minutes. Remove from the heat and pour into a bowl. To serve, pour a little of the chokecherry syrup onto each peach. Place two halves of the grilled peaches onto each plate. Garnish with the toasted pine nuts.

Serve immediately.

Note:

If using store-bought peaches, allow them to ripen for several days before grilling for optimal flavor as store bought peaches are unripe when purchased. When using farmers' market peaches, you don't have to allow them to ripen as they are usually sold already ripened.

VANILLA MELON SALAD

The Southwest is abundant with many varieties of melons. Technically, melons are an introduced food from Africa and Southwest Asia, but in almost every Pueblo and across the Navajo Nation, Native American communities grow melons. Chef Walter's dad, Thomas Mike, always grew a variety of melons with corn, squash, and sunflowers. Watermelon is probably the most typical, and they are now found at every Feast, many Ceremonies, and almost all large family gatherings.

This combination of a perfectly ripened cantaloupe and a mini seedless watermelon is my favorite, but feel free to use whatever melons are available in your area. The most important thing to remember is that you want to use perfectly ripened melons, whether grown yourself, purchased from your local farmers' market, or store-bought.

MAKES 4 TO 6 SERVINGS

1 small red watermelon or ½ medium
    watermelon
1 small cantaloupe or muskmelon
1 tablespoon vanilla bean paste or extract
¾ cup prickly pear syrup (see source guide)
    or chokecherry syrup (page 271)
¼ cup chiffonade or finely chopped fresh mint
    leaves

Carefully prepare both melons by cutting off the ends of each side of the melon. First the top and then the bottom. Set the melon up on one of the flat sides, and using a knife, cut away the rind, working your way around the fruit until all the rind is cut off and can be discarded. Slice the watermelon into 1-inch rounds. Then slice the rounds in half and cut each half into three wedges. Trim the edge of each wedge, as needed, making them into triangles, and reserve.

Slice the cantaloupe in half lengthwise, scoop out the seeds, and cut into long slices approximately ½ inch thick. Arrange both melons on a large platter, or plate individually. Combine the vanilla and the prickly pear syrup and drizzle on top of the melons. Finally, sprinkle on the mint.

Serve immediately.

VANILLA PEACH SAUCE

Peach sauce can accompany a variety of dishes. I use it with Peach Bread Pudding (page 212), Dried Fruit & Vanilla Dessert Tamales (page 218), and Chocolate Piñon Cake (page 243). You can use frozen peaches as directed below. If you have very ripe and sweet fresh peaches, you may just want to peel, pit, and then blend them with vanilla and serve. If you find yourself with a bunch of peaches at peak season, double or triple the batch and freeze; you'll have the best-tasting vanilla peach sauce all year round.

MAKES APPROXIMATELY 2½ CUPS

4 cups or 1 pound fresh or frozen peaches, peeled, pitted, and sliced

4 tablespoons agave sweetener, or to taste, divided

2 teaspoons freshly squeezed lemon juice

2 teaspoons vanilla bean paste

Place all the ingredients into a blender using half of the agave and blend on high speed for approximately 3 minutes to make a smooth purée. Taste. If you want a sweeter sauce, add the remaining agave and blend again. Adjust sweetness or acidity, if needed. Pour into a squeeze bottle or container.

Peach sauce can be kept in the refrigerator for approximately 3 to 5 days or frozen for later use.

PEACH BREAD PUDDING

Almost every Pueblo in New Mexico and several tribes throughout the Southwest have their own version of bread pudding, and it is a common Pueblo Feast Day dessert. Feast Days are the designated day of each Pueblo's Patron Saint, given to them by the Spanish. Pueblo households host visitors to their Pueblo on the day of their Patron Saint and may feed up to several hundred people in a day. I have never tasted a bread pudding I didn't like, but they do vary slightly in how they are made from Native community to Native community. This version uses fresh grated ginger for a zesty flavor while vanilla adds an aroma and subtle essence to the peaches that pairs perfectly with the bread. The Vanilla Peach Sauce complements each serving. You can use fresh or frozen peaches in this dish.

MAKES APPROXIMATELY 9 SERVINGS

1 loaf of farm bread or Pueblo oven bread
  (see Note), cut into 1-inch cubes
  (approximately 8 cups)
1 pound fresh or frozen peaches (approximately
  3 cups when chopped)
2 cups warm water
4 tablespoons cornstarch
¾ cup unsweetened almond milk
2 tablespoons low-sugar apricot or peach
  preserves (organic if possible)
½ teaspoon ground cinnamon
¼ teaspoon ground nutmeg
¼ teaspoon kosher salt
1 tablespoon vanilla bean paste or extract
1 cup unfiltered apple juice or apple cider
1 tablespoon finely grated fresh ginger
¾ cup golden raisins
1 recipe Vanilla Peach Sauce (page 211)

Preheat the oven to 350°F. Place the bread on a large, dry sheet pan, or two smaller ones, and toast for approximately 30 minutes, or until golden brown.

If you are using frozen peaches, place them in a bowl, add the warm water, and let them sit for at least 15 minutes or until the peaches are completely defrosted. Strain out the liquid and reserve, making sure to save it for later, and cut the peaches into 1-inch pieces. If using fresh peaches, peel, remove the pit, and chop into small chunks. Place the chunks of peaches in cold water just enough to cover, and let sit for 15 minutes. Then reserve the liquid and set aside the chopped peaches.

In a separate mixing bowl, whisk together the cornstarch and almond milk until there are no lumps. Add the water from the soaked peaches, apricot preserves, cinnamon, nutmeg, salt, vanilla, apple juice, and ginger. Mix well. Fold in the raisins, peach chunks, and toasted bread.

Let this mixture sit for 5 minutes to allow the bread to soak up the liquid. Then transfer to a 9 x 9-inch glass baking pan. Bake for 55 minutes, or until the top is golden brown and it gently springs back when touched. Remove from the oven and let cool for 5 minutes to cut. Serve warm with the Vanilla Peach Sauce (page 211).

Note:

Pueblo oven bread is a round-loaf yeasted bread made in the outdoor Pueblo adobe ovens here in the Southwest. If you can't get this bread in your area, use a yeasted non-sourdough bread, which is sometimes called a farm bread (our farmers' market sells a Native Wheat Bread), which will work perfectly for this recipe.

BAKED BERRY VANILLA CRISP

This lovely berry dessert is not too sweet and not too tart. The vanilla adds a wonderful flavor component and is an integral ingredient to this dessert.

I serve it with a little Chokecherry Syrup (page 271) and then add a little Coconut Whipped Cream (page 273). Because it is not overly sweet, it is also a perfect breakfast dish slightly warmed.

MAKES 6 TO 8 SERVINGS

10 cups frozen mixed sweet cherries, raspberries,
    blackberries, and blueberries
    (three 1-pound frozen bags)
½ cup gluten-free flour
½ cup finely ground white cornmeal
1½ cups rolled oats
1 cup packed brown sugar
¼ teaspoon salt
½ cup sunflower oil
1 tablespoon vanilla bean paste or extract
1 recipe coconut whipped cream (page 273)
1 cup chokecherry syrup (page 271)

In an ovenproof baking dish (approximately 10 x 12 inches), place the frozen berries evenly spread out, and set aside. Preheat the oven to 350°F.

In a separate medium mixing bowl, combine the flour, cornmeal, oats, brown sugar, and salt and mix with a spoon. Add the sunflower oil and vanilla, and using a spoon or your hands, mix until you have a moist, sandy mixture that resembles a crumble topping. Evenly place the crumble over the frozen berries, spreading it out so that it covers the entire top of the berries in the baking dish.

Bake for 45 minutes. Rotate the pan in the oven and bake for another 45 minutes, or until the crisp top is golden brown and the berries have completely baked together and they don't move when gently touching the baking dish. You will notice that the berries are bubbling around the edges of the dessert, and this will release the pectin from the fruit, making the dessert set.

Remove from the heat and serve either warm and family style with the coconut whipped cream (page 273) on the side or let cool to room temperature so that you can cut it. Using a round cookie cutter, cut circles in the pan and place a round piece of the crisp on top of a little chokecherry syrup drizzled onto each plate. Serve with a dollop of the coconut whipped cream.

I don't like to waste anything, so any of the crisp that is left over from cutting the circles, we scrape out of the baking dish and put in an airtight plastic container to enjoy for breakfast the following day.

Note:
I buy local, organic fresh berries from the Santa Fe Farmers' Market when they are in season or from a local grocery when they are on sale and freeze them in bags or containers for use throughout the off-season months.

VANILLA & CACAO SUNFLOWER SKILLET CAKES

This is a modern version from a traditional recipe that was made with just ground sunflower seeds and water that I learned how to make many years ago. The traditional recipe originates from an Ancestral cake that was made using sunflower seeds from plants that grow all over the Southwest. These plants grow quickly here and need very little care. Sometimes sunflower seeds were parched and eaten whole, but they were also ground and mixed with cornmeal. I call them cakes because they remind me of hotcakes, but they also resemble a moist cookie. My version is packed with protein, easy to make, and will last for several days once cooked. Perfect for breakfast on the go or a healthy snack, I also like to serve these skillet cakes for dessert with Chokecherry Syrup (page 271) or Vanilla Peach Sauce (page 211), but they are also tasty with just a little maple syrup drizzled on top.

MAKES APPROXIMATELY 14 COOKIE CAKES FOR EACH BATCH

For the Vanilla Skillet Cakes:

3 cups sunflower seeds, shelled, roasted, no added salt
5 tablespoons finely ground blue cornmeal
4 tablespoons unbleached sugar
½ teaspoon kosher salt
2 tablespoons vanilla bean paste
1 cup water
1 tablespoon sunflower oil (for cooking), divided
To make the cacao version of the skillet cakes.
 Add 1 tablespoon of cacao powder to the skillet cake mix.

For the vanilla skillet cakes, place the sunflower seeds in a food processor. Add the cornmeal, sugar, and salt and process for at least 3 minutes. Use a rubber spatula to scrape the bowl of the food processor and push the ingredients back down to the bottom to ensure they are completely processed. Add the vanilla and then slowly add the water and process until the seeds are completely ground. If there are still whole seeds around the edges of the food processor, scrape them into the center with a spatula and process again until they are ground, about 1 more minute. The dough will be quite thick, resembling a nut butter consistency. With your hands or a small ice-cream scoop, shape the dough into round cakes about the size of silver dollars.

In a large cast-iron skillet, evenly rub 1½ teaspoons of the sunflower oil onto the pan and heat until it is hot but not smoking. Place the cakes in the pan and brown them for 2 to 3 minutes on each side, turning once. Remove them from the pan and set aside. Add the remaining 1½ teaspoons of the sunflower oil and cook the remainder of the cookie cakes.

For the cacao version of these cakes, add 1 tablespoon of cacao powder to the skillet cake mix and follow as per the instructions above.

Serve warm with your favorite sauce or syrup.

DRIED FRUIT & VANILLA DESSERT TAMALES

These tamales feature a dried fruit compote with coconut and vanilla. They are not too sweet, have a lovely texture, and are a rare treat, as most tamales are savory. I like to make them in advance, and freeze, so that all I have to do is steam the tamales and serve them with my favorite sauce. The best way to make these is with family and friends and to make a large amount so that everyone gets to take some home. This recipe makes approximately twenty-six tamales, but you can easily double or triple the recipe. I freeze them in freezer bags, and cook them when needed. I like to serve these with the Vanilla Peach Sauce (page 211); this dessert is always a huge hit.

MAKES APPROXIMATELY 26 TAMALES

1 recipe Vanilla Peach Sauce (page 211)
1 Basic Tamale Masa (page 31)
2 tablespoons vanilla bean paste
1 tablespoon agave sweetener
30 dried corn husks
52 corn husk ties (see directions)

For the Tamale Filling:
2 cups dried apricots, diced
1 cup golden raisins
4 tablespoons unfiltered apple juice or cider
2 cups water
1 tablespoon vanilla bean paste
2 tablespoons agave sweetener
6 tablespoons low-sugar apricot jam
   (organic if possible)
¼ cup unsweetened, dried, organic shredded
   coconut

First prepare the Vanilla Peach Sauce (page 211) and set aside. Next prepare the Basic Tamale Masa (page 31), adding the vanilla and agave during the preparation process. Cover with plastic wrap to keep it moist before setting it aside.

Soak the corn husks in hot water until soft, for approximately 10 minutes, keeping them immersed in the hot water. Remove them from the warm water and place in a bowl.

To make the ties, tear a few corn husks into long strips, approximately 8 inches long by about ¼ inch wide.

To prepare the filling, heat a medium saucepan over high heat. Add the apricots, raisins, apple juice, water, and vanilla. Bring mixture to a boil, stirring frequently to prevent burning. Add the agave, apricot jam, and coconut and lower heat to simmer for 15 minutes, stirring occasionally until the mixture thickens and the dried fruit plumps. Remove from heat, place in a bowl, and set aside.

Open a corn husk lengthwise, spread about 2 tablespoons of the prepared masa onto the corn husk, and press evenly in the middle of the husk, leaving at least 1 inch of husk on each side (left and right side) uncovered. Spoon approximately 1 heaping tablespoon of the cooked fruit filling on the center of the pressed-down masa and then fold each side of the corn husk over the filling, rolling it together so that the masa wraps around the filling. Holding and bringing up both sides of the husk, gently press the masa up and around the filling as much as possible. Fold the left side, then the right side of the corn husk covering the masa so that the tamale is sealed inside the corn husk and fully wrapped. Twist the end of the corn husk and then tie it with a piece of corn husk. Next twist the other end of the corn husk and tie that end. The tamale should resemble a candy wrapper. This style of wrapping and tying tamales is commonly used for sweet or dessert tamales.

Repeat the process with the rest of the ingredients until all the tamales are filled and tied.

Next, using a pasta pot with an insert or a large pot with a steamer basket, add water and fill to the bottom of the insert or steamer basket. Bring to a boil, then place the tied tamales into the insert or steamer basket. Take a clean kitchen towel and run under hot water, then wring it out and lay over the top of the tamales inside the pot. Cover with a lid and steam for approximately 35 minutes or approximately 45 minutes for frozen tamales. Turn off the heat and let rest for 5 minutes. Remove the towel, then remove the tamales and serve with the Vanilla Peach Sauce.

HOMINY CORN & CHOKECHERRY SORBET

I've planted an edible landscape outside my home that includes a small-growing tree commonly called chokecherry, *Prunus virginiana*, that produces anywhere from twenty to over thirty-five pounds of chokecherries each year. This recipe pairs the chokecherry syrup that I make each year with the white hominy corn that is produced by our local farmers here in Northern New Mexico. While you might not think to use hominy corn in a dessert, it has a lovely corn essence that pairs wonderfully with the chokecherries. I leave some of the corn hominy in small pieces to give this sorbet some nice texture and bring out the lovely corn hominy flavor in this dessert. It makes a beautifully colored and unique chokecherry sorbet flavored with the perfect amount of vanilla.

MAKES 1 QUART OF SORBET

3 cups cooked hominy corn (page 259)
1½ cups chokecherry syrup (page 271)
1 cup water
¼ teaspoon kosher salt
2 teaspoons vanilla bean paste

Break up 1 cup of the hominy corn with your hands into small pieces and reserve in a bowl. Blend the remaining 2 cups of hominy corn with the chokecherry syrup, water, salt, and vanilla in a high-speed blender, for approximately 2 minutes, or until completely smooth. Transfer to a bowl and fold in the small pieces of hominy.

Place the mixture in an ice-cream machine and process for approximately 25 minutes or as per the instructions for your machine.

Remove from the ice-cream maker, put into a plastic quart container, and freeze. Temper the sorbet at room temperature before serving for approximately 20 minutes to be able to scoop out. Scoop several small balls of the chokecherry sorbet, and serve alone or drizzle with additional chokecherry syrup.

VANILLA ALMOND MILK

In the Ancestral past, culinary ash used in many Native recipes was a great source of calcium, and milk was never needed, nor a part of the Indigenous diets in the Americas. Also, many Native Americans are lactose intolerant and cannot process animal-based milks even though milk powder was and still is distributed through the Food Distribution Program on Indian Reservations (FDPIR). Milk can be made from almost any nut, and many Native Americans have been making milks from indigenous nuts for millennia.

Today, plant-based milks can be found in most supermarkets; however, this is an easy-to-make homemade almond milk for those of you who want to make your own. I use vanilla and dates for flavor and sweetness; you can adjust the sweetness to your own liking.

YIELDS 6 CUPS

1 cup raw almonds, soaked in 3 cups filtered
    water overnight in the fridge

3 dates, pitted

2 teaspoons vanilla bean paste

5 cups filtered water

Drain and rinse the soaked almonds.

Add the almonds, dates, vanilla, and water to a blender. Blend on high for approximately 1 minute until all the ingredients are completely blended.

Drain the blended milk through a fine-mesh strainer, cheesecloth, or a nut milk bag (my preference). Make sure all the liquid is removed from the blended nut mixture and then place it in a glass jar or storage container.

Refrigerate and enjoy for up to 3 days.

Note:
I would advocate for you to buy organic almonds if you can find an affordable source. This way you will be guaranteed that there are no pesticides on the nuts, and of course, it's better for the environment.

I think that organic almonds also have better flavor, making a better tasting almond milk.

VANILLA, LAVENDER & LEMON SPRITZER

Chef Walter and I get asked all the time for healthy alternatives to sodas; we use this at many of our Red Mesa Cuisine dinners. Vanilla is the star of this syrup; even though the lavender and lemon didn't originate in the Americas, they enhance the flavor of the vanilla, making a delicious spritzer. By making a syrup and storing it in the fridge separately, you can make this many times without worrying about your sparkling water going flat. Try using wild mint in the summer for a refreshing alternative to the lavender in this recipe.

MAKES 4 APPROXIMATELY 6-OUNCE SERVINGS

½ cup agave sweetener
½ cup water
1 tablespoon dried culinary lavender leaves
Zest and juice of 2 lemons (zest and juice kept
    separately)
2 teaspoons vanilla bean paste or extract
1 large (750 ml) bottle of sparkling water

In a medium saucepan bring agave, water, lavender, and lemon zest (not juice) to a simmer. Turn off the heat and let this mixture sit for 10 minutes. Strain through a fine-mesh strainer. Whisk in the lemon juice and vanilla. Let the mixture cool completely before storing it in a glass jar in the fridge.

To serve, whisk together the syrup with an entire bottle of sparkling water and serve over ice. For individual servings, add ¼ of the total amount of syrup to approximately 6 ounces of sparkling water.

Notes:
You can make a spritzer with sparkling water and a splash of any kind of juice or syrup for a healthier drink. Try adding 1 ounce prickly pear syrup, chokecherry syrup (page 271), cherry juice, citrus juice, cucumbers, fresh citrus, and fresh herbs to 6 to 8 ounces of sparkling water for a healthy alternative to soda pop and sugary drinks.

Fruit-flavored sparkling water beverages are a great beverage for children as well. Everyone we have served them to loves them.

You can also purchase your own sodastream machine to make your own sparkling bubbly water.

I recommend using an organic lime for the lime zest as then you can be sure that the lime skin is pesticide-free.

Cacao

Cacao beans, from the cacao tree, are the principal ingredient in chocolate and another major food that many of us eat every day with its origin in the Americas. Cacao has a long, intricate, and rich history in Mesoamerican Native cultures. Traces of this food of the gods date back to over four thousand years ago. It gained its divine and revered status among the Olmecs, Izapan, Maya, Toltecs, Aztecs, and the Incas. The Maya built large cities in the tropical rain forests of present-day Mexico, Guatemala, and Honduras, which were, and still are, regions ideal for cultivating cacao, and this became, and still is, an important plant to the Maya. The Aztecs believed that it was a gift of the god Quetzalcoatl, who was considered to be the patron of agriculture.[29]

Cacao was used as a highly prized drink primarily consumed by the elite—the chiefs and their royal courts within these Native communities. The word cacao stems from the Olmec and Mayan word kakaw. Its Latin name Theobroma translates to "food of the gods," as Theo means "god" and broma means "food." Considered a sacred drink that connects one to the divine and has been and continues to be used in Ceremonies, rituals, and offerings, it was shared among tribes and served to honored guests. Some references say that it was served by the Aztec emperor Montezuma to Hernán Cortés, and it is believed that Cortés was one of the first Europeans to have been offered an Indigenous cacao drink.[30]

In "A Brief History of Botany of Cacao," John West notes that "The early history of cacao and of chocolate culture is obscure, in part because conquistadors and Catholic missionaries in Latin America destroyed records wholesale in their haste to eradicate native religious and social systems."[31] One of the few and most important documents that survived this destruction is the Codex Mendoza, famous for the renderings of large sacks of cacao beans along with other goods that were paid to the Aztecs, and produced by an Aztec artist for the Spanish viceroy of Mexico, Antonio de Mendoza. The drawings in this Codex are simply spectacular. In the Aztec Nahuatl language, cacahuatl directly refers to the cacao bean, and it is believed that the Spanish word cacao is derived from that Nahuatl word.[32]

The Spanish took control of much of the Mayan agriculture and trade, which gave them a monopoly on the production of cacao. Once the beans were taken by the Spanish, they became one of the most important crop exports during the sixteenth and early seventeenth centuries. The Spanish controlled its trade and consumption not only in Europe but also in the colonies in the United States.[33] And once chocolate became fashionable among European royalty, the demand increased from the French, English, and Dutch. This is when the bean was planted in other regions of the world, including Brazil, the Philippines, the Ivory Coast of Africa, Java, and other sites in Indonesia.

You may be wondering how we got from "cacao" to "cocoa." To simplify it, cacao is the seed (most of us know it as a bean) from which chocolate is made, and cocoa is an ingredient in processed chocolate products and bars.

Most recipes using cacao start with the cacao nibs, which are the dried and fermented beans ground into pieces or a powder. These have some very impressive health benefits, including containing many antioxidants.

Truthfully, I'd never seen a fresh cacao pod until I ordered some of them as research for this book and began to work with the fresh whole fruit that encases the prized beans. The cacao fruit has a hard outer shell, which turns from yellow to orange to a dark brown when ripe; inside the pod, there are seeds, usually called beans, that are embedded in an edible white pulp inside the fruit's hard outer shell. Each pod contains approximately fifty beans, about enough to make a chocolate bar that is 100 grams, which is the equivalent of about a half a cup. The seeds are the main ingredient in chocolate while the pulp is used in some regions where it grows, and is readily available, and people have access to it to prepare fresh juices and smoothies.

When the fresh cacao pods arrived, we opened the fruits and ate the white pulp, which had a texture similar to a peach; it was slightly sweet and a little sour all at the same time. We then fermented and roasted the cacao beans, processed the cacao nibs, and ground the nibs into a powder. The whole experience helped me to truly appreciate these beans and the amount of work it takes to process them. See page (234) for instructions if you want to try this time-intensive but fascinating process yourself.

Of course, another—easier—way to enjoy the benefits of cacao is to make the recipes in this section. One of my favorites is the Chocolate Piñon Cake (page 243), but all the recipes in this chapter—from the simple Chocolate-Dipped Strawberries (235) to Chocolate Bread Pudding (241), to the decadent Dark Chocolate Torte (245)—feature chocolate at its best. Cacao is also used here in savory dishes: mole is a sauce that features chocolate and chiles; you'll find my favorite mole recipe on page 228.

After working with the fresh cacao beans, learning how to process them, and then creating desserts, rubs, and sauces that feature this magical ingredient, I fully understand why historically it was considered a food of the gods. I think it still is. At least for me.

MOLE SAUCE

Mole comes from the Indigenous Nahuatl word *mōlli*, meaning "sauce." It is a traditional sauce used in Mexican cuisine, originating from different regions throughout Mexico. While the true story of mole is not known—some say that it was an Aztec delicacy served to the Spanish conquistadors, and others say that it was created by Hispanic nuns in the sixteenth century—however it was created, this amazing sauce has made its way into kitchens all over the world. It can be defined by the variety of chile or by its color—*negro, rojo, amarillo*, and *verde*—but also by its region, such as Puebla, Oaxaca, Mexico City (notably San Pedro Atocpan, which is one of the communities that makes up the borough of Milpa Alta in Mexico City), Veracruz, and elsewhere.

Moles are different in color, flavor, sweetness, and heat but almost always contain fruits, nuts, chile peppers, and spices. Some moles contain chocolate, and some do not. Whatever the exact ingredients, mole is a complex sauce rich and deep in its flavor profile yet bright and robust at the same time. I love the chocolate undertones and fruit flavors, along with the subtle or pungent heat that comes from the use of different chiles.

It is a time-consuming sauce to make but well worth the effort. This recipe makes 2 quarts; you can halve it or, even better, make some to eat right away and freeze the rest for later use.

MAKES 2 QUARTS

4 dried ancho chiles

3 dried guajillo chiles

4 Roma tomatoes (approximately 2 cups diced)

2 tablespoons sunflower oil

1 medium white onion, finely chopped (approximately 1½ cups)

1 tablespoon blackened garlic (page 253)

½ cup pecans, toasted and chopped

2 tablespoons tahini or ¼ cup sesame seeds, toasted

¼ cup pumpkin seeds, toasted

½ teaspoon ground *canela* (see Notes) or cinnamon

2 teaspoons kosher salt

¼ teaspoon freshly ground black pepper

½ cup chopped dried apricots

½ cup dried tart cherries

½ cup dark raisins

3 ounces Mexican chocolate (a little over ½ cup chopped) (see Notes)

2 ounces 72 percent dark chocolate (a little under ½ cup chopped)

7 cups water

Toast the chiles in a 350°F oven for 3 minutes. Then stem, seed them, and break them into small pieces. Using a Cast Iron Cooking Grill (see source guide) or open flame, roast the Roma tomatoes until the outer skin is blackened, then dice them once they are cool enough to handle.

In a large saucepan over medium heat, heat the oil until it is hot but not smoking. Add the onions and sauté until they are clear, for 4 to 5 minutes. Stir occasionally to prevent the onions from burning. Add the garlic and cook for another 1 to 2 minutes. Add the ancho and guajillo chile pieces and cook for another 2 minutes, stirring to prevent burning. Add the pecans, tahini, pumpkin seeds, *canela*, salt, and pepper. Continue to cook, stirring occasionally to prevent burning, for another 5 minutes. Next add the apricots, cherries, raisins, Mexican chocolate, and dark chocolate. Stir. Cook for another 3 minutes, stirring constantly to prevent burning. Add the water and bring to a boil. Reduce heat to low and cook, uncovered, for 30 minutes, stirring occasionally to prevent burning.

Working in batches so as not to overcrowd your blender, blend the mole on high until it is completely blended. Return the mole to a saucepan, and over low heat, simmer, uncovered, for 15 minutes, stirring occasionally to prevent burning. If the mole seems to be too thick, you can add a little additional water to thin it out. Once you have a nice sauce consistency, remove from heat, and use as per the recipe or allow to cool and then freeze in an airtight container.

Notes:

Ancho and guajillo chiles can be purchased online (see source guide) or in the Latin food section of your grocery. Our supermarkets here in Santa Fe carry both of these dried chiles. I prefer the Ibarra brand of Mexican chocolate; it can also be ordered online or found in the Latin food section of your grocery.

Known as canela *in Mexico, this spice is milder, less spicy, and more floral than its counterpart cinnamon, or cassia. The bark is much softer than cinnamon and can be crumbled with your fingers, and that is an easy way to tell the two apart. Canela is primarily found in the Latin food section of your supermarket or it can be purchased online, or it can be substituted by cinnamon in the recipe above, although I would use a little less if using cinnamon.*

MOLE ENCHILADAS WITH MUSHROOMS & POTATOES

Featuring Mole Sauce (page 228), this is a traditional enchilada, with vegetables that are rolled inside corn tortillas. You can make the mole sauce the day before and then compile the enchiladas the day of your dinner. Because this is such a rich and complex-flavored dish, I recommend serving either the Green Chile Herbed Rice (page 140) or a simple salad as the side.

MAKES ONE CASSEROLE DISH WITH 12 MOLE ENCHILADAS

For the Potatoes:

1 large or 2 medium russet potatoes, diced into
   ¼-inch cubes (approximately 1 pound)
1 teaspoon New Mexico red chile powder, mild
1 tablespoon sunflower oil
½ teaspoon kosher salt
¼ teaspoon freshly ground black pepper
¼ teaspoon garlic powder

For the Mushrooms:

1 tablespoon sunflower oil
8 ounces portobello mushrooms, gills removed,
   and diced into ¼-inch cubes (2 to 3
   mushrooms, depending on their size)
½ teaspoon kosher salt
¼ teaspoon freshly ground black pepper,
   or to taste
1 tablespoon blackened garlic (page 253)

For the Enchiladas:

12 White Corn Tortillas (page 27),
   or use store-bought
½ batch Mole Sauce (page 228)
4 scallions, sliced on a bias, for garnish
   (optional)
Cilantro, sprigs or chopped, for garnish
   (optional)

Preheat the oven to 350°F and line a sheet tray with parchment paper. In a large bowl, toss together the potatoes, chile powder, sunflower oil, salt, pepper, and garlic powder. Transfer this mixture to the sheet tray and roast until the potatoes are golden and crispy, around 40 minutes. Remove from the oven and transfer the potatoes to a large bowl.

While the potatoes are roasting, cook the mushrooms. In a large skillet over medium-high heat, add the sunflower oil. Once the oil is hot but not smoking, add the mushrooms, salt, and pepper, cooking for 10 to 12 minutes until all the water has evaporated and the mushrooms are nicely caramelized. Add the garlic and cook for another minute, stirring frequently. Transfer the mushrooms to the large bowl with the potatoes. Add just enough mole sauce to lightly coat the mixture.

Lightly warm the tortillas over an open flame or in a seasoned hot skillet. Place in a basket lined with a clean kitchen towel to hold and keep warm. When ready to assemble, place a tortilla onto your work surface and spread approximately 2 tablespoons of the potato mixture evenly across the center of each tortilla. Roll the tortilla around the mixture and place in a lightly oiled baking pan or casserole dish with the seam side down. Repeat the process for all the tortillas. Pour 2 cups of mole sauce on top of the rolled enchiladas and bake, uncovered, in a 350°F preheated oven for 30 to 40 minutes, or until they are hot all the way through.

Pour the remaining mole in a small saucepan and keep warm over low heat until ready to serve. When the enchiladas come out of the oven, serve family style or place two enchiladas onto a plate, cover with some additional mole sauce, and garnish with scallions and cilantro.

Serve immediately.

CACAO SPICE RUB

I keep a jar of this spice rub in my pantry to use at any time. Its flavors are not too overpowering; it makes a wonderful addition to roasted vegetables, popcorn, soups, and stews. And it's adaptable to your palate; while I've made this recipe to be savory and not too spicy, you can tailor this blend to different spice levels by using mild, medium, or hot New Mexico red chile powder. While cacao is a key ingredient, which can be purchased at most specialty supermarkets, health food stores, or online, the rub, so to speak, is in the chile powder. There is a difference between *red chile powder* and *chili powder* (the common grocery store spice blend). Red chile powder is a pulverized, pure blended chile powder from one chile, usually a red chile pod, with no additives. Chili powder is typically a blend of ground chile peppers and other spices; the ingredients vary from brand to brand, so I recommend that you check the label for the ingredients so that you know exactly what is in the blend before you use it in your recipes. I use pure New Mexico red chile powder (see source guide).

MAKES 1 CUP

5 tablespoons New Mexico red chile powder,
    mild
5 tablespoons cacao powder
3 tablespoons ground coriander
2 tablespoons garlic powder
1 tablespoon freshly ground black pepper

Stir together the chile powder, cacao powder, ground coriander, garlic powder, and pepper. Store in a glass jar or an airtight container for up to 1 year.

CACAO NIBS

Cacao nibs are highly nutritious. They are dried and fermented bits of cacao beans. And the texture of cacao nibs is a little like roasted coffee beans. They have a rich, deep, chocolate flavor that is both bitter and nutty at the same time.

Note that this is a labor-intensive recipe; I encourage you to order pods and try the full experience if you are interested in the origins of chocolate. Of course, if you don't want to make your own cacao nibs, they are available on the internet from a variety of sources. You can use them to sprinkle on top of smoothies for a chocolaty crunch, in trail mix, on plant-based yogurt, on top of Chocolate Nice Cream (page 247), and on baked goods.

8 fresh cacao pods

To begin, open the cacao pod. Using a sharp knife, carefully make a cut lengthwise along one of the grooves of the pod on each side downward from the stem. Once you cut through the skin, you will feel the resistance lessen. Put your knife down, and using your hands, pry the pod open, almost as if you are opening a book. Inside, you will see the white fruit pulp surrounding the cacao beans. Remove all the beans from the pods.

At this point, you can remove the fluffy white pulp from each bean to eat or blend with a little water to make cacao juice (this is great in smoothies), or you can simply remove the white pulp and continue to the next step.

Set a dehydrator to 105°F. Spread out the cacao beans (that have the white pulp removed from them) in single layers. Let them dehydrate for 5 days to both ferment and dry out. If you don't have a dehydrator, you can dehydrate the cacao beans in your oven, at the very lowest temperature; however, you will need to watch the cacao beans more closely and it will take a shorter amount of time. If you think you will do this process often, I recommend you purchase a dehydrator as it is a great way to preserve a variety of fruits and vegetables.

Once they have fermented and dehydrated, transfer them to a sheet tray, in a single layer. Preheat the oven to 250°F and, using a convection setting if your oven has one, roast the beans for 20 minutes. If you don't have a convection setting on your oven,

increase the cooking time by approximately 5 minutes. Remove them from the oven and let them cool.

Then press them between your fingers to loosen the shell from the bean, separating the shell from the cacao nibs. Reserve the nibs and discard the shells or put them in your compost.

Place all the nibs in a heavy-duty plastic bag and pound them with a rolling pin into small pieces. Transfer nibs into an airtight glass container and store in a cool, dark, and dry place for up to 1 year. They can be sprinkled on Hominy Corn and Chokecherry Sorbet (page 220), Chocolate Nice Cream (page 247), used in smoothies, and much more.

CHOCOLATE-DIPPED STRAWBERRIES

This recipe is an American classic. But what many people don't know is that it combines two ingredients that originated in the Americas. Wild strawberries are indigenous to North America and grow across the United States and into parts of Canada. Many tribes on the East Coast celebrate the importance of the strawberry with Ceremonies and powwows to show their reverence to these berries when they ripen in the spring. Wild strawberries are much smaller and sweeter than cultivated varieties, making them unpopular as a cultivated crop. When purchasing commercially available strawberries, I highly recommend purchasing locally grown strawberries from your farmers' market or buying organic strawberries from your supermarket, to avoid the pesticides commercial strawberries have on them. However, for any of you who have ever eaten wild strawberries, there is nothing like the sweet taste of these tiny fruits, especially when dipped in a rich, dark cacao chocolate.

You can skip adding the chile, if you want, for a more substantial chocolate flavor and sweeter dessert. You can also use other fruits, fresh or dried: try pineapple, dried apples, dried apricots, fresh or dried figs, or bananas. Adding coconut oil makes the chocolate a little harder, almost like a shell.

MAKES APPROXIMATELY 25 CHOCOLATE-COVERED STRAWBERRIES, DEPENDING ON THEIR SIZE

1 pound fresh strawberries, washed and allowed to air-dry (organic if possible)
1 cup dark chocolate, cut into small pieces, or high-quality baking chips (63 to 72 percent dark chocolate works well here) (approximately 5 ounces)
1 tablespoon coconut oil
1 teaspoon New Mexico red chile powder, mild to medium

Place a piece of parchment paper or a Silpat nonstick silicone mat on the bottom of a large sheet tray. Have the washed and dried strawberries ready to go in a bowl.

Next create a double boiler setup. Place a medium saucepan filled with 2 inches of water over medium heat. Place a heatproof stainless steel bowl that nestles into the pot so it sits well above the water. Once the water comes to a simmer, add the chocolate pieces and coconut oil to the dry bowl until the chocolate melts. Gently whisk together the melted chocolate and coconut oil until they are completely combined. Then stir in the red chile powder.

Carefully transfer the bowl of melted chocolate to the counter. I like to place the bowl on a clean kitchen towel. One at a time, holding the green part of the strawberry, dip each piece into the chocolate, leaving some room uncovered for holding. Transfer dipped strawberries to a lined sheet tray. Once all the strawberries are dipped, move the sheet tray to the fridge for 30 minutes or until chocolate is hardened and set.

Serve on its own or as a part of a dessert platter with Grilled Pineapple with Chocolate (page 236).

GRILLED PINEAPPLE WITH CHOCOLATE

This is a dessert that I have been making for a long time, with Chef Walter, at Red Mesa Cuisine, and in the Indigenous Concepts of Native American Food class at IAIA, and as part of the culinary training for chefs and cooks in Native community kitchens. Grilling the pineapple caramelizes the pieces to bring out the natural sweetness and reduce any extra tartness. The secret, however, is to purchase the pineapple in advance and allow it to ripen for several days for the most flavor. I use the Cast Iron Cooking Grill (see source guide) that works on your stove top for this recipe, but you can also use a gas grill or cast-iron pan. All these methods work fine for searing and grilling the pineapple pieces.

MAKES 4 TO 6 SERVINGS

For the Grilled Pineapple:
1 ripe pineapple, skin trimmed, cored, and sliced
    lengthwise

For the Chocolate Sauce:
8 ounces 72 percent dark chocolate, cut into
    small pieces (approximately 1⅔ cups)

Preheat a cast-iron pan, a cast-iron cooking grill, or outdoor grill over high heat. Place the pineapple slices in the pan or on the grill. Grill for approximately 1 to 2 minutes, then turn over and grill the other side. Once both sides of the pineapple pieces have nice grill marks and are blackened from grilling, remove from heat and set aside on a parchment-lined sheet pan.

Next create a double boiler setup. Place a medium saucepan filled with 2 inches of water over medium heat. Insert a heatproof stainless steel bowl that sits on top of, yet still nestles inside, the pot so it sits well above the water. Once the water comes to a simmer, add the chocolate to the dry bowl until it melts. Once the chocolate has melted, remove from the heat and place the bowl on a kitchen towel on a dry, flat surface. Using a spoon, drizzle the melted chocolate over the grilled pineapple slices on a

platter or individual plates. This is the fun part, so have fun and enjoy creating a design with the chocolate drizzle.

Serve immediately.

CHOCOLATE SAUCE

This Chocolate Sauce can accompany a variety of dessert dishes. I use it with the Chocolate, Coconut & Dried Cherry Tamales (page 239), Chocolate Bread Pudding (page 241), and Chocolate Piñon Cake (page 243), but you can be creative, as it is a delicious and rich sauce and will go with many recipes. If you add some additional almond milk, oat milk, or other nut-based milk, this will make a luscious cup of hot chocolate. This is a very easy-to-make chocolate sauce that is full of flavor but not too sweet.

MAKES APPROXIMATELY 2 CUPS

1 can (13.5 ounces) organic coconut milk
½ cup chopped 72 percent dark chocolate
    (approximately 3 ounces)

In a small saucepan over medium heat, bring coconut milk to a simmer. Then remove from heat and add the dark chocolate. Let the chocolate sit in the heated coconut milk for 5 minutes (do not stir) and then whisk together.

Serve immediately with your favorite dessert.

Chocolate Sauce with Chocolate Bread Pudding (page 241)

CHOCOLATE, COCONUT & DRIED CHERRY TAMALES

Dark chocolate, coconut, vanilla, and dried cherries combine with basic tamale corn masa for a delicious dessert. It is a time-consuming recipe, but one that can be made in advance and frozen. When you're ready to serve, all you have to do is steam the tamales. Serve them with Chocolate Sauce (page 237) for a decadent dessert everyone will love.

MAKES APPROXIMATELY 26 TAMALES

1 Basic Tamale Masa recipe (page 31)
1 cup chopped 72 percent dark chocolate
    (around 5 ounces in weight)
2 teaspoons vanilla bean paste
½ cup unsweetened, dried, organic shredded
    coconut
1½ cups dried tart cherries
30 dried corn husks
52 corn husk ties (see directions)
1 recipe Chocolate Sauce (page 237)

Make the Basic Tamale Masa (page 31), following the instructions up to the final step. Next create a double boiler setup. Place a medium saucepan filled with 2 inches of water over medium heat. Insert a heatproof stainless steel bowl that nestles inside the pot so it sits well above the water. Once the water comes to a simmer, add the chocolate to the dry bowl until it melts.

Then add the melted chocolate and the vanilla to the final step of the basic masa, mixing them in well. Gently fold in the coconut and the dried cherries to the masa using the lowest setting on the stand mixer or mix in by hand. The dough will be moist and chocolate colored with the dried cherries spread evenly throughout the masa. Once the dough is completely mixed, place it in a plastic freezer bag to keep it moist. Set aside.

Soak the corn husks in hot water until soft, for approximately 10 minutes. I place a dinner plate on top of the soaking husks to keep them immersed in the hot water. Then remove them from the warm water and place in a mixing bowl.

To make the ties, tear a few corn husks into long strips, approximately 8 inches in length by about ¼ inch wide.

Open a corn husk lengthwise and spread about 2 tablespoons of the prepared masa onto the corn husk and press evenly in the middle of the husk, leaving at least 1 inch of husk on each side (left and right side) uncovered. Fold each side of the corn husk over the masa-flavored filling, rolling it together so that the corn husk wraps entirely around the masa. Fold the left side, then the right side of the corn husk, covering the masa so that the tamale is sealed inside the corn husk and fully wrapped. Twist the end of the corn husk and then tie it with a piece of corn husk. Next twist the other end of the corn husk and tie that end. The tamale should resemble a candy wrapper.

Tie each strip into a knot and trim any excess corn husk hanging out from the piece that is tucked in. Repeat the process with the rest of the ingredients until all the tamales are shaped and tied.

Next, using a pasta pot with an insert or a large pot with a steamer basket, add water and fill to the bottom of the insert or steamer basket. Bring to a boil, then place the tied tamales into the insert or steamer basket. Take a clean kitchen towel and run under hot water, then wring it out and lay over the top of the tamales inside the pot. Cover with a lid. Steam for 45 minutes for frozen tamales or 35 minutes for fresh tamales. Then turn off the heat and let rest, covered in the pot, for 5 minutes. Remove the towel, then remove the tamales and serve plated with the Chocolate Sauce (page 237) or place in a bowl and serve family style with the chocolate sauce on the side.

Serve immediately.

Note:
This recipe makes approximately twenty-six tamales, which you can serve all at once, or steam only the ones you want to serve and freeze the additional tamales in a plastic freezer bag for future use.

CHOCOLATE BREAD PUDDING

I love bread pudding. When we created the Peach Bread Pudding recipe (page 212), we pulled out all the stops, making multiple versions in our journey to the perfect plant-based bread pudding. Along the way, we added melted dark chocolate to one of the versions and this recipe was born. It is not only delightful but also unique in that most bread pudding recipes don't use chocolate. This version is richer than the fruit version, yet because we use a 72 percent dark chocolate, it is not too sweet.

MAKES 8 TO 10 SERVINGS

1 loaf farm bread or 1 Pueblo Oven bread (around 1 pound), cut into 1-inch cubes (approximately 8 cups)

1 cup chopped 72 percent dark chocolate (approximately 5 ounces)

4 cups vanilla unsweetened oat milk

¼ cup flax seeds

½ teaspoon ground cinnamon

½ teaspoon ground nutmeg

½ teaspoon kosher salt

1 tablespoon vanilla bean paste or extract

1 tablespoon freshly grated ginger

½ cup packed brown sugar

1 recipe Chocolate Sauce (page 237)

Preheat the oven to 350°F. On a dry sheet pan, place the cubed bread and toast in the oven for approximately 30 minutes until golden brown. Allow to cool and then transfer to a large mixing bowl.

Next create a double boiler setup. Place a medium saucepan filled with 2 inches of water over medium heat. Insert a heatproof stainless steel bowl that nestles inside the pot so it sits well above the water. Once the water comes to a simmer, add the chocolate to the dry bowl until it melts.

Then remove it from the heat and place it in a blender with the oat milk, flax seeds, cinnamon, nutmeg, salt, vanilla, ginger, and brown sugar. Blend on high for 1 minute to ensure that all the ingredients are completely mixed. Pour the chocolate mixture over the cooked bread in the large mixing bowl and stir to combine. Let sit for 5 minutes to allow the mixture to absorb into the bread. Place mixture into an approximately 9 x 9-inch baking dish. Bake for 55 minutes, uncovered, or until the top is crispy and gently springs back to the touch.

Remove from the oven, let rest for approximately 5 to 10 minutes. Spoon onto individual plates or bowls and serve with about 1 ounce of the Chocolate Sauce (page 237).

Serve warm.

Note:
Pueblo Oven bread is a round-loaf yeasted bread made in the outdoor Pueblo adobe ovens here in the Southwest. If you can't get this bread in your area, use a yeasted non-sourdough bread, which is sometimes called a farm bread (our farmers' market sells a Native Wheat Bread), all of which will work perfectly for this recipe.

CHOCOLATE PIÑON CAKE

I've been making a version of a chocolate and piñon nut cake recipe for many years now. In my first cookbook, *Foods of the Southwest Indian Nations*, the recipe calls for egg yolks and butter, and it was called a Feast Day Torte, in honor of the tortes I tasted at different Pueblos during their Feast Day celebrations. Feast Days are a Pueblo celebration that honors each Pueblo's Patron Saint, where Native homes from each Pueblo invite relatives and visitors into their homes for a meal.

This plant-based version is a rich and moist cake—and is now my go-to cake for many of the events we do at Red Mesa Cuisine. If piñon (pine) nuts are not available or too expensive, you can easily substitute raw pecans. Serve this cake individually plated with Vanilla Peach Sauce (page 211), chokecherry syrup (page 271), or Chocolate Sauce (page 237). Chef Walter and I like to individually stencil a design on each piece, using a store-bought or handmade stencil design with powdered sugar, and then paint the sauce we use onto the plate, placing the stenciled piece of cake on top, adding fresh berries and mint, and serving each person their own art creation, or stencil and serve as pictured.

MAKES 1 9-INCH ROUND CAKE, 12 TO 14 SERVINGS

Vegan baking spray

1 cup all-purpose flour, plus more to dust

½ cup raw piñon nuts

1 tablespoon finely ground blue cornmeal

1 cup finely chopped 72 percent dark chocolate (approximately 5 ounces)

⅓ cup organic unbleached granulated sugar

¼ cup sunflower oil

2 teaspoons vanilla bean paste or extract

1 cup vanilla almond milk

1 teaspoon baking powder

¾ teaspoon baking soda

¼ teaspoon kosher salt

1 to 2 tablespoons powdered sugar for decoration (optional)

Spray a 9-inch round cake pan with a nonstick vegan baking spray or grease with vegan butter and dust with flour. Preheat the oven to 350°F. In a food processor, grind the piñon nuts to a very moist nut butter, scraping down the sides frequently to make sure all the nuts are creamed together, similar to the consistency of peanut butter. This will take several minutes. Add the blue cornmeal and blend again for about 30 seconds, just long enough to combine.

Next create a double boiler setup. Place a medium saucepan filled with 2 inches of water over medium heat. Insert a heatproof stainless steel bowl that nestles inside the pot so it sits well above the water. Once the water comes to a simmer, add the chocolate to the dry bowl until it melts. Stir occasionally so that it melts evenly. Then remove from the heat, and using a kitchen towel, hold the bowl with the melted chocolate over the food processor while using a rubber spatula to carefully add the chocolate to the piñon mixture. Blend about 1 minute until smooth, scraping the sides to ensure that it is completely mixed.

In a separate bowl, whisk together the sugar, sunflower oil, vanilla, and almond milk, and add this to the chocolate mixture. Process again until smooth, pulsing slowly, and scraping the sides with a flat rubber spatula, until it is completely mixed, for 15 to 30 seconds.

In a medium-size mixing bowl, combine the dry ingredients, reserving the powdered sugar for the stencil design. Pour the wet ingredients from the food processor into the dry ingredients, and using a spoon, rubber spatula, or whisk, fold them together, making sure there are no lumps. You will need to mix the dry and wet ingredients completely, stirring in a circular motion until it is a smooth and creamy cake texture.

Transfer the batter into the prepared cake pan and make sure it is spread evenly in the pan. The batter will resemble a thick pancake batter. Bake for 48 to 50 minutes, depending on your oven, or until the cake springs back when the center is touched and a toothpick or small knife pushed into the center of the cake comes up clean.

Remove from the oven and place on a wire rack to cool for 15 minutes. Then remove it from the pan and be creative for the decorating process. You can do individual stencils on each slice or decorate the entire cake. To make the Southwestern motif pictured, cut a stencil out of cardboard or purchase from a hobby store. Carefully place the stencil onto the cake's surface, without moving it. Using a small strainer, with a little powdered sugar in it, gently hit the strainer and cover the cake or piece of cake so that the powdered sugar has lightly dusted the surface. Carefully remove the stencil without disrupting the design.

Serve with Vanilla Peach Sauce (page 211), hand-harvested prickly pear syrup (see source guide), Chokecherry Syrup (page 271), or Chocolate Sauce (page 237) (pictured).

DARK CHOCOLATE TORTE

This indulgent, rich, and creamy torte is the perfect dessert for any chocolate lovers. The filling is our version of a vegan ganache (like the inside of a chocolate truffle) that is smooth, luscious, and I serve it with coconut whipped cream (page 273), but for extra decadence, try it with Chocolate Sauce (page 237). It is also wonderful with Vanilla Peach Sauce (page 211) and Chokecherry Syrup (page 271). However you decide to serve this showstopper, all your family and friends will be amazed that it is not only dairy-free but also gluten-free.

MAKES ONE 9-INCH DESSERT (ABOUT 12 SERVINGS)

For the Crust:

1 cup pecan pieces

1 cup piñon (pine) nuts

¼ cup unbleached granulated sugar

1 teaspoon ground cinnamon

1 teaspoon kosher salt

4 tablespoons sunflower oil

For the Torte Filling:

1¼ cans (13.5 ounces) organic coconut milk

½ cup brown sugar

¼ cup sunflower oil

1 teaspoon vanilla bean paste or extract

2 cups finely chopped 72 percent dark chocolate (9 to 10 ounces in weight)

Preheat the oven to 350°F. To prepare the crust, pulse the pecans, piñon nuts, sugar, cinnamon, and salt in a food processor. Add the sunflower oil and pulse again. Transfer this mixture and press evenly with your fingers onto the bottom and up the sides of a pie dish. Then use the bottom of a ramekin or flat-bottomed cup to make sure the crust is evenly spread out over the entire pie pan. Bake for 15 minutes, or until it is lightly caramelized. Remove the piecrust from oven and let it cool.

To prepare the filling, bring the coconut milk, brown sugar, sunflower oil, and vanilla to a boil in a medium, heavy-bottomed saucepan. Place chocolate in a large bowl. Pour the hot mixture over the chocolate and let sit for 5 minutes, then whisk until it is completely combined. Let cool to room temperature.

Pour mixture into the pie dish and refrigerate uncovered until cool for at least 4 hours, or let it set overnight, which is what I like to do. Letting it set overnight is my preferred method because then I know for sure that it will completely set. Serve chilled with the coconut whipped cream (page 273) and the Chocolate Sauce (page 237) or the Vanilla Peach Sauce (page 211) and Chokecherry Sauce (page 271).

Pictured on page 245: Dark Chocolate Torte with Vanilla Peach Sauce (page 211), Chokecherry Syrup (page 271), and fresh raspberries.

CHOCOLATE NICE CREAM

This frozen treat makes great use of overly ripened bananas that are sitting on your counter, when they have small black spots all over the yellow skin. Just peel the overripe bananas and place in a freezer bag or airtight container and freeze. I like to freeze them in batches of four bananas at a time, as that is what this recipe calls for.

I make this dessert two ways, one with peanut butter and chocolate chips, which is the method below. However, you can also make a berry version of this recipe, using both fresh and frozen berries (see Note). The best part of this dessert is that it is dairy-free, delicious, nutritious, and inexpensive because you are using bananas that most people will no longer eat, and it is easy to make.

MAKES 4 TO 6 SERVINGS

4 perfectly overripe bananas, peeled and frozen
2 tablespoons smooth peanut butter, nonhydrogenated if possible
½ cup vanilla almond milk
1 teaspoon vanilla bean paste
¼ cup semisweet or dark chocolate chips

Break frozen bananas into pieces and place in the food processor. Process until smooth. I usually process for approximately 30 seconds, then with a flat plastic spatula push any unbroken pieces of banana to the bottom and process again for approximately 30 seconds. Add the peanut butter and process again for another 30 seconds to mix with the bananas. Add the almond milk and vanilla and process again until it has a smooth consistency. Finally, add the chocolate chips and pulse lightly (a couple of seconds at a time) until the chips are mixed in, but not broken.

Put into small cups and top with Cacao Nibs (page 233) or coconut whipped cream (page 273) or just as it is, and serve immediately. You can also place in the freezer until ready to serve.

Note:

To make the berry version, omit the peanut butter and chocolate chips and add 1½ cups of frozen blueberries or other type of frozen berry (my favorites are blueberries, blackberries, or cherries as I find that raspberries have too many tiny seeds in them) and then proceed with the instructions as noted.

Pantry Staples

FIRE-ROASTED GREEN CHILES

New Mexico is known for its chiles, which are some of the best chiles in the United States (and according to some, the best in the world). An important part of the modern-day New Mexico economy and culture, chiles have been used by Native Americans in this region for millennia, and many Pueblos pride themselves on their chile crop.

Any kind of green chile can be roasted; red bell peppers are also commonly roasted, and this technique works perfectly for them as well. There are various techniques for roasting chiles; I roast my chiles using the open flame method, which can be done on your gas-burning stove top using the Cast Iron Cooking Grill (see source guide) or on your exterior gas grill. The Cast Iron Cooking Grill will work on an electric coiled element on the highest setting (although not as good as gas), but it will not work on a ceramic cooktop.

4 Anaheim or New Mexico green chiles
1 tablespoon water

Place the chiles on the Cast Iron Cooking Grill or exterior gas grill, over a medium to high flame. Let the skin blacken and char. Use kitchen tongs to rotate the chile every 2 to 3 minutes, so that all the skin gets evenly charred and turns black, but doesn't burn. You may have to hold specific parts of the chiles over the flame to blacken them, especially since some chiles are not perfectly smooth and contain curves that can be hard to blacken. There is a fine line between roasting and over-roasting a chile, so you will need to watch them, rotating each chile as each section of the skins chars and turns black until it is charred all over the exterior.

Then remove them from the heat and place in a large metal or glass bowl, add the water, and cover with plastic wrap to allow them to steam as they cool down, for 5 to 7 minutes until they are cool enough to handle.

Remove the cooled chiles from the bowl, and using your hands, gently push the blackened skin away from the flesh. It should come off easily and can be composted. If you find that there are some parts of the chile where the skin is difficult to remove, place it under a little cold running water, then rub the charred skins off and discard. Make a small incision from the top of the chile (where the stem is) straight down to the bottom of the chile (where the tip is). Gently pull out the veins and seeds; if you have difficulty, place the chile under running water to remove.

If you are stuffing the chiles, you will want to keep them whole (with just the slit in them) and use as per the instructions in the recipe. This method is the best for making stuffed chiles; however, if you are going to chop them, cut off the top and place on a flat work surface or cutting board. Chop or dice the chiles as per the instructions in the recipe. Four chiles will make approximately 1 cup of chopped or diced chiles depending on their size.

Note:
Pick the freshest chiles possible; the skin should be smooth and firm to the touch. Before using, wash the chiles to remove any dirt. Whenever you handle chiles, always take precautions to avoid skin irritation. If you are sensitive to the capsaicin (what causes the heat in chiles), then I recommend you use kitchen gloves. Never rub your eyes and always wash your hands before and after handling chiles.

BLACKENED CORN

This is another must-have, go-to recipe in my kitchen. I blacken corn a lot to bring out the roasted flavor, especially when it is not at its perfect peak flavor as during the summer season. You can blacken fresh or frozen corn kernels with the same results.

MAKES APPROXIMATELY ½ CUP OF BLACKENED CORN

1 cup corn kernels, fresh or frozen

Preheat a dry, seasoned medium cast-iron pan over high heat until it is hot but not smoking. Place corn kernels in the pan and cook, stirring occasionally until the corn begins to blacken on all sides. The kernels will pop a bit while they are browning. Cook for approximately 4 to 5 minutes depending on your flame. It is important to keep the corn rotating in the pan by stirring it so that it evenly blackens on all sides, but it should not be completely black. You should still have some parts of the corn that retain their original color. Remove from the heat and place in a bowl to cool for about 5 minutes. Once the corn has cooled, place in a container. Use as needed or follow the instructions in the recipe. You can store the corn in the refrigerator for 1 to 2 days, but I always blacken corn as needed.

BLACKENED GARLIC

This is another must-have, go-to recipe in my kitchen. I blacken garlic almost every time I cook with it as it softens the flavor of raw garlic and brings an earthy quality to almost every recipe. I highly recommend making a batch of this blackened garlic before you begin cooking and use it throughout the week.

MAKES APPROXIMATELY ½ CUP OF BLACKENED GARLIC

1 cup raw garlic cloves, peeled and brown end
    cut off

Preheat a dry, seasoned medium cast-iron pan over high heat until it is hot but not smoking. Place the raw peeled garlic in the pan and cook, stirring occasionally, until the garlic begins to blacken on all sides. Cook for approximately 6 minutes depending on your flame. It is important to keep the garlic rotating in the pan by stirring it so that it evenly blackens on all sides, but it should not be completely black. You should still have some parts of the garlic that retain their original color.

Remove from heat and place in a bowl to cool for about 5 minutes. Then place in a food processor and process on pulse until the garlic is finely chopped. Scrape down the sides of the food processor, and then pulse once more, ensuring that the garlic is evenly minced. Remove from the food processor and place in a container for use. If you do not have a food processor, the garlic can be finely chopped by hand. Store in the refrigerator for 3 to 4 days.

Note:
If you would like to extend the life of the garlic by several days, add just enough organic sunflower or olive oil to cover it in the container. The oil will keep the garlic moist and retain the flavor without letting it dry out.

CHILE GARLIC OIL

This recipe was originally created as a garnish for the Butternut Squash Soup (page 101), but it is so good that I fell in love with it and I felt it needed to be included in the cookbook as its own recipe. It can be used with the Perfect Baked Potato with All the Fixings (page 194), drizzled over the Sweet Potato, Kale & Wild Rice Bowl (page 195), or even used in salad dressings. I've also used it drizzled on top of all three bean spreads (pages 69, 70, and 71).

MAKES APPROXIMATELY 1 CUP

4 dried New Mexico red chiles, mild, stemmed,
    seeded, and broken into pieces
1 cup sunflower oil
3 cloves of garlic, peeled and left whole

In a dry saucepan over medium heat, sear the pieces of chile for approximately 10 seconds on each side. Add the sunflower oil and garlic. Then simmer for 10 minutes.

Turn the heat off and let sit for 30 minutes to infuse all the flavors together. Place the warm oil in a blender (being careful that it's not too hot) and mix for approximately 1 minute until all the ingredients are completely blended. Pass through a fine-mesh strainer and discard or compost the contents of the strainer. The oil will keep for up to 1 week in the fridge.

Note:
Because this recipe involves hot oil, it is very important to keep your pan, your utensils, and hands dry throughout the entire process. Water and hot oil are a dangerous combination, and you must be careful so you don't burn yourself.

CULINARY ASH

Culinary ash dates back thousands of years and has been used by Native communities throughout the Americas for millennia. It is primarily made from shrubs and trees growing near or around the Native communities that use it. For instance, the Navajo primarily use juniper ash. Chef Walter Whitewater and his family have been using juniper ash in their traditional dishes since he was a little boy.

Juanita Tiger Kavena, who has since passed, author of *Hopi Cookery*, talks in her cookbook about the Hopi using the ash from corncobs, corn silk, and corn husks, as well as the four-winged saltbush (*Atriplex canescens*), which is also called chamisa. Her son, Wilmer Kavena Junior, whom I know as Chibbon (which is Creek for little boy), prepared some ash for me to use for the recipes in this cookbook. He said that the four-wing saltbush is the preferred bush for the Hopi but that ash can be made from burning any bushes. He prefers to make ash from the four-wing saltbush since these bushes are more alkaline and work better with the corn. And Brandon Baugh from San Felipe Pueblo, my student from the Indigenous Concepts of Native American Food class at the Institute of America Indian Arts (IAIA), did research on using ash in his community and at San Felipe Pueblo for his final paper and presentation and found that in his community they use juniper, four-wing saltbush, and onion ash. Other Native communities all over the United States use various materials, including the ash from certain types of wood.

With the increase in culinary ash use, it is important to think about the purity of the ashes you are using. Ashes made from chemically treated wood, newspapers, magazines, or commercially purchased logs that burn all night are not suitable for making culinary ash as they may be toxic. It is always best to use pesticide-free, preservative-free, and chemical-free natural bushes or wood not sprayed with any chemicals. If you don't want to make your own ash, it is available from several different sustainable sources (see source guide).

The practice of adding culinary ash to corn dishes raises the already-substantial mineral content of the corn, increasing the nutritional value. In an interview from NPR in 2017, Daniel Begay, who is Navajo and was a student at Northern Arizona University at the time, analyzed the amount of calcium in twenty-seven samples of juniper ash from juniper trees all over the reservation. Begay stated that "for every gram of ash that I was able to sample, I was getting roughly 280–300 milligrams of calcium." This amount of calcium is about the same as in a glass of milk, and the body absorbs the calcium from the juniper ash more readily. More and more research is being done on traditional Ancestral Native American foods showing that the nutritional value in many of them is extremely high. Ash is one of these ingredients that provides nutrients and is an important part of an Ancestral diet for health and wellness.

6 small branches from a juniper tree,
   completely dried

Using the empty bottom of a charcoal grill, carefully burn the branches completely, so the blackened wood part of the branches has turned to white and completely burned down to an ash. After the branches are thoroughly charred and have stopping smoking, and there is only ash left in the bottom of the grill, allow them to completely cool so that you can handle them. Then scoop up the ashes into a metal bowl.

Using a fine-mesh strainer, sieve the ashes into a separate bowl or container, making sure that only the white powder goes through the strainer. Any pieces of wood or branches that did not completely burn will be left in the strainer. Discard or compost those. Transfer the strained ash to a glass jar and use as per the recipe. Ash can be stored for several months in an airtight container or glass jar.

BASIC COOKED BEANS

There are many ways to cook beans. You can cook them on the stove top, in a slow cooker, in a Crockpot, or in an Instant Pot. I like to cook them in a Crockpot. In my opinion, cooked beans are superior to canned beans. They have a better flavor and are less expensive than canned beans.

MAKES APPROXIMATELY 6 CUPS COOKED BEANS AND ABOUT 4 CUPS BEAN JUICE DEPENDING ON THE BEANS

2 cups dried beans (any kind of bean will work)
10 cups warm water

Place beans and water in a Crockpot on the low heat setting. Cook approximately 7 hours, or until the beans are tender. I usually do this overnight or during the day if I am at home working. I don't leave the beans cooking on their own, however, if I'm not at home. Check to make sure that they are done before removing them from the Crockpot.

Then strain the beans over a container to catch all the liquid, which I save and use in soups and stews. If I'm making a soup or stew with the cooked beans, I add the bean juice as flavoring. If I'm not using the beans right away, I allow the beans and liquid to cool completely and

then place them back together in an airtight container to store them in the refrigerator. If you have any leftover bean juice, this can be stored in its own glass jar or airtight container. Cooked beans and bean juice will last several days in the refrigerator. Cooked beans can also be frozen, but because I use beans so often, I don't usually freeze them. I make them as I need them and store in the refrigerator to use during the week in that week's recipes.

Note:
If you want to halve the recipe (1 cup of dried beans will yield 3 cups cooked beans), note that you will use 6 cups of water to 1 cup of dried beans to account for evaporation with the smaller batch.

COOKED HOMINY CORN

Hominy corn is a dried corn that has been cooked with wood ash, baking soda, or a diluted solution of lye (potassium hydroxide) or of slaked lime (calcium hydroxide from limestone). Most people buy the treated corn dried (the most common way to purchase it) in either white, blue, or red. It can also be purchased frozen here in New Mexico in many of our supermarkets.

There are many ways to cook hominy corn: stove top, slow cooker, Crockpot, or Instant Pot. I like to cook them in a Crockpot.

MAKES APPROXIMATELY 6 CUPS COOKED HOMINY CORN AND ABOUT 4 CUPS CORN LIQUID DEPENDING ON THE COLOR OF CORN YOU COOK

1½ cups dried treated hominy corn
    (white, blue, or red)
8 cups warm water

Place hominy corn and water in a slow cooker or Crockpot on the low heat setting. Cook approximately 7 hours, or until the corn has puffed and the kernels are tender. I usually do this overnight or during the day if I am at home working. I don't leave the corn cooking unattended, however, if I'm not at home. Check to make sure that the kernels have puffed and are done before removing them from the Crockpot.

Then strain over a container to catch all the liquid, which I save and use in soups, stews, smoothies, sorbet, and even for making overnight oats. The corn liquid adds nutrients and flavor, and there are so many ways to use and not waste the liquid. If I'm making a soup or stew with the cooked corn, I add the corn liquid as flavoring. If I'm not using the cooked hominy corn right away, I allow the cooked corn and the corn liquid to cool completely and then place the cooked corn with some of the corn liquid in an airtight container to store it in the refrigerator. Leftover corn liquid can be stored in its own glass jar or airtight container. Cooked corn and corn liquid will last several days in the refrigerator, or it can be frozen for future use.

COOKED PUMPKIN PURÉE

There is nothing like the taste of fresh pumpkin purée to make soups, pies, scones, or any other recipe that requires pumpkin. I make pumpkin purée every fall when the pumpkins are plentiful and inexpensive. The purée can be frozen for use throughout the year. Smaller "pie pumpkins," or pumpkins specifically grown for cooking, make the best purée. I use Cinderella pumpkins, which are widely available during the fall and make a perfect purée for all kinds of recipes including the Pumpkin Pie with Piñon Pecan Crust (page 119). And don't discard the seeds; they make a delightful snack of Toasted Pumpkin Seeds (page 261).

MAKES APPROXIMATELY 4 QUARTS

For the Pumpkin Purée:
1 pumpkin (I used an 11.9-pound pumpkin)
3 cups water

Preheat the oven to 350°F. Cut the pumpkin in half and remove the seeds, pull off any pumpkin pulp or stringy flesh, and set the cleaned pumpkin on a sheet tray to bake. For the seeds, place them on a sheet tray to dry for several days in an undisturbed place until they are completely dry. It may take less time for the seeds to dry in dryer climates.

Place the pumpkin halves cut side down on a sheet tray or in a roasting pan and add 2 cups of the water, being careful it does not spill over the sides of the pan. Cook for 30 minutes, turn tray around in oven, and cook for another 30 minutes to ensure the pumpkin cooks evenly throughout. Then add another cup of water and bake for another 30 minutes or until the pumpkin flesh is soft when poked with a small knife. Remove from the oven and allow to cool.

When the pumpkin is cool enough to handle, peel off the skin and place about ¼ of the pumpkin in the food processor to process until

it is smooth. Repeat until all the pumpkin is puréed. Place in airtight containers or freezer bags, label, and date, and then transfer to the refrigerator or freezer for future use. The purée will last for approximately 3 to 4 days in the refrigerator or several months in the freezer.

TOASTED PUMPKIN SEEDS

There are two options for toasting pumpkin seeds. You can toast and use seeds straight from fresh pumpkins (in which case you need to hull them), or you can buy raw hulled seeds that have the outer covering removed and the green inner seed exposed, which of course is much easier. Either way, this is a simple, nutritious snack. Below, I address how to toast the seeds both ways.

MAKES 2 CUPS

2 cups pumpkin seeds
1 teaspoon sunflower oil
Kosher or sea salt, to taste

If you have purchased hulled pumpkin seeds (green without the white hull still on), skip this step. If you have gathered seeds from the inside of a pumpkin, you will need to hull them. To do this, bring 6 cups of water to a boil. Let the seeds boil for 10 minutes. Drain and spread them on a clean kitchen towel. When they are cool enough to handle, gently roll a rolling pin over the seeds. Using your fingers, squeeze the sides of the seed until the green seed pops out of the hull. Make sure the green pumpkin seeds are dry before moving on to the next step.

Once the white hull has been removed and the seeds have completely dried, they are now ready for toasting. In a large sauté pan over medium heat, add the pumpkin seeds and sunflower oil. Stir frequently as you'll hear them pop, and they will turn a golden brown and begin to toast. As they cook, sprinkle salt on top and continue to toast and stir for 12 to 15 minutes, or until they have all turned a light golden brown. Let them cool completely before transferring them to an airtight container. Store at room temperature for up to 1 week.

MUSHROOM STEM BRUSCHETTA

I don't like to waste anything, especially when I am buying locally sourced produce. Chef Walter says that traditionally everything was used in the Ancestral past when something was harvested, and nothing was ever wasted. This is a great recipe for using the mushroom stems from the Tomato & Mushroom Medley (page 173) and the Chile Empañaditas (page 137) or any other recipe that has mushrooms in it. This makes a wonderful appetizer or snack. Chef Marianne and I made this dish using both oregano and thyme and it tasted great both ways. Chef Walter likes thyme better than oregano, and I like oregano better than thyme. Use whichever herb you like better or try it both ways. The mushroom mixture can also be served as a topping on almost anything.

MAKES 4 TO 6 SERVINGS

For the Mushroom Bruschetta:

1 tablespoon sunflower oil
2 cups mushroom stems, finely diced
1 tablespoon blackened garlic (page 253)
½ teaspoon kosher salt
¼ teaspoon freshly ground black pepper
1 tablespoon finely chopped fresh thyme
    or oregano
1 tablespoon freshly squeezed lemon juice
    (about ½ small lemon)

For the Whole Sliced Croutons:

1 tablespoon sunflower oil
8 slices of baguette bread
¼ teaspoon kosher salt

Heat the sunflower oil in a sauté pan over medium to high heat until hot but not smoking. You will see ripples in the bottom of the pan. Add the mushroom stems, garlic, salt, and pepper. Cook for approximately 10 minutes, until the mushroom stems are tender and have caramelized. Reduce the heat to low and add the thyme and lemon juice. Cook for 1 minute, stirring to ensure that the thyme is completely mixed into the other ingredients. Transfer the mushroom mixture to a bowl and reserve.

For the whole sliced croutons, heat the sunflower oil over medium to high heat until hot but not smoking. Once you see ripples in the oil, add the bread slices and cook until toasted, approximately 5 minutes. Flip over and cook for another 5 minutes until the slices turn brown and are completely toasted. Sprinkle with the salt.

Place the mushroom stem bruschetta onto the whole sliced croutons and serve immediately.

VEGETABLE BROTH

Broth is different from stock, as stock is darker with stronger flavors. This is an aromatically fragrant broth that adds a light flavor to soups and stews. I like to use vegetable broth when I want some flavor and nutrients but not so much that it masks or overwhelms the dish I am preparing. It will work well in any recipe that requires water. If you can get organic or grow your own vegetables, use the skins but if not, discard the skins and follow the recipe below.

MAKES 8 CUPS

1 large yellow onion, quartered
  (approximately 2 cups)
1 head of garlic, outer peel and
  bottom cut off, then sliced in half
4 large carrots, sliced (approximately 2 cups)
4 large celery stalks, sliced
  (approximately 2 cups)
1 cup of fresh herbs
  (thyme, rosemary, parsley)
2 teaspoons kosher salt
9 cups water

Place all the ingredients in a large, heavy-bottomed pot over high heat. As soon as it comes to a boil, reduce the heat to low and simmer for 30 minutes.

Strain through a fine-mesh strainer to remove the vegetables and let cool. Pour into glass jars or airtight containers. Stock will last for several days in the refrigerator or can be frozen for later use. Freeze in containers for the amount you think you will use because once it has defrosted, it cannot be frozen again. Use as per the recipe, or instead of water in any recipe that uses water.

VEGETABLE STOCK

This lovely vegetable stock works well in any recipe that requires water, adding additional flavor as well as nutrients. Stock is different from vegetable broth, as stock is darker with a stronger taste. With stock, you sauté and caramelize the vegetables, giving them a rich and more robust flavor, and because you caramelize the vegetables, the stock becomes a darker color. I make stocks a lot but don't like to add them to delicate soups or stews because they might overpower them. But both vegetable stock and vegetable broth contain nutrients. If you can get organic or grow your own vegetables, use the skins but if not, discard the skins and follow the recipe below. Use instead of water in any recipe where you want a more robust flavor profile, or serve with your favorite pasta for a homemade vegetable noodle soup.

YIELDS 6 CUPS

2 teaspoons sunflower oil

1 large yellow onion, loosely chopped (approximately 2 cups)

4 large carrots, sliced (approximately 2 cups)

4 large celery stalks, sliced (approximately 2 cups)

1 head of garlic, outer peel and bottom cut off and broken into cloves (approximately ½ cup)

1 cup of fresh herbs (thyme, rosemary, parsley)

9 cups water

2 teaspoons kosher salt

In a stock-size heavy-bottomed pot over medium to high heat, heat the sunflower oil until hot but not smoking. Add the onion, carrots, and celery and cook for approximately 10 minutes. Stir occasionally to prevent burning but avoid stirring so much that the vegetables don't start to turn brown. Reduce the heat to medium, add the garlic, and cook for an additional 3 minutes. Add the herbs and cook for an additional 3 minutes, stirring to prevent burning but again not overstirring so that the ingredients don't brown. You want them to brown and begin to stick to the bottom of the stockpot. This is part of the caramelization. Once the vegetables have caramelized, add the water, stir, then add the salt.

Bring to a boil, then reduce the heat and simmer for 30 minutes. Strain to remove the vegetables and compost or discard. Pour into glass jars or airtight containers. Stock will last for several days in the refrigerator or can be frozen in containers for future use. Freeze in containers for the amount you think you will use because once it has defrosted, it cannot be frozen again.

NO FRY FRYBREAD

Almost every Native American community has a recipe for frybread. Frybread is delicious but not something that we recommend be eaten every day; Chef Walter and I call it a "sometimes food." These No Fry Frybreads are a healthier version of the same dough that is fried. Traditionally frybread was made by hand; some aunties and grandmas who are expert frybread makers shape the bread with their hands. This takes time to master, so you may want to use a rolling pin at first to make sure the breads are the desired thickness and diameter and round in shape. However you decide to make the breads, stretch or roll the dough out so that it is 5 to 6 inches in diameter and the thickness is ⅛ to ¼ inch. That's the most important thing to remember.

Chef Walter has gotten really good at making a great No Fry Frybread dough over the years and makes it now whenever we use it at Red Mesa Cuisine. These breads can be cooked on an open flame with the Cast Iron Cooking Grill (see source guide) or in a seasoned cast-iron pan instead of fried. Some community members on some of the Pueblos call these tortilla breads. They are a wonderful accompaniment to many soups and stews and are the base for Healthy Indian Tacos (page 86).

MAKES APPROXIMATELY 20 TORTILLA BREADS

4 cups unbleached flour, plus ¼ cup flour to roll out the breads

2 tablespoons baking powder

1 teaspoon kosher salt

1⅔ cups warm water

In a medium mixing bowl, combine the flour, baking powder, and salt. Gradually stir in the water with a spoon or your hands until the dough becomes soft and pliable without sticking to the bowl. If the dough feels too dry, add a little more water. If it feels too wet, add a little more flour.

Remove the bread from the bowl and knead the dough on a lightly floured cutting board or surface (using a little of the additional flour) for 3 to 4 minutes, folding the outer edges of the dough toward the center until the dough is soft and pliable. Return the dough to the bowl, cover with plastic wrap, and let rest for at least 30 minutes to allow it to rise. I usually try to let it rest for an hour if I have the time.

Then shape the dough into small-size balls (about the size of a golf ball) and roll out, using a little of the flour and a rolling pin, to ⅛ to ¼ inch in thickness and 5 to 6 inches in diameter on a lightly floured surface.

Preheat a dry, seasoned cast-iron skillet over high heat until very hot or use a Cast Iron Cooking Grill (see source guide). If you are using the open flame grill, you will want to cook the breads over medium to low heat so as not to burn them.

Place your shaped dough circle onto the hot pan or open flame grill, and let it cook for approximately for 2 to 3 minutes on each side until it bubbles and begins to turn brown, then turn the bread over and cook for another 2 to 3 minutes until it bubbles again, and the bread is completely done. It will puff a little, bubble, and somewhat resemble a pita bread.

Repeat this process, rolling each piece of dough out with a little flour so that it doesn't stick to the surface. Keep the cooked breads warm between two clean kitchen towels or place them in a basket lined with a clean kitchen towel. Flour sack towels work perfectly for this. Serve immediately with your favorite stew or use as the base for the Healthy Indian Tacos (page 86).

BLUE CORN NO FRY FRYBREAD

This blue corn version of the No Fry Frybread is a little denser than the all-purpose flour version but healthier because we've incorporated blue cornmeal into it. It has a lovely color and is a delicious alternative to the flour version.

MAKES APPROXIMATELY 20 NO FRY OR GRILLED TORTILLA BREADS

4 cups unbleached flour, plus ¼ cup flour to roll out the breads
1 cup finely ground blue cornmeal
2 tablespoons baking powder
1 teaspoon kosher salt
2 cups warm water

In a medium mixing bowl, combine the flour, cornmeal, baking powder, and salt. Gradually stir in the water with a spoon or your hands until the dough becomes soft and pliable without sticking to the bowl. If the dough feels too dry, add a little more water. If it feels too wet, add a little more flour.

Remove the bread from the bowl and knead the dough on a lightly floured cutting board or surface (using a little of the additional flour) for 3 to 4 minutes, folding the outer edges of the dough toward the center until the dough is soft and pliable.

Then return the dough to the bowl, cover with plastic wrap, and let rest for at least 30 minutes to allow it to rise. I usually try to let it rest for an hour if I have the time.

Shape the dough into small-size balls (about the size of a golf ball) and roll out, using a little of the flour and a rolling pin, to ⅛ to ¼ inch in thickness and 5 to 6 inches in diameter on a lightly floured surface.

Preheat a dry, seasoned cast-iron skillet until very hot over high heat or use a Cast Iron Cooking Grill (see source guide). If you are using the open flame grill, you will want to cook the breads over medium to low heat so as not to burn them.

Place your shaped dough circle onto the hot pan or open flame grill, and let it cook for 2 to 3 minutes on each side until it bubbles and begins to turn brown, then turn the bread over and cook for another 2 to 3 minutes until it bubbles again and the bread is completely done. It will puff a little and somewhat resemble a pita bread.

Repeat this process, rolling each piece of dough out with a little flour so that it doesn't stick to the surface. Keep the cooked breads warm between two clean kitchen towels or place them in a basket lined with a clean kitchen towel. Flour sack towels work perfectly for this. Serve immediately with your favorite stew or use as the base for the Healthy Indian Tacos (page 86).

RED CHILE AGAVE

This recipe is a great go-to for a glaze for any kind of vegetable and an ingredient in the salad dressing for the Three Bean Salad (page 73). This agave can be drizzled over any kind of potato including sweet potatoes and Yukon gold potatoes, as well as used over fresh fruit in the summer months. Another favorite use of this is to put it in ramekins for my guests to drizzle onto the Blue Corn No Fry Frybread (page 268), the Poblano Corn Bread (page 151), or the Gluten-Free Blue Corn Bread (page 29) instead of any kind of butter, which is a healthy alternative.

MAKES APPROXIMATELY ½ CUP

4 teaspoons New Mexico red chile powder, mild
6 tablespoons agave sweetener

Mix ingredients with a whisk. Place in ramekins as a side or use as per the instructions in the recipe. Store at room temperature for up to 1 week.

CHOKECHERRY SYRUP

The common chokecherry (*Prunus virginiana*) is indigenous to parts of Canada, most of the United States, and parts of northern Mexico and has been used by Native American tribes for millennia. This small tree produces green berries (not eaten and only used for dye) that ripen in the summer months to deep red-purple, almost black, berries (harvested and eaten fresh or dried for later use) that are quite sour and have a large pit. Many tribes have traditionally used the ripened fruit that is eaten fresh, as well as dried in large quantities for winter use; Chef Walter says that the Navajo use both the green and ripened purple berries for dye, and they use the chokecherry wood Ceremonially. Many other tribes have used this plant as both food and medicine. Chokecherries have been used medicinally for centuries with some new data showing that they have been successful with the reduction of certain cancer cells.[34] They are an ingredient in the Plains dish pemmican, a staple traditional food.

I grow chokecherries on the land that surrounds the north side of my house and have for years now. I call this an edible landscape or a form of acceptance gardening (accepting what nature offers and assisting it to grow) and use the chokecherries that grow here every year, while still leaving some for the birds and other creatures as well as leaving enough for the plant to repropagate itself. Whenever Chef Walter and I use hand-harvested wild foods, we are very careful, and we not only thank the wild plant for letting us use it for food and medicine but also always give back any unused parts of the plant or seeds to the earth with a prayer of gratitude.

MAKES APPROXIMATELY 1 QUART OF JUICE OR 2 CUPS OF SYRUP

For the Chokecherry Juice:

4 cups (1 quart) fresh ripened chokecherries, washed and cleaned

8 cups water

For the Chokecherry Syrup:

4 cups (1 quart) chokecherry juice

¾ cup agave sweetener

1 teaspoon freshly squeezed lemon juice (approximately ½ small lemon)

To make the juice, bring the chokecherries and water to boil in a heavy-bottomed saucepan over high heat. Reduce the heat to medium and simmer for 1 hour, skimming off any foam that forms on the top of the pan. Remove from the heat. In small batches, pass the berries and cooking liquid through a fine-mesh strainer, using a wooden smasher, mallet, or heavy kitchen spoon to mash the berries, removing all the juice and leaving only the pits and skins behind.

This takes some time to do and gives you a great upper-arm workout. I smash the cooked berries for approximately 5 minutes until no juice comes out the bottom of the strainer. Tap the strainer to remove any pulp. Continue this process until all the boiled berries and liquid have passed through the fine sieve. Either compost the seeds and pits, or give them back to the earth, with gratitude, and then reserve the juice. You should have 1 quart of juice.

To make the syrup, combine the chokecherry juice and agave in a heavy-bottomed saucepan and bring to boil. Reduce the heat to low and simmer for 60 minutes, uncovered. Add the lemon juice, stir, and cook for an additional 5 minutes. Remove from heat. Pass through a fine-mesh strainer.

Allow the syrup to cool and then freeze in hard plastic containers. Or can in jars, following hot-water-bath canning instructions from your favorite canning cookbook, making sure the jar are properly sealed. Then store in a pint jar for up to a year.

COCONUT WHIPPED CREAM

This is another must-have recipe for serving a dollop of whipped cream with many of the desserts in this cookbook. Be sure to use full-fat coconut milk for this recipe as the fat content and solidified cream are essential here (I like to use the 365 brand of coconut milk). You can whip this up easily as is or halve the recipe for a smaller batch. It will last for several days in the refrigerator.

MAKES APPROXIMATELY 1 CUP

2 cans (13.5 ounces each) coconut milk,
    refrigerated overnight
1 tablespoon agave sweetener
1 teaspoon vanilla bean paste

Open the cold cans of coconut milk that have been in the refrigerator overnight, and then using a spoon, poke a hole through the solidified coconut, and with a fine strainer, gently strain the liquid from the can without pushing any of the solids through. Keep the coconut liquid for another use, and use within a few days or freeze it for later use.

Transfer the solids left in the can to the bowl of a stand mixer with the whisk attachment (or to a bowl for use with a handheld mixer). Add the agave and vanilla and whip until you have stiff peaks, for 2 to 3 minutes, just as if you are making whipped cream.

Place in a container and store in the refrigerator until ready to use. I often put it into a plastic disposable pastry bag or a plastic freezer bag to hold it in, and then I cut off one end of the pastry or freezer bag and squeeze out a nice dollop for plating my desserts when I'm ready to use it. Basically, I'm creating a pastry bag out of the plastic freezer bag so as to easily squeeze the coconut whipped cream onto my desserts.

THE CULTURAL CONSERVANCY

The Cultural Conservancy (TCC) has been supporting and advocating for Indigenous food systems and food sovereignty since our origins. Maintaining and renewing our Ancestral food systems is deeply tied to our mission to protect and revitalize Indigenous cultures, empowering them in the direct application of their traditional knowledge and practices on Ancestral lands.

TCC supports Indigenous food sovereignty through local farms, a growing Native Foodways Program, national and international networks, a podcast series, and global grant making. Our long-term commitment is to Mend the Circle of Indigenous health and wellness through the revitalization of Native lands, agriculture, and foodways—from seed to plate, soil to sky, song to recipe, and ancestors to future generations.

TCC is deeply rooted in Turtle Island (North America) with strong connections to Hawai'i and Abya Yala, the greater Pacific, and internationally across the Americas. We focus much of our work with California Indian communities, including recognized tribes/ sovereign nations, unrecognized tribes, Native organizations, and urban, intertribal Indian communities.

Our focus on biocultural diversity aims to renew and restore the health of traditional knowledge, foodways, landscapes, and practices of Indigenous cultures that were substantially damaged by the last five hundred years of colonialism in the Americas and the Pacific. Our intertribal and intercultural team fosters these connections by honoring the self-determination of Indigenous Peoples in the implementation of our vision. We operate as pollinators among local communities, funders, allies, traditional knowledge holders, and regional and global movements. By working diligently to open and maintain dialogue between varying global communities, we promote productive connections that cultivate awareness of diverse ways of knowing related to the stewardship of the earth.

For more information, please visit:
The Cultural Conservancy
www.nativeland.org
www.nativeseedpod.org

SOURCE GUIDE FOR NATIVE FOODS

BINESHII
Phone: 218-335-8461
Website: www.bineshiiwildrice.store
Email: bineshii@bineshiiwildrice.com
Wild rice products, corn products

BLUE CORN CUSTOM DESIGNS
Rochelle L. Garcia
Phone: 602-679-5801
Website: www.bccdofficial.com
Email: bccdofficial@outlook.com
Culinary ash and blue cornmeal

CHE'IL MAYAN CHOCOLATE
Julio Saqui
Phone: 501-637-6521
Email: juliosaqui@gmail.com
Facebook: Che'il Mayan Products
Homemade chocolate, chocolate making
  sessions, Belizean chocolate, and Cacao Farm
  Tours.

CLC PECANS, LLC
Tami Cavitt
Phone: 575-318-9220
Website: www.clcpecans.com
Email: tami@clcpecans.com
New Mexico pecans

DYNAMITE HILL FARMS
Phone: 906-235-6177
Email: dynamitehillfarms@gmail.com
Wild rice and maple products

GRACE TRACY
Phone: 928-781-2366
Email: gtracy45@gmail.com
Culinary ash

KING ARTHUR BAKING COMPANY
Phone: 800-827-6836
Website: www.kingarthurbaking.com
Email: customercare@kingarthurbaking.com
Organic masa harina, all-purpose flour, organic
  all-purpose flour

LOS CHILEROS
Phone: 505-768-1100
Toll-Free: 888 EAT CHILE
Website: www.loschileros.com
Dried chiles, corn products, corn husks,
  epazote, herbs, spices, blue corn posole,
  white corn posole

MADE IN NEW MEXICO
Jonathan Rinkevich
Phone: 575-758-7709 Store
Website: www.madeinnewmexico.com
Email: minmtaos@gmail.com
New Mexico chile products, dried chiles,
  ristras, prickly pear syrup

**NATIVE HARVEST OJIBWE PRODUCTS,
A SUBDIVISION OF WHITE EARTH LAND
RECOVERY PROJECT**
Phone: 218-375-4602
Website: www.nativeharvest.com
Email: WhiteEarthNativeHarvest@gmail.com
Wild rice products, chokecherry syrup, maple
  syrup, wild plum syrup

NEW MEXICO CONNECTION
Grocery Store
Phone: 800-933-2736
Website: www.newmexicanconnection.com
Email: nmbestchile@gmail.com
New Mexico frozen chiles, New Mexico chile
  products, sauces, spices, posole, and beans

RAMONA FARMS
Phone: 520-418-0900
Email: cs@ramonafarms.com
Website: www.ramonafarms.com
Heirloom white tepary beans, heirloom brown
  tepary beans, and heritage corn products

RED MESA CUISINE, LLC
Phone: 505-466-6306
Website: www.redmesacuisine.com
Email: redmesacuisine@gmail.com
Cast Iron Cooking Grills, blue cornmeal,
  white cornmeal, azafran, tepary beans,
  Anasazi beans, white corn posole, blue corn
  posole, red chile powder, Mexican oregano

SANTA FE SCHOOL OF COOKING
Phone: 505-983-4511
Toll-Free: 800-982-4688
Website: www.santafeschoolofcooking.com
Email: cookin@nets.com
New Mexico chiles, New Mexico chile products,
  salsas, cookware, Santa Fe School of Cooking
  grills, cookbooks, and posters

**SÉKA HILLS, YOCHA DEHE WINTUN
NATION**
Phone: 530-796-2810
Website: www.SekaHills.com
Email: SekaHills@SekaHills.com
Olive oil, elderberry balsamic vinegar

SHIMÁ OF NAVAJOLAND
Phone: 928-729-5540
Website: www.shimaofnavajoland.com
Email: info@shimaofnavajoland.com
Blue cornmeal, culinary ash

STOKLI
Marianne Sundquist
Website: www.stokli.com
Email: hello@stokli.com
New Mexico chile products, dried fruit, jam

TROPICAL FRUIT BOX
Phone: 786-758-4787
Website: www.tropicalfruitbox.com
Email: hello@tropicalfruitbox.com
Fresh seasonal cacao pods

WILMER KAVENA
Phone: 928-613-5177
Email: kavenawilmer@yahoo.com
Culinary Ash

NOTES

INTRODUCTION

1 Please note that the Americas is referred to as the "Old World" because history has traditionally been told from a Eurocentric perspective and that history is never objective but always subjective depending on who is telling the story.

2 New evidence from footprints found in White Sands National Park now suggests that people existed in the Southwest over twenty thousand years ago. Jeff Pigati and Kathleen Springer, research geologists with the US Geological Survey, radiocarbon-dated seeds from under newly discovered footprints at somewhere between twenty-one thousand and twenty-three thousand years ago. These are now the oldest footprints in the United States. See https://www.npr.org/2021/09/24/1040381802/ancient-footprints-new-mexico-white-sands-humans and https://www.youtube.com/watch?v=dFk7o6C2kV8.

3 Patricia L. Crown and W. Jeffrey Hurst, "Evidence of Cacao Use in the Prehispanic American Southwest," *Proceedings of the National Academy of Sciences of the United States of America*, PNAS, February 2, 2009, doi: 10.1073/pnas.0812817106.

4 Richard I. Ford, "Inter-Indian Exchange in the Southwest," in *Handbook of North American Indians, Volume 10: Southwest*, William C. Sturtevant, general ed., and Alfonso Ortiz, Southwest ed. (Washington, DC: Smithsonian Institution, 1983), 711–722.

5 Linda Murray Berzok, *American Indian Foods* (Westport, CT: Greenwood Press, 2005), and Lois Ellen Frank, *The Discourse and Practice of Native American Cuisine: Native American Chefs and Native American Cooks in Contemporary Southwest Kitchens*, PhD diss. (Albuquerque, NM: University of New Mexico, 2011).

6 Frank, *The Discourse and Practice of Native American Cuisine*.

7 Berzok, *American Indian Foods*, and Frank, *The Discourse and Practice of Native American Cuisine*.

8 Stephen C. Jett and John Thompson, "The Destruction of Navajo Orchards in 1864," *Journal of the Southwest* 16, no. 4 (1974): 365–378.

9 There is a new permanent interpretive exhibition entitled *Bosque Redondo: A Place of Suffering . . . A Place of Survival* at the Bosque Redondo Memorial at Fort Sumner Historic Site, which tells the true story of the internment of Diné (Navajo) and Ndé (Mescalero Apache) tribal members at Bosque Redondo in the mid-1860s and how that

tragedy continues to affect these communities today. Bosque Redondo Memorial at Fort Sumner chronicles a dark history: the forced relocation of an estimated 9,500 Diné (Navajo) and 500 Ndé (Mescalero Apache) from their traditional tribal homelands to the Bosque Redondo Indian Reservation.

Fort Sumner, a US Army internment camp, stood at the reservation's center according to the Museum of New Mexico Foundation and the Friends of Bosque Redondo Memorial, who co-sponsored the public opening for this exhibition on May 28, 2022. The exhibit is framed from a Native American perspective and is eye-opening. Chef Walter and I visited it in the fall of 2021 while writing this cookbook, and it had a tremendous impact on both of us to learn the actual history of what happened at Bosque Redondo. The permanent exhibition's ultimate goal is to serve as a place of dialogue, where visitors can draw connections between the site's history with contemporary global issues of ethnic cleansing, genocide, and reconciliation, according to the website.

10 Berzok, *American Indian Foods.*

11 For more information on this program, visit https://www.fns.usda.gov/fdpir/food -distribution-program-indian-reservations.

12 Readers seeking to learn more about TEK might start with the Wikipedia article: https://en.wikipedia.org/wiki/Traditional _ecological_knowledge.

13 Melissa K. Nelson, "Re-Indigenizing Our Bodies and Minds Through Native Foods," in *Original Instructions: Indigenous Teachings for a Sustainable Future* (Rochester, VT: Bear & Company, 2008), 180.

14 Devon A. Mihesuah, *Recovering Our Ancestors' Gardens: Indigenous Recipes and Guide to Diet and Fitness* (Lincoln: University of Nebraska Press, 2020), 3.

15 See "Food Sovereignty," La Via Campesina International Peasants' Movement origin story of food sovereignty, https:// viacampesina.org/en/food-sovereignty/, accessed May 19, 2022.

16 Joseph Owle, "Healthy Roots Project, Eastern Band of Cherokee Indians," in Centers for Disease Control and Prevention, *Traditional Foods in Native America—Part III: A Compendium of Stories from the Indigenous Food Sovereignty Movement in American Indian and Alaska Native Communities* (Atlanta, GA: CDC, 2015), 28–29, https://www .cdc.gov/diabetes/ndwp/pdf/part-iii ---compendium-of-traditional-foods -stories-june-9-508.pdf.

CORN

17 The New World has been historically used to describe the Americas that Columbus encountered because history was told from a Eurocentric perspective. It is important to remember that history is always subjective and not objective. I use the bicycle wheel analogy with any historic event: the center of the bicycle wheel and all the spokes represent all the differing perspectives of the same historic event.

18 Jack Weatherford, *Native Roots: How the Indians Enriched America* (New York: Crown Publishers, 1991).

BEANS

19 Richard S. MacNeish, "Preliminary Archaeological Investigations in the Sierra de Tamaulipos, Mexico," *Transactions of the American Philosophical Society* 48 (Philadelphia, 1958).

SQUASH

20 Centers for Disease Control and Prevention. *Traditional Foods in Native America: A Compendium of Stories from the Indigenous Food Sovereignty Movement in American Indian and Alaska Native Communities --Part I: Mvskoke Food Sovereignty Initiative (MFSI) Muscogee (Creek) Nation,* (Atlanta, GA: CDC, 2013) 12-15 https://www.cdc.gov/diabetes/ndwp/pdf/part-i- traditional-foods-in-native-america-april-21.pdf.

CHILES

21 Sophie D. Coe, *America's First Cuisines* (Austin: University of Texas Press, 1994).

22 Bernardino de Sahagún, *General History of the Things of New Spain*, trans. Arthur J. O. Anderson and Charles E. Dibble (Santa Fe, NM: School of American Research, and the University of Utah, 1950–1982), 8:37 and 10:70.

TOMATOES

23 Bernardino de Sahagún, *General History of the Things of New Spain*, trans. Arthur J. O. Anderson and Charles E. Dibble (Santa Fe, NM: School of American Research, and the University of Utah, 1950–1982), 10:70.

24 Sylvia A. Johnson, "Tomatoes Forbidden Fruit," in *Tomatoes, Potatoes, Corn, and Beans: How the Foods of the Americas Changed Eating Around the World* (New York: Antheneum Books for Young Readers 1997), 90.

POTATOES

25 John Reader, "Potato: A History of the Propitious Esculent," in *Part 1: South America 3. Domestication* (New Haven, CT, and London: Yale University Press, 2011), 38–39.

26 Noel Vietmeyer, "Forgotten Roots of the Incas," in *Chilies to Chocolate: Food the Americas Gave the World*, Nelson Foster and Linda Cordell, eds. (Tucson: University of Arizona Press, 1992), 95–104.

VANILLA

27 Rebecca Rupp, "The History of Vanilla," *National Geographic*, October 23, 2014, https://www.nationalgeographic.com/culture/article/plain-vanilla?loggedin =true.

28 Rupp, "The History of Vanilla."

CACAO

29 Sylvia A. Johnson, "Chocolate: Food of the Gods," in *Tomatoes, Potatoes, Corn, and Beans: How the Foods of the Americas Changed Eating Around the World* (New York: Antheneum Books for Young Readers, 1997), 96.

30 Pure Kakaw, accessed April 13, 2022, https://purekakaw.com/pages/history-of-cacao.

31 John A. West, "A Brief History and Botany of Cacao," in *Chilies to Chocolate: Food the Americas Gave the World*, Nelson Foster and Linda Cordell, eds. (Tucson: University of Arizona Press, 1992), 105.

32 West, "A Brief History and Botany of Cacao," 105–106.

33 West, "A Brief History and Botany of Cacao," 108.

PANTRY STAPLES

34 Sarah Sunshine Manning, "Native American Student Proves Traditional Chokecherry Pudding Is Medicine," ICT (updated September 13, 2018), https://indiancountrytoday.com/archive/bringing-science-culture-together-chokecherry-pudding.

BIBLIOGRAPHY

"Ancient Grains—Chia Seeds." https://www .ancientgrains.com/, accessed February 20, 2022.

Andrews, Jean. 1984. *Peppers: The Domesticated Capsicums.* Austin: University of Texas Press.

Berzok, Linda Murray. 2005. *American Indian Food.* Westport, CT: Greenwood Press.

Betancourt, Marian, Michael O'Dowd, Jack Strong, and Ron Manville. 2009. *The New Native American Cuisine: Five-Star Recipes from the Chefs of Arizona's Kai Restaurant.* Guilford, CT: Three Forks.

Bitsoie, Freddie, and James O. Fraioli. 2021. *New Native Kitchen: Celebrating Modern Recipes of the American Indian.* New York: Abrams.

Byrant, Barbara, and Betsy Rentress. 2019. *Pecans: Recipes and History of an American Nut.* New York: Rizzoli International Publications.

Castelló Yturbide, Teresa. 1987. *Comida Prehispanica.* México, D.F. C.P.: Banamex Fomento Cultural Banamex, A.C.

Cobo, Bernabe. 1979. *History of the Inca Empire.* Translated and edited by Roland Hamilton. Austin: University of Texas Press.

Coe, Sophie D. 1994. *America's First Cuisines.* Austin: University of Texas Press.

Coe, Sophie D., and Michael D. Coe. 1996. *The True History of Chocolate.* London: Thames and Hudson.

Crown, Patricia L., and W. Jeffrey Hurst. 2009. "Evidence of Cacao Use in the Prehispanic American Southwest." *Proceedings of the National Academy of Sciences of the United States of America*, PNAS. February 2, 2009. doi: 10.1073/pnas.0812817106.

Edible New Mexico. 2017. "An Interview with Matt Romero." https://www.ediblenm.com /best-farm-romero-farms/. Accessed March 29, 2022.

Farb, Peter. 1968. *Man's Rise to Civilization as Shown by the Indians of North America from Primeval Times to the Coming of the Industrialist State.* New York: E. P. Dutton.

Ford, Richard I. 1981. "Gardening and Farming Before A.D. 1000: Patterns of Prehistoric Cultivation North of Mexico." *Journal of Ethnobiology* 1, no. 1: 6–27.

———. 1983. "Inter-Indian Exchange in the Southwest." In *Handbook of North American Indians, Volume 10: Southwest.* General Editor, William C. Sturtevant. Southwest Editor, Alfonso Ortiz, 711–722. Washington, DC: Smithsonian Institution.

———. 1985. "Pattern of Prehistoric Food Production in North America." In *Prehistoric Food Production in North America*, 341–364. Ann Arbor: Museum of Anthropology, University of Michigan.

———. 1994. "Corn Is Our Mother." In *Corn & Culture: In the Prehistoric New World.* Sisseel Johannessen and Christine Ann Hastorf, eds., 513–525. Boulder, CO: Westview Press.

Foster, Nelson, and Linda S. Cordell, eds. 1992. *Chiles to Chocolate: Food the Americas Gave the World.* Tucson: University of Arizona Press.

Frank, Lois Ellen. 2002. *Foods of the Southwest Indian Nations: Traditional and Contemporary Native American Recipes.* Berkeley, CA: Ten Speed Press.

———. 2011. *The Discourse and Practice of Native American Cuisine: Native American Chefs and Native American Cooks in Contemporary Southwest Kitchens.* PhD diss., Albuquerque, New Mexico: University of New Mexico. https://digitalrepository.unm .edu/anth_etds/24.

Fussell, Betty Harper. 2004. *The Story of Corn.* Albuquerque: University of New Mexico Press.

Galinat, Walton C. 1992. "Maize: Gift from America's First Peoples." In *Chilies to Chocolate: Food the Americas Gave to the World.* Nelson Foster and Linda Cordell, eds., 47–60, Tucson: University of Arizona Press.

Hart, Tashia. 2021. *The Good Berry Cookbook: Harvesting and Cooking Wild Rice and Other Wild Foods.* St. Paul: Minnesota Historical Society Press.

Hoover, Elizabeth. 2017. "'You Can't Say You're Sovereign If You Can't Feed Yourself': Defining and Enacting Food Sovereignty in American Indian Community Gardening." *American Indian Culture and Research Journal* 41, no. 3: 31–70. doi: 10.17953 /aicrj.41.3.hoover.

Isaac, Gwyneira, Symma Finn, Jennie R. Joe, Elizabeth Hoover, Joseph P. Gone, Clarita Lefthand-Begay, and Stewart Hill. 2018. "Native American Perspectives on Health and Traditional Ecological Knowledge." *Environmental Health Perspectives* 126, no. 12: 125002. doi: 10.1289/EHP1944.

Jett, Stephen C., and John Thompson. 1974. "The Destruction of Navajo Orchards in 1864." *Journal of the Southwest* 16, no. 4: 365–378.

Johnson, Sylvia A. 1997. *Tomatoes, Potatoes, Corn, and Beans: How the Foods of the Americas Changed Eating Around the World.* New York: Antheneum Books for Young Readers.

Kavena, Juanita Tiger. 1980. *Hopi Cookery.* Tucson: University of Arizona Press.

Kennedy, Diana. 1990. *Mexican Regional Cooking.* New York: Harper Perennial.

Kimmerer, Robin Wall. 2013. *Braiding Sweetgrass: Indigenous Wisdom, Scientific Knowledge, and the Teachings of Plants.* Minneapolis, MN: Milkweed Editions.

Manning, Sarah Sunshine. 2018. "Native American Student Proves Traditional Chokecherry Pudding Is Medicine," ICT (updated September 13, 2018). https://indiancountrytoday.com/archive/bringing-science-culture-together-chokecherry-pudding.

McDougall, Christopher. 2011. *Born to Run: A Hidden Tribe, Superathletes, and the Greatest Race the World Has Never Seen.* New York: Vintage Books.

Mihesuah, Devon A. 2020. *Recovering Our Ancestors' Gardens: Indigenous Recipes and Guide to Diet and Fitness.* Lincoln: University of Nebraska Press.

Miller, Mark, with John Harrisson. 1991. *The Great Chile Book.* Berkeley, CA: Ten Speed Press.

Moerman, Daniel E. 1998. *Native American Ethnobotany.* Portland, OR: Timber Press.

Morales, Laurel. August 21, 2017. "To Get Calcium, Navajos Burn Juniper Branches to Eat the Ash." *NPR Morning Edition.* https://www.npr.org/sections/thesalt/2017/08/21/544191316/to-get-calcium-navajos-burn-juniper-branches-to-eat-the-ash. Accessed February 28, 2022.

Mullins, G. W., and C. L. Hause. 2017. *The Native American Cookbook: Recipes from Native American Tribes.* Carbondale, CO: Light of the Moon Publishing.

Murphy, Hugh. *Foods Indigenous to the Western Hemisphere,* American Indian Health and Diet Project. https://aihd.ku.edu/foods/strawberry.html. Accessed January 9, 2022.

Murray, Jennifer. 2019. "The Difference Between Cocoa and Cacao." The Spruce Eats. https://www.thespruceeats.com/difference-between-cocoa-and-cacao-3376438.

Nabhan, Gary Paul. 1989. *Enduring Seeds: Native American Agriculture and Wild Plant Conservation.* New York: North Point Press.

———. 2002. *Coming Home to Eat: The Pleasures and Politics of Local Foods.* New York: Norton.

Nabhan, Gary Paul, ed., Ashley Rood, and Deborah Madison. 2008. *Renewing American's Food Traditions: Saving and Savoring the Continent's Most Endangered Foods.* White River Junction, VT: Chelsea Green.

Naranjo, Norma. 2021. *The Four Sisters: Keeping Family Traditions Alive; Recipes from the Pueblo.* Ohkay Owingeh Pueblo, NM: Feasting Place.

Nelson, Melissa K. 2008. "Re-Indigenizing Our Bodies and Minds Through Native Foods." In *Original Instructions,* 180–195. Rochester, VT: Bear & Company.

NPR.org. "Ancient Footprints in White Sands National Park." https://www.npr.org/2021/09/24/1040381802/ancient-footprints-new-mexico-white-sands-humans. Accessed May 18, 2022.

NPR.org. "To Get Calcium, Navajos Burn Juniper Branches to Eat the Ash." https://www.npr.org/sections

/thesalt/2017/08/21/544191316/to-get-calcium -navajos-burn-juniper-branches-to-eat-the -ash. Accessed April 9, 2022.

O'Loughlin, Ed, and Mihir Zaveri. May 5, 2020. "Irish Return an Old Favor, Helping Native Americans Battling the Virus." https://www.nytimes.com/2020/05/05 /world/coronavirus-ireland-native-american -tribes.html. Accessed March 31, 2022.

Owle, Joseph. 2015. "Healthy Roots Project, Eastern Band of Cherokee Indians." In *Traditional Foods in Native America—Part III: A Compendium of Stories from the Indigenous Food Sovereignty Movement in American Indian and Alaska Native Communities*, 28–29. Atlanta, GA: CDC. https://www.cdc.gov/diabetes/ndwp/pdf /part-iii---compendium-of-traditional-foods -stories-june-9-508.pdf.

PBS.org. "Ancient Footprints in White Sands National Park." https://www.youtube.com /watch?v=dFk7o6C2kV8. Accessed May 18, 2022.

Rain, Patricia. 2003. *Vanilla: The Cultural History of the World's Favorite Flavor and Fragrance*. New York: Tarcher/Pequin.

Reader, John. 2011. "Potato: A History of the Propitious Esculent." In *Part 1: South America 3. Domestication*, 38–39. New Haven, CT, and London: Yale University Press.

Roach, John. 2002. "Saving the Potato in Its Andean Birthplace." *National Geographic*, June 2002.

Root, Wavery, and Richard De Rochemont. 1995. *Eating in America: A History*. Hopewell, NJ: Ecco Press.

Sahagún, Bernardino de. 1950–1982. *General History of the Things of New Spain*. Translated by Arthur J. O. Anderson and Charles E. Dibble, in thirteen parts. Santa Fe, NM: School of American Research and the University of Utah.

Sherman, Sean, with Beth Dooley. 2017. *The Sioux Chef's Indigenous Kitchen*. Minneapolis: University of Minnesota Press.

Spruce Eats. "What Is Epazote?" https://www. thespruceeats.com/what-is-epazote-4126810. Accessed February 24, 2022.

Swentzell, Roxanne, and Patricia M. Perea. 2016. *The Pueblo Food Experience Cookbook: Whole Food of Our Ancestors*. Santa Fe, NM: Museum of New Mexico Press.

Washington University in St. Louis. "Deep History of Coconuts Decoded: Origins of Cultivation, Ancient Trade Routes, and Colonization of the Americas." Science Daily. www.sciencedaily.com /releases/2011/06/110624142037.htm. Accessed July 21, 2022.

Weatherford, Jack. 1991. *Native Roots: How the Indians Enriched America*. New York: Crown Publishers.

Wesner, Chelsea. 2008–2014. "Traditional Food Stories." "Part I—Traditional Foods in Native America, Part II—Good Food Is Power, Part III—Compendium of Traditional Food Stories, Part IV—Traditional Foods in

Native America, Part V—Traditional Foods in Native America." Centers for Disease Control and Prevention, Native Diabetes Wellness Program. https://www.cdc.gov/diabetes /ndwp/traditional-foods/.

Wikipedia. "Dysphania Ambrosioides." https://en.wikipedia.org/wiki/Dysphania _ambrosioides. Accessed February 24, 2022.

Wikipedia. "Hominy." https://en.wikipedia.org /wiki/Hominy. Accessed February 6, 2022.

INDEX

Note: Page references in *italics* indicate photographs.

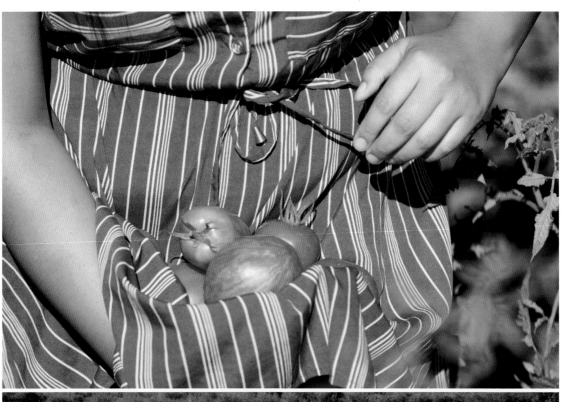